Official Product Do
from Macromedia

Powerful design and development tools require authoritative technical documentation. With the release of Macromedia Studio 8, there is no more authoritative source than the development and writing teams who created the product. Now their official documentation is available to you in printed book form, to help you evaluate the software or to advance your capabilities as you take advantage of the powerful features in this release.

Developing Extensions for Macromedia Flash 8
Learn firsthand how to extend the capabilities of the Web's most popular authoring platform, using JavaScript. Create commands and extensible tools for use in this authoring environment.
0-321-39416-X, $44.99

Using ActionScript 2.0 Components with Macromedia Flash 8
The resource for developers and ActionScript users who want to use components to speed development.
0-321-39539-5, $54.99

Learning Actionscript 2.0 for Macromedia Flash 8
A detailed introduction to coding with ActionScript to add interactivity and produce high-impact Web experiences. Includes extensive reusable code examples.
0-321-39415-1, $49.99

Macromedia Flash 8: A Tutorial Guide
A collection of step-by-step tutorials that teach both beginning and advanced Flash techniques.
0-321-39414-3, $29.99

ActionScript 2.0 Language Reference for Macromedia Flash 8
Dictionary-style reference covers valuable syntax and usage information; detailed descriptions of classes, functions, properties, and events; and code samples for every element in the ActionScript language.
0-321-38404-0, $39.99

Developing Extensions for Macromedia Dreamweaver 8
Extend the capabilities of Dreamweaver 8 using JavaScript. Write your own objects, behavior actions, and commands that affect Dreamweaver 8 documents and the elements within them.
0-321-39540-9, $54.99

macromedia®
PRESS
www.macromediapress.com

Visit www.peachpit.com/MacromediaDocs for details and special promotions on these new books.

Developing Extensions for Macromedia® FLASH® 8

Barbara Snyder

macromedia®
PRESS

Developing Extensions for Macromedia Flash 8

Barbara Snyder

Macromedia Press books are published by:
Peachpit
1249 Eighth Street
Berkeley, CA 94710
510/524-2178 510/524-2221 (fax)
Find us on the World Wide Web at:
www.peachpit.com www.macromedia.com

To report errors, please send a note to errata@peachpit.com

ISBN 0-321-39416-X

9 8 7 6 5 4 3 2 1

Printed and bound in the United States of America

Credits

Macromedia

Project Management: Sheila McGinn

Writing: Jay Armstrong

Managing Editor: Rosana Francescato

Lead Editor: Lisa Stanziano

Editing: Geta Carlson, Evelyn Eldridge, Mark Nigara

Production Management: Patrice O'Neill, Kristin Conradi, Yuko Yagi

Media Design and Production: Adam Barnett, Aaron Begley, Paul Benkman. John Francis, Geeta Karmarkar, Masayo Noda, Paul Rangel, Arena Reed, Mario Reynoso

Special thanks to Jody Bleyle, Mary Burger, Lisa Friendly, Stephanie Gowin, Bonnie Loo, Mary Ann Walsh, Erick Vera, the beta testers, and the entire Flash and Flash Player engineering and QA teams.

Macromedia Press

Macromedia Press Editor: Angela C. Kozlowski

Production Editor: Pat Christenson

Product Marketing Manager: Zigi Lowenberg

Cover Design: Charlene Charles Will

Dedication

The Studio 8 Documentation Team recognizes and honors Patrice O'Neill, who inspires all of us with her dedication and commitment.

Contents

Introduction

As a Macromedia Flash user, you may be familiar with ActionScript, which lets you create scripts that execute at runtime in Macromedia Flash Player. The Flash JavaScript application programming interface (JavaScript API) is a complementary programming tool that lets you create scripts that run in the authoring environment.

This document describes the objects, methods, and properties available in the JavaScript API. It assumes that you know how to use the documented commands when working in the authoring environment. If you have a question about what a particular command does, use other documents in Flash Help, such as *Using Flash*, to find that information.

This document also assumes that you are familiar with JavaScript or ActionScript syntax and with basic programming concepts such as functions, parameters, and data types.

This chapter contains the following sections:

Overview of the Macromedia Flash JavaScript API

The ActionScript language lets you write scripts to perform actions in the Flash Player environment (that is, while a SWF file is playing). The Flash JavaScript API lets you write scripts to perform several actions in the Flash authoring environment (that is, while a user has the Flash program open). These scripts can be used to help streamline the authoring process. For example, you can write scripts to automate repetitive tasks, add custom tools to the Tools panel, or add timeline effects.

The Flash JavaScript API is designed to resemble the Macromedia Dreamweaver and Macromedia Fireworks JavaScript API (which were designed based on the Netscape JavaScript API). The Flash JavaScript API is based on a Document Object Model (DOM), which allows Flash documents to be accessed using JavaScript objects. The Flash JavaScript API includes all elements of the Netscape JavaScript API, plus the Flash DOM. These added objects and their methods and properties are described in this document. You can use any of the elements of the native JavaScript language in a Flash script, but only elements that make sense in the context of a Flash document will have an effect.

The JavaScript API also contains a number of methods that let you implement extensibility using a combination of JavaScript and custom C code. For more information, see Chapter 3, "C-Level Extensibility," on page 533.

The JavaScript interpreter in Flash is the Mozilla SpiderMonkey engine, version 1.5, which is available on the web at www.mozilla.org/js/spidermonkey/. SpiderMonkey is one of the two reference implementations of the JavaScript language developed by Mozilla.org. It is the same engine that is embedded in the Mozilla browser.

SpiderMonkey implements the core JavaScript language as defined in the ECMAScript (ECMA-262) edition 3 language specification and it is fully compliant with the specification. Only the browser-specific host objects, which are not part of the ECMA-262 specification, are not supported. Similarly, many JavaScript reference guides distinguish between core JavaScript and client-side (browser-related) JavaScript. Only core JavaScript applies to the Flash JavaScript interpreter.

Creating JSFL files

You can use Macromedia Flash 8 or your preferred text editor to write and edit Flash JavaScript (JSFL) files. If you use Flash, these files have a .jsfl extension by default.

You can also create a JSFL file by selecting commands in the History panel and then clicking the Save button in the History panel or selecting Save As Command from the options pop-up menu. The command (JSFL) file is saved in the Commands folder (see "Saving JSFL files" on page 7). You can then open the file and edit it the same as any other script file.

The History panel provides some other useful options as well. You can copy selected commands to the Clipboard, and you can view JavaScript commands that are generated while you are working in Flash.

To copy commands from the History panel to the Clipboard:

1. Select one or more commands in the History panel.

2. Do one of the following:

   - Click the Copy button.

   - Select Copy Steps from the options pop-up menu.

To view JavaScript commands in the History panel:

- Select View > JavaScript in Panel from the options pop-up menu.

Saving JSFL files

You can have JSFL scripts available within the Flash authoring environment by storing them in one of several folders within the Configuration folder. By default, the Configuration folder is in the following location:

- Windows 2000 or Windows XP:

  boot drive\Documents and Settings*user*\Local Settings\Application Data\Macromedia\\
  Flash 8*language*\Configuration\

- Mac OS X:

  Macintosh HD/Users/*userName*/Library/Application Support/Macromedia/Flash 8/
  language/Configuration/

To determine the location of the Configuration folder, use `fl.configDirectory` or `fl.configURI`.

Within the Configuration folder, the following folders can contain scripts that you can access in the authoring environment: Behaviors, Commands (for scripts that appear on the Commands menu), Effects (for timeline effects), JavaScript (for scripts used by Script Assist), Tools (for extensible tools in the Tools panel), and WindowSWF (for panels that appear in the Windows menu). This document focuses on scripts used for commands, effects, and tools.

If you edit a script in the Commands folder, the new script is immediately available in Flash. If you edit a script for an effect or extensible tool, you have to close and restart Flash, or else use the `fl.reloadEffects()` or `fl.reloadTools()` command. However, if you used a script to add an extensible tool to the Tools panel and you then edit the script, you must either remove and then add the tool to the Tools panel again, or else close and restart Flash for the revised tool to be available.

There are three locations where you can store command, effect, and tool files so they can be accessed in the authoring environment.

- For scripts that will appear as items in the Commands menu, save the JSFL file in the Commands folder in the following location:

  - Windows 2000 or Windows XP:

    boot drive\Documents and Settings*user*\Local Settings\Application Data\Macromedia\ Flash 8*language*\Configuration\Commands

  - Mac OS X:

    Macintosh HD/Users/*userName*/Library/Application Support/Macromedia/Flash 8/*language*/Configuration/Commands

- For scripts that will appear as extensible tools in the Tools panel, save the JSFL file in the Tools folder in the following location:

  - Windows 2000 or Windows XP:

    boot drive\Documents and Settings*user*\Local Settings\Application Data\Macromedia\Flash 8\ *language*\Configuration\Tools

  - Mac OS X:

    Macintosh HD/Users/*userName*/Library/Application Support/Macromedia/Flash 8/*language*/Configuration/Tools

- For scripts that will appear as timeline effects in the Effects panel, save the JSFL file in the Effects folder in the following location:

  - Windows 2000 or Windows XP:

    boot drive\Documents and Settings*user*\Local Settings\Application Data\Macromedia\Flash 8\ *language*\Configuration\Effects

  - Mac OS X:

    Macintosh HD/Users/*userName*/Library/Application Support/Macromedia/Flash 8/*language*/Configuration/Effects

If a JSFL file has other files that go with it, such as XML files, they should be stored in the same directory as the JSFL file.

Running JSFL files

There are several ways to run JSFL files. The most common ways are discussed in this section.

To run a script that is in the Commands folder, do one of the following:

- Select Commands > *Script Name*.
- Use a keyboard shortcut that you have assigned to the script. To assign a keyboard shortcut, use Edit > Keyboard Shortcuts and select Drawing Menu Commands from the Commands pop-up menu. Expand the Commands node in the menu tree to view a list of available scripts.

To run a command script that is not in the Commands folder, do one of the following:

- From the authoring environment, select Commands > Run Command, and then select the script to run.
- From within a script, use the `fl.runScript()` command.
- From the file system, double-click the script file.

To add a tool implemented in a JSFL file to the Tools panel:

1. Copy the JSFL file for the tool and any other associated files to the Tools folder (see "Saving JSFL files" on page 7).
2. Select Edit > Customize Tools Panel (Windows) or Flash > Customize Tools Panel (Macintosh).
3. Add the tool to the list of available tools.
4. Click OK.

You can add individual JavaScript API commands to ActionScript files by using the `MMExecute()` function, which is documented in the *ActionScript 2.0 Language Reference*. However, the `MMExecute()` function has an effect only when it is used in the context of a custom user-interface element, such as a component Property inspector, or a SWF panel within the authoring environment. Even if called from ActionScript, JavaScript API commands have no effect in Flash Player or outside the authoring environment.

To issue a command from an ActionScript script:

- Use the following syntax (you can concatenate several commands into one string):

  `MMExecute(Javascript command string);`

You can also run a script from the command line

To run a script from the command line on Windows:

■ Use the following syntax (add path information as required):

```
"flash.exe" myTestFile.jsfl
```

To run a script from the command line on the Macintosh:

■ Use the following syntax (add path information as required):

```
osascript -e 'tell application "flash" to open alias "Mac OS
  X:Users:user:myTestFile.jsfl" '
```

The osascript command can also run AppleScript in a file. For example, you could put the following text in a file named myScript:

```
tell application "flash"
  open alias "Mac OS X:Users:user:myTestFile.jsfl"
end tell
```

Then, to invoke the script, you would use this command:

```
osascript myScript
```

What's new in the JavaScript API

In Flash 8, several new top-level functions and objects have been added. In addition, some existing objects now have new methods or properties. These additions, along with other changes, are summarized below. Also, new samples are provided; see "Sample implementations" on page 19.

If you have not used the JavaScript API before, you might want to skip this section and go directly to "The Flash Document Object Model" on page 14.

New top-level methods

The following top-level method is new in Flash 8:

```
confirm()
```

The following top-level methods were implemented in Flash MX 2004 but are newly documented in this release:

```
alert()
```

```
prompt()
```

New objects

The following objects are new in Flash 8:

Filter object

Project object

ProjectItem object

The following object was implemented in a Flash MX 2004 update release, but is newly documented in this release:

FLfile object

New methods and properties

The following methods and properties are new in Flash 8:

```
componentsPanel.reload()
document.addFilter()
document.changeFilterOrder()
document.crop()
document.deleteEnvelope()
document.disableAllFilters()
document.disableFilter()
document.disableOtherFilters()
document.enableAllFilters()
document.enableFilter()
document.exportPNG()
document.getBlendMode()
document.getFilters()
document.getMetadata()
document.importFile()
document.intersect()
document.punch()
document.removeAllFilters()
document.removeFilter()
document.setBlendMode()
document.setFilterProperty()
document.setFilters()
```

```
document.setMetadata()
document.swapStrokeAndFill()
document.union()
document.zoomFactor
element.layer
element.selected
fill.focalPoint
fill.linearRGB
fill.overflow
fl.browseForFolderURL()
fl.closeProject()
fl.contactSensitiveSelection
fl.createProject()
fl.objectDrawingMode
fl.getAppMemoryInfo()
fl.getProject()
fl.objectDrawingMode
fl.showIdleMessage()
frame.getCustomEase()
frame.hasCustomEase
frame.setCustomEase()
frame.useSingleEaseCurve
shape.isDrawingObject
stroke.capType
stroke.joinType
stroke.miterLimit
stroke.strokeHinting
stroke.scaleType
stroke.shapeFill
symbolInstance.blendMode
symbolInstance.cacheAsBitmap
symbolInstance.filters
symbolItem.scalingGrid
```

```
symbolItem.scalingGridRect
text.antiAliasSharpness
text.antiAliasThickness
textAttrs.letterSpacing
text.fontRenderingMode
videoItem.sourceFilePath
videoItem.videoType
xmlui.getControlItemElement()
xmlui.getEnabled()
xmlui.getVisible()
xmlui.setControlItemElement()
xmlui.setControlItemElements()
xmlui.setEnabled()
xmlui.setVisible()
```

Other changes

The following items have new parameters, additional acceptable values for existing parameters, or other implementation changes in Flash 8:

```
document.setSelectionBounds()
document.setSelectionRect()
instance.instanceType
outputPanel.save()
fl.openProject()
text.border, text.useDeviceFonts, textAttrs.autoKern
```
(no longer apply only to static text)

Deprecated properties

The following property is deprecated in this release:

`textAttrs.characterSpacing` (recommended property to use is `textAttrs.letterSpacing`)

The Flash Document Object Model

The Flash Document Object Model (DOM) for the Flash JavaScript API consists of a set of top-level functions (see "Top-Level Functions and Methods" on page 23) and two top-level objects—the FLfile object and the flash object (fl). Each object is guaranteed to be available to a script because it always exists when the Flash authoring environment is open. For more information, see FLfile object and flash object (fl).

When referring to the flash object, you can use flash or fl. For example, to close all open files, you can use either of the following statements:

```
flash.closeAll();
fl.closeAll();
```

The flash object contains the following *child* objects:

Object	How to access
componentsPanel object	Use fl.componentsPanel to access the componentsPanel object. This object corresponds to the Components panel in the Flash authoring environment.
Document object	Use fl.documents to retrieve an array of all the open documents; use fl.documents[index] to access a particular document; use fl.getDocumentDOM() to access the current document (the one with focus).
drawingLayer object	Use fl.drawingLayer to access the drawingLayer object.
Effect object	Use fl.effects to retrieve an array of effect descriptors that corresponds to the effects registered when Flash starts; use fl.effects[index] to access a particular effect; use fl.activeEffect to access the effect descriptor for the current effect being applied.
Math object	Use fl.Math to access the Math object.
outputPanel object	Use fl.outputPanel to access the outputPanel object. This object corresponds to the Output panel in the Flash authoring environment.
Project object	Use fl.getProject() to return a Project object for the currently open project.
Tools object	Use fl.tools to access an array of Tools objects.
XMLUI object	Use fl.xmlui to access an XML User Interface (XMLUI) object. The XMLUI object provides the ability to get and set properties of an XMLUI dialog box.

The Document object

An important property of the top-level flash object is the `fl.documents` property. (See `fl.documents` property.) The `fl.documents` property contains an array of Document objects that each represent one of the FLA files currently open in the authoring environment. The properties of each Document object represent most of the elements that a FLA file can contain. Therefore, a large portion of the DOM is composed of child objects and properties of the Document object. For more information, see Document object.

To refer to the first open document, for example, use the statement `flash.documents[0]` or `fl.documents[0]`. The first document is the first Flash document that was opened during the current session in the authoring environment. When the first opened document is closed, the indexes of the other open documents are decremented.

To find a particular document's index, use `flash.findDocumentIndex(nameOfDocument)` or `fl.findDocumentIndex(nameOfDocument)`. See `fl.findDocumentIndex()`.

To access the document that is currently focused, use the statement `flash.getDocumentDOM()` or `fl.getDocumentDOM()`. See `fl.getDocumentDOM()`. The latter is the syntax used in most of the examples in this document.

To find a particular document in the `fl.documents` array, iterate through the array and test each document for its `document.name` property. See `fl.documents` and `document.name`.

All the objects in the DOM that aren't listed in the previous table (see "The Flash Document Object Model" on page 14) are accessed from the Document object. For example, to access the library of a document, you use the `document.library` property, which retrieves a library object:

```
fl.getDocumentDOM().library
```

To access the array of items in the library, you use the `library.items` property; each element in the array is an Item object:

```
fl.getDocumentDOM().library.items
```

To access a particular item in the library, you specify a member of the `library.items` array:

```
fl.getDocumentDOM().library.items[0]
```

In other words, the library object is a child of the Document object, and the Item object is a child of the library object. For more information, see `document.library`, library object, `library.items`, and Item object.

Specifying the target of an action

Unless otherwise specified, methods affect the current focus or selection. For example, the following script doubles the size of the current selection because no particular object is specified:

```
fl.getDocumentDOM().scaleSelection(2, 2);
```

In some cases, you might want an action to specifically target the currently selected item in the Flash document. To do this, use the array that the document.selection property contains (see document.selection). The first element in the array represents the currently selected item, as shown in the following example:

```
var accDescription = fl.getDocumentDOM().selection[0].description;
```

The following script doubles the size of the first element on the Stage that is stored in the element array, instead of the current selection:

```
var element =
  fl.getDocumentDOM().getTimeline().layers[0].frames[0].elements[0];
if (element) {
  element.width = element.width*2;
  element.height = element.height*2;
}
```

You can also do something such as loop through all the elements on the Stage and increase the width and height by a specified amount, as shown in the following example:

```
var elementArray =
  fl.getDocumentDOM().getTimeline().layers[0].frames[0].elements;
  for (var i=0; i < elementArray.length; i++) {
    var offset = 10;
    elementArray[i].width += offset;
    elementArray[i].height += offset;
  }
```

Summary of the DOM structure

The following list displays the DOM structure in outline format. Numbers at the beginning of each line represent the level of an object. For example, an object preceded by "03" is a child of next highest "02" object, which, in turn, is a child of the next highest "01" object.

In some cases, an object is available by specifying a property of its parent object. For example, the document.timelines property contains an array of Timeline objects (see document.timelines and Timeline object). These properties are noted in the following outline.

Finally, some objects are subclasses of other objects, rather than being children of other objects. An object that is a subclass of another object has methods and/or properties of its own in addition to the methods and properties of the other object (the superclass). Subclasses share the same level in the hierarchy as their superclass. For example, the Item object is a superclass of the BitmapItem object (see Item object and BitmapItem object). These relationships are illustrated in the following outline:

01 Top-Level Functions and Methods

01 FLfile object

01 flash object (fl)

  02 componentsPanel object

  02 Document object (`fl.documents` array)

    03 Filter object

    03 Matrix object

    03 Fill object

    03 Stroke object

    03 library object

      04 Item object (`library.items` array)

      04 BitmapItem object (subclass of Item object)

      04 folderItem object (subclass of Item object)

      04 fontItem object (subclass of Item object)

      04 SoundItem object (subclass of Item object)

      04 SymbolItem object (subclass of Item object)

      04 VideoItem object (subclass of Item object)

    03 Timeline object (`document.timelines` array)

      04 Layer object (`timeline.layers` array)

        05 Frame object (`layer.frames` array)

          06 Element object (`frame.elements` array)

            07 Matrix object (Element.matrix)

06 Instance object (abstract class, subclass of Element object)

06 BitmapInstance object (subclass of Instance object)

06 CompiledClipInstance object (subclass of Instance object)

06 ComponentInstance object (subclass of SymbolInstance object)

   07 Parameter object (`componentInstance.parameters`)

06 SymbolInstance object (subclass of Instance object)

06 Text object (subclass of Element object)

   07 TextRun object (`text.textRuns` array)

     08 TextAttrs object (`textRun.textAttrs` array)

06 Shape object (subclass of Element object)

   07 Contour object (`shape.contours` array)

     08 HalfEdge object

       09 Vertex object

       09 Edge object

   07 Edge object (`shape.edges` array)

     08 HalfEdge object

       09 Vertex object

       09 Edge object

   07 Vertex object (`shape.vertices` array)

     08 HalfEdge object

       09 Vertex object

       09 Edge object

03 ScreenOutline object

  04 Screen object (`screenOutline.screens` array)

    05 Parameter object (`screen.parameters` array)

02 drawingLayer object

  03 Path object

    04 Contour object

02 Effect object (`fl.effects` array)

02 Math object

02 outputPanel object

02 Project object

   03 ProjectItem object (project.items array)

02 Tools object (`fl.tools` array)

   03 ToolObj object (`tools.toolObjs` array)

02 XMLUI object

Sample implementations

Several sample JSFL implementations are included with Flash 8. You can review and install these files to familiarize yourself with the JavaScript API. The samples are installed in a folder named Samples/ExtendingFlash within the folder in which you installed Flash. For example, if you installed Flash using the default setting, the samples are placed in the following location:

- In Windows: *boot drive*\Program Files\Macromedia\Flash 8\Samples and Tutorials\Samples\ExtendingFlash
- On the Macintosh: Macintosh HD/Applications/Macromedia/Flash 8/Samples and Tutorials/Samples/ExtendingFlash

Sample Shape command

A sample JavaScript API script named Shape.jsfl is located in the ExtendingFlash/Shape folder (see "Sample implementations" above). This script displays information about the contours of the shape in the Output panel.

To install and run the Shape script:

1. Copy the Shape.jsfl file to the Configuration/Commands folder (see "Saving JSFL files" on page 7).
2. In a Flash document (FLA file), select a shape object.
3. Select Commands > Shape to run the script.

Sample get and set filters command

A sample JavaScript API script named filtersGetSet.jsfl is located in the ExtendingFlash/
filtersGetSet folder (see "Sample implementations" on page 19). This script adds filters to a
selected object and displays information about the filters being added in the Output panel.

To install and run the filtersGetSet script:

1. Copy the filtersGetSet.jsfl file to the Configuration/Commands folder (see "Saving JSFL
   files" on page 7).

2. In a Flash document (FLA file), select a text, movie clip, or button object.

3. Select Commands > filtersGetSet to run the script.

Sample PolyStar tool

A sample JavaScript API script named PolyStar.jsfl is located in the ExtendingFlash/PolyStar
folder (see "Sample implementations" on page 19).

The PolyStar.jsfl replicates the PolyStar tool that can be found in the Flash Tools panel. The
script demonstrates how to build the PolyStar tool using the JavaScript API, and includes
detailed comments describing what the code is doing. Read this file to gain a better
understanding of how the JavaScript API can be used. You should also read the PolyStar.xml
file in the Tools directory to learn more about how to build your own tool.

Flash includes an earlier (obfuscated) version of the PolyStar.jsfl script that you must remove
in order to use the sample PolyStar.jsfl file.

To remove the earlier version of the PolyStar.jsfl file that was installed with Flash:

1. Select Edit > Customize Tools Panel (Windows) or Flash > Customize Tools Panel (Macintosh).

2. In the Customize Tools Panel dialog box, click the Rectangle tool on the left side of the dialog box.

   The Rectangle tool and the PolyStar tool should now be listed in the Current Selection list on the right side of the dialog box.

3. Select the PolyStar tool in the Current Selection list.

4. Click Remove.

5. Click OK.

6. Quit Flash.

7. Remove only the PolyStar.jsfl file from the Configuration/Tools folder (see "Saving JSFL files" on page 7). The PolyStar.xml and PolyStar.png files are needed by the new PolyStar.jsfl file that you will install later. When you restart Flash, the PolyStar tool no longer appears in the Customize Tools Panel dialog box.

To install the updated PolyStar example files:

1. If Flash is running, exit the application.

2. Copy the new PolyStar.jsfl file to the Configuration/Tools folder (see "Saving JSFL files" on page 7). The PolyStar.xml and PolyStar.png files that you see in this folder are needed by the new PolyStar.jsfl file.

3. Restart Flash.

4. Select Edit > Customize Tools Panel (Windows) or Flash > Customize Tools Panel (Macintosh). You should see PolyStar tool in the available tools list.

5. Click the Rectangle tool at the left side of the Customize Tools Panel dialog box. The Rectangle Tool should appear in the Current Selection list at the right side of the dialog box.

6. Select the PolyStar tool from the Available Tools list.

7. Click Add.

8. Click OK.

   The PolyStar tool now appears in the Rectangle tool pop-up menu.

Sample Trace Bitmap panel

A set of files named TraceBitmap.fla and TraceBitmap.swf are located in the ExtendingFlash/TraceBitmapPanel folder (see "Sample implementations" on page 19). These files illustrate how to design and build a panel to control the functions of Flash. They also show the use of the `MMExecute()` function to call JavaScript commands from an ActionScript script.

To run the TraceBitmap sample:

1. If Flash is running, exit from Flash.

2. Copy the TraceBitmap.swf file to the Configuration/WindowSWF folder (see "Saving JSFL files" on page 7).

3. Start Flash.

4. Create or open a Flash document (FLA file), and import a bitmap or JPEG image into the file.

   You can use the flower.jpg file provided in the TraceBitmapPanel folder or another image of your choice.

5. With the imported image selected, select Window > Other Panels > TraceBitmap.

6. Click Submit.

   The image is converted into a group of shapes.

Sample DLL

A sample DLL implementation is located in the ExtendingFlash/dllSampleComputeSum folder (see "Sample implementations" on page 19). For more information about building DLLs, see Chapter 3, "C-Level Extensibility," on page 533.

CHAPTER 1
Top-Level Functions and Methods

1

This chapter describes the top-level functions and methods that are available when you use the Macromedia Flash JavaScript application programming interface (JavaScript API). For information about where to store JavaScript API files, see "Saving JSFL files" on page 7.

The following lists summarize the areas in the authoring environment that relate to each function or method. Following the lists, the functions and methods are listed in alphabetical order.

Global methods

The following methods can be called from any JavaScript API script:

```
alert()
confirm()
prompt()
```

Timeline effects

The following functions are specific to timeline effects:

```
configureEffect()
executeEffect()
removeEffect()
```

Extensible tools

The following functions are available in scripts that create extensible tools:

```
activate()
configureTool()
deactivate()
keyDown()
keyUp()
mouseDoubleClick()
mouseDown()
mouseMove()
mouseUp()
notifySettingsChanged()
setCursor()
```

activate()

Availability

Flash MX 2004.

Usage

```
function activate() {
  // statements
}
```

Parameters

None.

Returns

Nothing.

Description

Function; called when the extensible tool becomes active (that is, when the tool is selected in the Tools panel). Use this function to perform any initialization tasks the tool requires.

Example

The following example sets the value of `tools.activeTool` when the extensible tool is selected in the Tools panel:

```
function activate() {
  var theTool = fl.tools.activeTool
}
```

See also

`tools.activeTool`

alert()

Availability

Flash MX 2004.

Usage

`alert ( alertText )`

Parameters

`alertText`   A string that specifies the message you want to display in the Alert dialog box.

Returns

Nothing.

Description

Method; displays a string in a modal Alert dialog box, along with an OK button.

Example

The following example displays the message "Process Complete" in an Alert dialog box:

`alert("Process Complete");`

See also

`confirm(), prompt()`

configureEffect()

Availability

Flash MX 2004.

Usage

```
function configureEffect() {
  // Statements
}
```

Parameters

None.

Returns

Nothing.

Description

Function; called once when Flash loads; place any global initialization statements for your effect inside this function. The per instance parameter data for an effect cannot be accessed here.

See also

executeEffect( ), removeEffect( )

configureTool()

Availability

Flash MX 2004.

Usage

```
function configureTool() {
  // statements
}
```

Parameters

None.

Returns

Nothing.

Description

Function; called when Flash opens and the extensible tool is loaded into the Tools panel. Use this function to set any information Flash needs to know about the tool.

Example

The following examples show two possible implementations of this function:

```
function configureTool() {
  theTool = fl.tools.activeTool;
  theTool.setToolName("myTool");
  theTool.setIcon("myTool.png");
  theTool.setMenuString("My Tool's menu string");
  theTool.setToolTip("my tool's tool tip");
  theTool.setOptionsFile( "mtTool.xml" );
}

function configureTool() {
  theTool = fl.tools.activeTool;
  theTool.setToolName("ellipse");
  theTool.setIcon("Ellipse.png");
  theTool.setMenuString("Ellipse");
  theTool.setToolTip("Ellipse");
  theTool.showTransformHandles( true );
}
```

confirm()

Availability

Flash 8.

Usage

`confirm ( strAlert )`

Parameters

strAlert   A string that specifies the message you want to display in the Alert dialog box.

Returns

A Boolean value: `true` if the user clicks OK; `false` if the user clicks Cancel.

Description

Method; displays a string in a modal Alert dialog box, along with OK and Cancel buttons.

Example

The following example displays the message "Sort data?" in an Alert dialog box:

```
confirm("Sort data?");
```

See also

```
alert(), prompt()
```

deactivate()

Availability

Flash MX 2004.

Usage

```
function deactivate() {
    // statements
}
```

Parameters

None.

Returns

Nothing.

Description

Function; called when the extensible tool becomes inactive (that is, when the active tool changes from this tool to another one). Use this function to perform any cleanup the tool needs.

Example

The following example displays a message in the Output panel when the tool becomes inactive:

```
function deactivate() {
    fl.trace( "Tool is no longer active" );
}
```

executeEffect()

Availability

Flash MX 2004.

Usage

```
function executeEffect() {
  // statements
}
```

Parameters

None.

Returns

Nothing.

Description

Function; called when the user first applies an effect or changes an effect's properties. The code contained in this function modifies the original object(s) to create the desired effect. It is also responsible for copying the original to a hidden layer if necessary for the `removeEffect` function.

See also

`configureEffect()`, `removeEffect()`

keyDown()

Availability

Flash MX 2004.

Usage

```
function keyDown() {
  // statements
}
```

Parameters

None.

Returns

Nothing.

Description

Function; called when the extensible tool is active and the user presses a key. The script should call `tools.getKeyDown()` to determine which key was pressed.

Example

The following example displays information about which key was pressed when the extensible tool is active and the user presses a key.

```
function keyDown() {
  fl.trace("key " + fl.tools.getKeyDown() + " was pressed");
}
```

See also

`keyUp()`, `tools.getKeyDown()`

keyUp()

Availability

Flash MX 2004.

Usage

```
function keyUp() {
  // statements
}
```

Parameters

None.

Returns

Nothing.

Description

Function; called when the extensible tool is active and a key is released.

Example

The following example displays a message in the Output panel when the extensible tool is active and a key is released.

```
function keyUp() {
  fl.trace("Key is released");
}
```

See also

```
keyDown()
```

mouseDoubleClick()

Availability

Flash MX 2004.

Usage

```
function mouseDoubleClick() {
  // statements
}
```

Parameters

None.

Returns

Nothing.

Description

Function; called when the extensible tool is active and the mouse button is double-clicked on the Stage.

Example

The following example displays a message in the Output panel when the extensible tool is active and the mouse button is double-clicked.

```
function mouseDoubleClick() {
  fl.trace("Mouse was double-clicked");
}
```

mouseDown()

Availability

Flash MX 2004.

Usage

```
function mouseDown( [ pt ] ) {
  // statements
}
```

Parameters

pt   A point that specifies the location of the mouse when the button is pressed. It is passed to the function when the mouse button is pressed. This parameter is optional.

Returns

Nothing.

Description

Function; called when the extensible tool is active and the mouse button is pressed while the pointer is over the Stage.

Example

The following examples show how this function can be used when the extensible tool is active. The first example displays a message in the Output panel that the mouse button was pressed. The second example displays the *x* and *y* coordinates of the mouse's location when the button was pressed.

```
function mouseDown() {
  fl.trace("Mouse button has been pressed");
}
function mouseDown(pt) {
  fl.trace("x = "+ pt.x+" :: y = "+pt.y);
}
```

mouseMove()

Availability

Flash MX 2004.

Usage

```
function mouseMove( [ pt ] ) {
  // statements
}
```

Parameters

pt   A point that specifies the current location of the mouse. It is passed to the function whenever the mouse moves, which tracks the mouse location. If the Stage is in edit or edit-in-place mode, the point coordinates are relative to the object being edited. Otherwise, the point coordinates are relative to the Stage. This parameter is optional.

Returns

Nothing.

Description

Function; called whenever the extensible tool is active and the mouse moves over a specified point on the Stage. The mouse button can be down or up.

Example

The following examples show how this function can be used. The first example displays a message in the Output panel that the mouse is being moved. The second example displays the *x* and *y* coordinates of the mouse's location as it moves.

```
function mouseMove() {
  fl.trace("moving");
}

function mouseMove(pt) {
  fl.trace("x = "+ pt.x + " :: y = " + pt.y);
}
```

mouseUp()

Availability

Flash MX 2004.

Usage

```
function mouseUp() {
  // statements
}
```

Parameters

None.

Returns

Nothing.

Description

Function; called whenever the extensible tool is active and the mouse button is released after being pressed on the Stage.

Example

The following example displays a message in the Output panel when the extensible tool is active and the mouse button is released.

```
function mouseUp() {
  fl.trace("mouse is up");
}
```

notifySettingsChanged()

Availability

Flash MX 2004.

Usage

```
function notifySettingsChanged() {
  // statements
}
```

Parameters

None.

Returns

Nothing.

Description

Function; called when the extensible tool is active and the user changes its options in the Property inspector. You can use the `tools.activeTool` property to query the current values of the options (see `tools.activeTool`).

Example

The following example displays a message in the Output panel when the extensible tool is active and the user changes its options in the Property inspector.

```
function notifySettingsChanged() {
  var theTool = fl.tools.activeTool;
  var newValue = theTool.myProp;
}
```

prompt()

Availability

Flash MX 2004.

Usage

```
prompt( promptMsg, [ text ] )
```

Parameters

promptMsg   A string to display in the Prompt dialog box (limited to 256 characters on Macintosh OS X).

text   An optional string to display as a default value for the text field.

Returns

The string the user typed if the user clicks OK; `null` if the user clicks Cancel.

Description

Method; displays a prompt and optional text in a modal Alert dialog box, along with OK and Cancel buttons.

Example

The following example prompts the user to enter a user name. If the user types a name and clicks OK, the name appears in the Output panel.

```
var userName = prompt("Enter user name", "Type user name here");
fl.trace(userName);
```

See also

alert( ), confirm( )

removeEffect()

Availability

Flash MX 2004.

Usage

```
function removeEffect() {
  // statements
}
```

Parameters

None.

Returns

Nothing.

Description

Function; called when the user changes an effect's properties or uses the Remove Effect menu item. The code contained in this function returns the object(s) to their original state. For example, if the effect broke a text string apart, the removeEffect( ) method would remove the text string that was broken apart and replace it with the original string.

See also

configureEffect( ), executeEffect( )

setCursor()

Availability

Flash MX 2004.

Usage

```
function setCursor() {
  // statements
}
```

Parameters

None.

Returns

Nothing.

Description

Function; called when the extensible tool is active and the mouse moves, to allow the script to set custom pointers. The script should call `tools.setCursor()` to specify the pointer to use. For a list that shows which pointers correspond to which integer values, see `tools.setCursor()`.

Example

```
function setCursor() {
  fl.tools.setCursor( 1 );
}
```

## CHAPTER 2

Objects

This chapter briefly describes each of the objects available in the Flash JavaScript application programming interface (JavaScript API). The objects are listed in alphabetical order in the following table:

Object	Description
BitmapInstance object	The BitmapInstance object is a subclass of the Instance object and represents a bitmap in a frame.
BitmapItem object	A BitmapItem object refers to a bitmap in the library of a document. The BitmapItem object is a subclass of the Item object.
CompiledClipInstance object	The CompiledClipInstance object is a subclass of the Instance object.
ComponentInstance object	The ComponentInstance object is a subclass of the SymbolInstance object and represents a component in a frame.
componentsPanel object	The componentsPanel object, which represents the Components panel, is a property of the flash object (fl) and can be accessed by `fl.componentsPanel`.
Contour object	A Contour object represents a closed path of half edges on the boundary of a shape.
Document object	The Document object represents the Stage.
drawingLayer object	The drawingLayer object is accessible from JavaScript as a child of the flash object.
Edge object	The Edge object represents an edge of a shape on the Stage.
Effect object	The Effect object represents an instance of a timeline effect.
Element object	Everything that appears on the Stage is of the type Element.
Fill object	The Fill object contains all the properties of the Fill color setting of the Tools panel or of a selected shape.

Object	Description
Filter object	The Filter object contains all the properties for all filters.
flash object (fl)	The flash object represents the Flash application.
FLfile object	The FLfile object lets you write Flash extensions that can access, modify, and remove files and folders on the local file system.
folderItem object	The folderItem object is a subclass of the Item object.
fontItem object	The fontItem object is a subclass of the Item object.
Frame object	The Frame object represents frames in the layer.
HalfEdge object	Directed side of the edge of a Shape object.
Instance object	The Instance object is a subclass of the Element object.
Item object	The Item object is an abstract base class.
Layer object	The Layer object represents a layer in the timeline.
library object	The library object represents the Library panel.
Math object	The Math object is available as a read-only property of the flash object; see `fl.Math`.
Matrix object	The Matrix object represents a transformation matrix.
outputPanel object	The outputPanel object represents the Output panel, which displays troubleshooting information such as syntax errors.
Parameter object	The Parameter object type is accessed from the `screen.parameters` array (which corresponds to the screen Property inspector in the Flash authoring tool) or by the `componentInstance.parameters` array (which corresponds to the component Property inspector in the authoring tool).
Path object	The Path object defines a sequence of line segments (straight, curved, or both), which you typically use when creating extensible tools.
Project object	The Project object represents a Flash Project (FLP) file.
ProjectItem object	The ProjectItem object represents an item (file on disk) that has been added to a project.
Screen object	The Screen object represents a single screen in a slide or form document.
ScreenOutline object	The ScreenOutline object represents the group of screens in a slide or form document.

Object	Description
Shape object	The Shape object is a subclass of the Element object. The Shape object provides more precise control than the drawing APIs for manipulating or creating geometry on the Stage.
SoundItem object	The SoundItem object is a subclass of the Item object. It represents a library item used to create a sound.
Stroke object	The Stroke object contains all the settings for a stroke, including the custom settings.
SymbolInstance object	The SymbolInstance object is a subclass of the Instance object and represents a symbol in a frame.
SymbolItem object	The SymbolItem object is a subclass of the Item object.
Text object	The Text object represents a single text item in a document.
TextAttrs object	The TextAttrs object contains all the properties of text that can be applied to a subselection. This object is a subclass of the Text object.
TextRun object	The TextRun object represents a run of characters that have attributes that match all of the properties in the TextAttrs object.
Timeline object	The Timeline object represents the Flash timeline, which can be accessed for the current document by `fl.getDocumentDOM().getTimeline()`.
ToolObj object	A ToolObj object represents an individual tool in the Tools panel.
Tools object	The Tools object is accessible from the Flash object (`fl.tools`).
Vertex object	The Vertex object is the part of the shape data structure that holds the coordinate data.
VideoItem object	The VideoItem object is a subclass of the Item object.
XMLUI object	The XMLUI object provides the ability to get and set properties of an XMLUI dialog box, and accept or cancel out of one.

BitmapInstance object

Inheritance Element object > Instance object > BitmapInstance object

Availability

Flash MX 2004.

Description

The BitmapInstance object is a subclass of the Instance object and represents a bitmap in a frame (see Instance object).

Method summary for the BitmapInstance object

In addition to the Instance object methods, you can use the following methods with the BitmapInstance object:

Method	Description
bitmapInstance.getBits()	Lets you create bitmap effects by getting the bits out of the bitmap, manipulating them, and then returning them to Flash.
bitmapInstance.setBits()	Sets the bits of an existing bitmap element.

Property summary for the BitmapInstance object

In addition to the Instance object properties, you can use the following properties with the BitmapInstance object.

Property	Description
bitmapInstance.hPixels	Read-only; an integer that represents the width of the bitmap, in pixels.
bitmapInstance.vPixels	Read-only; an integer that represents the height of the bitmap, in pixels.

bitmapInstance.getBits()

Availability

Flash MX 2004.

Usage

```
bitmapInstance.getBits()
```

Parameters

None.

Returns

An object that contains `width`, `height`, `depth`, `bits`, and, if the bitmap has a color table, `cTab` properties. The `bits` element is an array of bytes. The `cTab` element is an array of color values of the form `"#RRGGBB"`. The length of the array is the length of the color table.

The byte array is meaningful only when referenced by a DLL or shared library. You typically use it only when creating an extensible tool or effect. For information on creating DLLs for use with Flash JavaScript, see Chapter 3, "C-Level Extensibility."

Description

Method; lets you create bitmap effects by getting the bits out of the bitmap, manipulating them, and then returning them to Flash. See also `bitmapInstance.setBits()`.

Example

The following code creates a reference to the currently selected object; tests whether the object is a bitmap; and traces the height, width, and bit depth of the bitmap:

```
var isBitmap = fl.getDocumentDOM().selection[0].instanceType;
if(isBitmap == "bitmap"){
    var bits = fl.getDocumentDOM().selection[0].getBits();
    fl.trace("height = " + bits.height);
    fl.trace("width = " + bits.width);
    fl.trace("depth = " + bits.depth);
}
```

See also

`bitmapInstance.setBits()`

bitmapInstance.hPixels

Availability

Flash MX 2004.

Usage

`bitmapInstance.hPixels`

Description

Read-only property; an integer that represents the width of the bitmap—that is, the number of pixels in the horizontal dimension.

Example

The following code retrieves the width of the bitmap in pixels:

```
// Get the number of pixels in the horizontal dimension.
var bmObj = fl.getDocumentDOM().selection[0];
var isBitmap = bmObj.instanceType;
if(isBitmap == "bitmap"){
    var numHorizontalPixels = bmObj.hPixels;
}
```

See also

bitmapInstance.vPixels

bitmapInstance.setBits()

Availability

Flash MX 2004.

Usage

bitmapInstance.setBits(*bitmap*)

Parameters

bitmap   An object that contains height, width, depth, bits, and cTab properties. The height, width, and depth properties are integers. The bits property is a byte array. The cTab property is required only for bitmaps with a bit depth of 8 or less and is a string that represents a color value in the form "#RRGGBB".

 The byte array is meaningful only when referenced by an external library. You typically use it only when creating an extensible tool or effect.

Returns

Nothing.

Description

Method; sets the bits of an existing bitmap element. This lets you create bitmap effects by getting the bits out of the bitmap, manipulating them, and then returning the bitmap to Flash.

Example

The following code tests whether the current selection is a bitmap, and then sets the height of the bitmap to 150 pixels:

```
var isBitmap = fl.getDocumentDOM().selection[0].instanceType;
if(isBitmap == "bitmap"){
  var bits = fl.getDocumentDOM().selection[0].getBits();
  bits.height = 150;
  fl.getDocumentDOM().selection[0].setBits(bits);
}
```

See also

bitmapInstance.getBits()

bitmapInstance.vPixels

Availability

Flash MX 2004.

Usage

bitmapInstance.vPixels

Description

Read-only property; an integer that represents the height of the bitmap—that is, the number of pixels in the vertical dimension.

Example

The following code gets the height of the bitmap in pixels:

```
// Get the number of pixels in the vertical dimension.
var bmObj = fl.getDocumentDOM().selection[0];
var isBitmap = bmObj.instanceType;
if(isBitmap == "bitmap"){
  var numVerticalPixels = bmObj.vPixels;
}
```

See also

bitmapInstance.hPixels

BitmapItem object

Inheritance   Item object > BitmapItem object

Availability
Flash MX 2004.

Description
A BitmapItem object refers to a bitmap in the library of a document. The BitmapItem object is a subclass of the Item object (see Item object).

Property summary for the BitmapItem object

In addition to the Item object properties, the BitmapItem object has following properties:

Property	Description
bitmapItem.allowSmoothing	A Boolean value that specifies whether to allow smoothing of a bitmap.
bitmapItem.compressionType	A string that determines the type of image compression applied to the bitmap.
bitmapItem.quality	An integer that specifies the quality of the bitmap
bitmapItem.useImportedJPEGQuality	A Boolean value that specifies whether to use the default imported JPEG quality.

bitmapItem.allowSmoothing

Availability
Flash MX 2004.

Usage
bitmapItem.allowSmoothing

Description
Property; a Boolean value that specifies whether to allow smoothing of a bitmap (true) or not (false).

Example

The following code sets the `allowSmoothing` property of the first item in the library of the current document to `true`:

```
fl.getDocumentDOM().library.items[0].allowSmoothing = true;
alert(fl.getDocumentDOM().library.items[0].allowSmoothing);
```

bitmapItem.compressionType

Availability

Flash MX 2004.

Usage

```
bitmapItem.compressionType
```

Description

Property; a string that determines the type of image compression applied to the bitmap. Acceptable values are `"photo"` or `"lossless"`. If the value of `bitmapItem.useImportedJPEGQuality` is `false`, `"photo"` corresponds to JPEG with a quality from 0 to 100; if `bitmapItem.useImportedJPEGQuality` is `true`, `"photo"` corresponds to JPEG using the default document quality value. The value `"lossless"` corresponds to GIF or PNG format. (See `bitmapItem.useImportedJPEGQuality`.)

Example

The following code sets the `compressionType` property of the first item in the library of the current document to `"photo"`:

```
fl.getDocumentDOM().library.items[0].compressionType = "photo";
alert(fl.getDocumentDOM().library.items[0].compressionType);
```

bitmapItem.quality

Availability

Flash MX 2004.

Usage

```
bitmapItem.quality
```

Description

Property; an integer that specifies the quality of the bitmap. To use the default document quality, specify -1; otherwise, specify an integer from 0 to 100. Available only for JPEG compression.

Example

The following code sets the `quality` property of the first item in the library of the current document to 65:

```
fl.getDocumentDOM().library.items[0].quality = 65;
alert(fl.getDocumentDOM().library.items[0].quality);
```

bitmapItem.useImportedJPEGQuality

Availability

Flash MX 2004.

Usage

```
bitmapItem.useImportedJPEGQuality
```

Description

Property; a Boolean value that specifies whether to use the default imported JPEG quality (`true`) or not (`false`). Available only for JPEG compression.

Example

The following code sets the `useImportedJPEGQuality` property of the first item in the library of the current document to `true`:

```
fl.getDocumentDOM().library.items[0].useImportedJPEGQuality = true;
alert(fl.getDocumentDOM().library.items[0].useImportedJPEGQuality);
```

CompiledClipInstance object

Inheritance   Element object > Instance object > CompiledClipInstance object

Availability
Flash MX 2004.

Description
The CompiledClipInstance object is a subclass of the Instance object. It is essentially an instance of a movie clip that has been converted to a compiled clip library item. (See Instance object.)

Property summary for the CompiledClipInstance object

In addition to the properties of the Instance object, the CompiledClipInstance object has the following properties:

Property	Description
compiledClipInstance.accName	A string that is equivalent to the Name field in the Accessibility panel.
compiledClipInstance.actionScript	A string that represents the ActionScript for this instance; equivalent to symbolInstance.actionScript.
compiledClipInstance.description	A string that is equivalent to the Description field in the Accessibility panel.
compiledClipInstance.forceSimple	A Boolean value that enables and disables the children of the object to be accessible.
compiledClipInstance.shortcut	A string that is equivalent to the Shortcut field in the Accessibility panel.
compiledClipInstance.silent	A Boolean value that enables or disables the accessibility of the object; equivalent to the inverse logic of the Make Object Accessible setting in the Accessibility panel.
compiledClipInstance.tabIndex	An integer that is equivalent to the Tab Index field in the Accessibility panel.

compiledClipInstance.accName

Availability

Flash MX 2004.

Usage

```
compiledClipInstance.accName
```

Description

Property; a string that is equivalent to the Name field in the Accessibility panel. Screen readers identify objects by reading the name aloud.

Example

The following example gets and sets the accessibility name of the first selected object:

```
// Get the name of the object.
var theName = fl.getDocumentDOM().selection[0].accName;
// Set the name of the object.
fl.getDocumentDOM().selection[0].accName = 'Home Button';
```

compiledClipInstance.actionScript

Availability

Flash MX 2004.

Usage

```
compiledClipInstance.actionScript
```

Description

Property; a string that represents the ActionScript for this instance; equivalent to `symbolInstance.actionScript`.

Example

The following code assigns ActionScript to specified elements:

```
// Assign some ActionScript to a specified Button compiled clip instance.
fl.getDocumentDOM().getTimeline().layers[0].frames[0].elements[0]
  .actionScript = "on(click) {trace('button is clicked');}";
// Assign some ActionScript to the currently selected Button compiled clip
  instance.
fl.getDocumentDOM().selection[0].actionScript =
  "on(click) {trace('button is clicked');}";
```

compiledClipInstance.description

Availability

Flash MX 2004.

Usage

```
compiledClipInstance.description
```

Description

Property; a string that is equivalent to the Description field in the Accessibility panel. The description is read by the screen reader.

Example

The following example illustrates getting and setting the `description` property:

```
// Get the description of the current selection.
var theDescription = fl.getDocumentDOM().selection[0].description;
// Set the description of the current selection.
fl.getDocumentDOM().selection[0].description =
  "This is compiled clip number 1";
```

compiledClipInstance.forceSimple

Availability

Flash MX 2004.

Usage

```
compiledClipInstance.forceSimple
```

Description

Property; a Boolean value that enables and disables the children of the object to be accessible. This is equivalent to the inverse logic of the Make Child Objects Accessible setting in the Accessibility panel. If `forceSimple` is `true`, it is the same as the Make Child Objects Accessible option being unchecked. If `forceSimple` is `false`, it is the same as the Make Child Object Accessible option being checked.

Example

The following example illustrates getting and setting the `forceSimple` property:

```
// Query if the children of the object are accessible.
var areChildrenAccessible = fl.getDocumentDOM().selection[0].forceSimple;
// Allow the children of the object to be accessible.
fl.getDocumentDOM().selection[0].forceSimple = false;
```

compiledClipInstance.shortcut

Availability

Flash MX 2004.

Usage

```
compiledClipInstance.shortcut
```

Description

Property; a string that is equivalent to the Shortcut field in the Accessibility panel. The shortcut is read by the screen readers. This property is not available for dynamic text fields.

Example

The following example illustrates getting and setting the shortcut property:

```
// Get the shortcut key of the object.
var theShortcut = fl.getDocumentDOM().selection[0].shortcut;
// Set the shortcut key of the object.
fl.getDocumentDOM().selection[0].shortcut = "Ctrl+I";
```

compiledClipInstance.silent

Availability

Flash MX 2004.

Usage

```
compiledClipInstance.silent
```

Description

Property; a Boolean value that enables or disables the accessibility of the object; equivalent to the inverse logic of Make Object Accessible setting in the Accessibility panel. That is, if silent is true, then Make Object Accessible is unchecked. If silent is false, then Make Object Accessible is checked.

Example

The following example illustrates getting and setting the silent property:

```
// Query if the object is accessible.
var isSilent =fl.getDocumentDOM().selection[0].silent;
// Set the object to be accessible.
fl.getDocumentDOM().selection[0].silent = false;
```

compiledClipInstance.tabIndex

Availability

Flash MX 2004.

Usage

```
compiledClipInstance.tabIndex
```

Description

Property; an integer that is equivalent to the Tab Index field in the Accessibility panel. Creates a tab order in which objects are accessed when the user presses the Tab key.

Example

The following example illustrates getting and setting the tabIndex property:

```
// Get the tabIndex of the object.
var theTabIndex = fl.getDocumentDOM().selection[0].tabIndex;
// Set the tabIndex of the object.
fl.getDocumentDOM().sele ction[0].tabIndex = 1;
```

ComponentInstance object

Inheritance   Element object > Instance object > SymbolInstance object >
ComponentInstance object

Availability
Flash MX 2004.

Description
The ComponentInstance object is a subclass of the SymbolInstance object and represents a
component in a frame. (See SymbolInstance object.)

Property summary for the ComponentInstance object

In addition to all the properties of the SymbolInstance object, the ComponentInstance object
has the following property:

Property	Description
componentInstance.parameters	Read-only; an array of ActionScript 2.0 properties that are accessible from the component Property inspector.

componentInstance.parameters

Availability
Flash MX 2004.

Usage
componentInstance.parameters

Description
Read-only property; an array of ActionScript 2.0 properties that are accessible from the
component Property inspector. See "Parameter object" on page 337.

Example
The following example illustrates getting and setting the parameters property:

```
var parms = fl.getDocumentDOM().selection[0].parameters;
parms[0].value = "some value";
```

See also
Parameter object

componentsPanel object

Availability

Flash MX 2004.

Description

The componentsPanel object, which represents the Components panel, is a property of the flash object (fl) and can be accessed by `fl.componentsPanel`. (See flash object (fl).)

Method summary for the componentsPanel object

You can use the following methods with the componentsPanel object:

Method	Description
`componentsPanel.addItemToDocument()`	Adds the specified component to the document at the specified position.
`componentsPanel.reload()`	Refreshes the Components panel's list of components.

componentsPanel.addItemToDocument()

Availability

Flash MX 2004.

Usage

`componentsPanel.addItemToDocument( position, categoryName, componentName )`

Parameters

position   A point (for example, {x:0, y:100}) that specifies the location at which to add the component. Specify *position* relative to the center point of the component—not the component's registration point.

categoryName   A string that specifies the name of the component category (for example, "Data"). The valid category names are listed in the Components panel.

componentName   A string that specifies the name of the component in the specified category (for example, "WebServiceConnector"). The valid component names are listed in the Components panel.

Returns

Nothing.

Description

Adds the specified component to the document at the specified position.

Examples

The following examples illustrate some ways to use this method:

```
fl.componentsPanel.addItemToDocument({x:0, y:0}, "User Interface",
    "CheckBox");
fl.componentsPanel.addItemToDocument({x:0, y:100}, "Data",
    "WebServiceConnector");
fl.componentsPanel.addItemToDocument({x:0, y:200}, "User Interface",
    "Button");
```

componentsPanel.reload()

Availability

Flash 8.

Usage

```
componentsPanel.reload()
```

Parameters

None.

Returns

A Boolean value of `true` if the Component panel list is refreshed, `false` otherwise.

Description

Method; refreshes the Components panel's list of components.

Example

The following example refreshes the Components panel:

```
fl.componentsPanel.reload();
```

Contour object

Availability

Flash MX 2004.

Description

A Contour object represents a closed path of half edges on the boundary of a shape.

Method summary for the Contour object

You can use the following method with the Contour object:

Property	Description
contour.getHalfEdge()	Returns a HalfEdge object on the contour of the selection.

Property summary for the Contour object

You can use the following properties with the Contour object:

Property	Description
contour.interior	Read-only: the value is true if the contour encloses an area; false otherwise.
contour.orientation	Read-only; an integer indicating the orientation of the contour.

contour.getHalfEdge()

Availability

Flash MX 2004.

Usage

contour.getHalfEdge()

Parameters

None.

Returns

A HalfEdge object.

Description

Method; returns a HalfEdge object on the contour of the selection.

Example

This example traverses all the contours of a selected shape and shows the coordinates of the vertices in the Output panel:

```
// with a shape selected

var elt = fl.getDocumentDOM().selection[0];
elt.beginEdit();

var contourArray = elt.contours;
var contourCount = 0;
for (i=0;  i<contourArray.length;  i++)
{
   var contour = contourArray[i];
   contourCount++;
   var he = contour.getHalfEdge();

   var iStart = he.id;
   var id = 0;
   while (id != iStart)
   {
      // get the next vertex.
      var vrt = he.getVertex();


      var x = vrt.x;
      var y = vrt.y;
      fl.trace("vrt: " + x + ", " + y);

      he = he.getNext();
      id = he.id;
   }
}
elt.endEdit();
```

contour.interior

Availability

Flash MX 2004.

Usage

```
contour.interior
```

Description

Read-only property; the value is `true` if the contour encloses an area; `false` otherwise.

Example

This example traverses all the contours in the selected shape and shows the value of the `interior` property for each contour in the Output panel:

```
var elt = fl.getDocumentDOM().selection[0];
elt.beginEdit();

var contourArray = elt.contours;

var contourCount = 0;
for (i=0;  i<contourArray.length;  i++) {
  var contour = contourArray[i];
  fl.trace("Next Contour, interior:" + contour.interior );
  contourCount++;
}
elt.endEdit();
```

contour.orientation

Availability

Flash MX 2004.

Usage

```
contour.orientation
```

Description

Read-only property; an integer indicating the orientation of the contour. The value of the integer is -1 if the orientation is counterclockwise, 1 if it is clockwise, and 0 if it is a contour with no area.

Example

The following example traverses all the contours of the selected shape and shows the value of the orientation property of each contour in the Output panel:

```
var elt = fl.getDocumentDOM().selection[0];
elt.beginEdit();

var contourArray = elt.contours;

var contourCount = 0;
for (i=0;  i<contourArray.length;  i++) {
  var contour = contourArray[i];
  fl.trace("Next Contour, orientation:" + contour.orientation);
  contourCount++;
}
elt.endEdit();
```

Document object

Availability

Flash MX 2004.

Description

The Document object represents the Stage. That is, only FLA files are considered documents.

Method summary for the Document object

You can use the following methods with the Document object.

Method	Description
document.addDataToDocument()	Stores specified data with a document.
document.addDataToSelection()	Stores specified data with the selected object(s).
document.addFilter()	Applies a filter to the selected objects.
document.addItem()	Adds an item from any open document or library to the specified Document object.
document.addNewLine()	Adds a new path between two points.
document.addNewOval()	Adds a new oval in the specified bounding rectangle.
document.addNewPublishProfile()	Adds a new publish profile and makes it the current one.
document.addNewRectangle()	Adds a new rectangle or rounded rectangle, fitting it into the specified bounds.
document.addNewScene()	Adds a new scene (Timeline object) as the next scene after the currently selected scene and makes the new scene the currently selected scene.
document.addNewText()	Inserts a new empty text field.
document.align()	Aligns the selection.
document.allowScreens()	Use this method before using the document.screenOutline property.
document.arrange()	Arranges the selection on the Stage.
document.breakApart()	Performs a break-apart operation on the current selection.

Method	Description
document.canEditSymbol()	Indicates whether Edit Symbols menu and functionality is enabled.
document.canRevert()	Determines whether you can use the document.revert() or fl.revertDocument() method successfully.
document.canTestMovie()	Determines whether you can use the document.testMovie() method successfully.
document.canTestScene()	Determines whether you can use the document.testScene() method successfully.
document.changeFilterOrder()	Changes the index of the filter in the Filter list.
document.clipCopy()	Copies the current selection from the document to the Clipboard.
document.clipCut()	Cuts the current selection from the document and writes it to the Clipboard.
document.clipPaste()	Pastes the contents of the Clipboard into the document.
document.close()	Closes the specified document.
document.convertLinesToFills()	Converts lines to fills on the selected objects.
document.convertToSymbol()	Converts the selected Stage item(s) to a new symbol.
document.crop()	Uses top selected drawing object to crop all selected drawing objects underneath it.
document.deleteEnvelope()	Deletes the envelope (bounding box that contains one or more objects) from the selected object.
document.deletePublishProfile()	Deletes the currently active profile, if there is more than one.
document.deleteScene()	Deletes the current scene (Timeline object) and, if the deleted scene was not the last one, sets the next scene as the current Timeline object.
document.deleteSelection()	Deletes the current selection on the Stage.
document.disableAllFilters()	Disables all filters on the selected objects.
document.disableFilter()	Disables the specified filter in the Filters list.
document.disableOtherFilters()	Disables all filters except the one at the specified position in the Filters list.
document.distribute()	Distributes the selection.

Method	Description
document.distributeToLayers()	Performs a distribute-to-layers operation on the current selection; equivalent to selecting Distribute to Layers.
document.documentHasData()	Checks the document for persistent data with the specified name.
document.duplicatePublishProfile()	Duplicates the currently active profile and gives the duplicate version focus.
document.duplicateScene()	Makes a copy of the currently selected scene, giving the new scene a unique name and making it the current scene.
document.duplicateSelection()	Duplicates the selection on the Stage.
document.editScene()	Makes the specified scene the currently selected scene for editing.
document.enableAllFilters()	Enables all the filters on the Filters list for the selected object(s).
document.enableFilter()	Enables the specified filter for the selected object(s).
document.enterEditMode()	Switches the authoring tool into the editing mode specified by the parameter.
document.exitEditMode()	Exits from symbol-editing mode and returns focus to the next level up from the editing mode.
document.exportPNG()	Exports the document as one or more PNG files.
document.exportPublishProfile()	Exports the currently active profile to an XML file.
document.exportSWF()	Exports the document in the Flash SWF format.
document.getAlignToDocument()	Identical to retrieving the value of the To Stage button in the Align panel.
document.getBlendMode()	Returns a string that specifies the blend mode for the selected object(s).
document.getCustomFill()	Retrieves the fill object of the selected shape or, if specified, the Tools panel and Property inspector.
document.getCustomStroke()	Returns the stroke object of the selected shape or, if specified, the Tools panel and Property inspector.
document.getDataFromDocument()	Retrieves the value of the specified data.
document.getElementProperty()	Gets the specified Element property for the current selection.

Method	Description
document.getElementTextAttr()	Gets a specified TextAttrs property of the selected text objects.
document.getFilters()	Returns an array that contains the list of filters applied to the currently selected object(s).
document.getMetadata()	Returns a string containing the XML metadata associated with the document.
document.getSelectionRect()	Gets the bounding rectangle of the current selection.
document.getTextString()	Gets the currently selected text.
document.getTimeline()	Retrieves the current Timeline object in the document.
document.getTransformationPoint()	Gets the location of the transformation point of the current selection.
document.group()	Converts the current selection to a group.
document.importPublishProfile()	Imports a profile from a file.
document.importFile()	Imports a file into the document.
document.importSWF()	Imports a SWF file into the document.
document.intersect()	Creates an intersection drawing object from all selected drawing objects.
document.match()	Makes the size of the selected objects the same.
document.mouseClick()	Performs a mouse click from the arrow tool.
document.mouseDblClk()	Performs a double mouse click from the arrow tool.
document.moveSelectedBezierPointsBy()	If the selection contains at least one path with at least one Bézier point selected, this method moves all selected Bézier points on all selected paths by the specified amount.
document.moveSelectionBy()	Moves selected objects by a specified distance.
document.optimizeCurves()	Optimizes smoothing for the current selection, allowing multiple passes, if specified, for optimal smoothing; equivalent to selecting Modify › Shape › Optimize.
document.publish()	Publishes the document according to the active Publish Settings (File › Publish Settings); equivalent to selecting File › Publish.

Method	Description
document.punch()	Uses top selected drawing object to punch through all selected drawing objects underneath it.
document.removeAllFilters()	Removes all filters from the selected object(s).<
document.removeDataFromDocument()	Removes persistent data with the specified name that has been attached to the document.
document.removeDataFromSelection()	Removes persistent data with the specified name that has been attached to the selection.
document.removeFilter()	Removes the specified filter from the Filters list of the selected object(s).
document.renamePublishProfile()	Renames the current profile.
document.renameScene()	Renames the currently selected scene in the Scenes panel.
document.reorderScene()	Moves the specified scene before another specified scene.
document.resetTransformation()	Resets the transformation matrix; equivalent to selecting Modify > Transform > Remove transform.
document.revert()	Reverts the specified document to its previously saved version; equivalent to selecting File > Revert.
document.rotateSelection()	Rotates the selection by a specified number of degrees.
document.save()	Saves the document in its default location; equivalent to selecting File > Save.
document.saveAndCompact()	Saves and compacts the file; equivalent to selecting File > Save and Compact.
document.scaleSelection()	Scales the selection by a specified amount; equivalent to using the Free Transform tool to scale the object.
document.selectAll()	Selects all items on the Stage; equivalent to pressing Control+A (Windows) or Command+A (Macintosh) or selecting Edit > Select All.
document.selectNone()	Deselects any selected items.
document.setAlignToDocument()	Sets the preferences for document.align(), document.distribute(),document.match(), and document.space() to act on the document; equivalent to enabling the To Stage button in the Align panel.

Method	Description
document.setBlendMode()	Sets the blend mode for the selected objects.
document.setCustomFill()	Sets the fill settings for the Tools panel, Property inspector, and any selected shapes.
document.setCustomStroke()	Sets the stroke settings for the Tools panel, Property inspector, and any selected shapes.
document.setElementProperty()	Sets the specified Element property on selected object(s) in the document.
document.setElementTextAttr()	Sets the specified TextAttrs property of the selected text items to the specified value.
document.setFillColor()	Changes the fill color of the selection to the specified color.
document.setFilterProperty()	Sets a specified filter property for the currently selected object(s).
document.setFilters()	Applies filters to the selected objects .
document.setInstanceAlpha()	Sets the opacity of the instance.
document.setInstanceBrightness()	Sets the brightness for the instance.
document.setInstanceTint()	Sets the tint for the instance.
document.setMetadata()	Sets the XML metadata for the specified document, overwriting any existing metadata.
document.setSelectionBounds()	Moves and resizes the selection in a single operation.
document.setSelectionRect()	Draws a rectangular selection marquee relative to the Stage, using the specified coordinates.
document.setStroke()	Sets the color, width, and style of the selected strokes.
document.setStrokeColor()	Changes the stroke color of the selection to the specified color.
document.setStrokeSize()	Changes the stroke size of the selection to the specified size.
document.setStrokeStyle()	Changes the stroke style of the selection to the specified style.
document.setTextRectangle()	Changes the bounding rectangle for the selected text item to the specified size.

Method	Description
document.setTextSelection()	Sets the text selection of the currently selected text field to the values specified by the *startIndex* and *endIndex* values.
document.setTextString()	Inserts a string of text.
document.setTransformationPoint()	Moves the transformation point of the current selection.
document.skewSelection()	Skews the selection by a specified amount.
document.smoothSelection()	Smooths the curve of each selected fill outline or curved line.
document.space()	Spaces the objects in the selection evenly.
document.straightenSelection()	Straightens the currently selected strokes; equivalent to using the Straighten button in the Tools panel.
document.swapElement()	Swaps the current selection with the specified one.
document.swapStrokeAndFill()	Swaps the Stroke and Fill colors.
document.testMovie()	Executes a Test Movie operation on the document.
document.testScene()	Executes a Test Scene operation on the current scene of the document.
document.traceBitmap()	Performs a trace bitmap on the current selection; equivalent to selecting Modify › Bitmap › Trace Bitmap.
document.transformSelection()	Performs a general transformation on the current selection by applying the matrix specified in the arguments.
document.unGroup()	Ungroups the current selection.
document.union()	Combines all selected shapes into a drawing object.
document.unlockAllElements()	Unlocks all locked elements on the currently selected frame.
document.xmlPanel()	Posts a XMLUI dialog box.

Property summary for the Document object

You can use the following properties with the Document object.

Property	Description
document.accName	A string that is equivalent to the Name field in the Accessibility panel.
document.autoLabel	A Boolean value that is equivalent to the Auto Label check box in the Accessibility panel.
document.backgroundColor	A string, hexadecimal value, or integer that represents the background color.
document.currentPublishProfile	A string that specifies the name of the active publish profile for the specified document.
document.currentTimeline	An integer that specifies the index of the active timeline.
document.description	A string that is equivalent to the Description field in the Accessibility panel.
document.forceSimple	A Boolean value that specifies whether the children of the specified object are accessible.
document.frameRate	A float value that specifies the number of frames displayed per second when the SWF file plays; the default is 12.
document.height	An integer that specifies the height of the document (Stage) in pixels.
document.library	Read-only; the library object for a document.
document.livePreview	A Boolean value that specifies if Live Preview is enabled.
document.name	Read-only; a string that represents the name of a document (FLA file).
document.path	Read-only; a string that represents the path of the document.
document.publishProfiles	Read-only; an array of the publish profile names for the document.
document.screenOutline	Read-only; the current ScreenOutline object for the document.
document.selection	An array of the selected objects in the document.
document.silent	A Boolean value that specifies whether the object is accessible.

Property	Description
document.timelines	Read-only; an array of Timeline objects (see Timeline object).
document.viewMatrix	Read-only; a Matrix object.
document.width	An integer that specifies the width of the document (Stage) in pixels.
document.zoomFactor	Specifies the zoom percent of the Stage at author time.

document.accName

Availability

Flash MX 2004.

Usage

```
document.accName
```

Description

Property; a string that is equivalent to the Name field in the Accessibility panel. Screen readers identify objects by reading the name aloud.

Example

The following example sets the accessibility name of the document to `"Main Movie"`:

```
fl.getDocumentDOM().accName = "Main Movie";
```

The following example gets the accessibility name of the document:

```
fl.trace(fl.getDocumentDOM().accName);
```

document.addDataToDocument()

Availability

Flash MX 2004.

Usage

```
document.addDataToDocument( name, type, data )
```

Parameters

name   A string that specifies the name of the data to add.

type   A string that defines the type of data to add. Acceptable values are *type* are
"integer", "integerArray", "double", "doubleArray", "string", and "byteArray".

data   the value to add. Valid types depend on the *type* parameter.

Returns

Nothing.

Description

Method; stores specified data with a document. Data is written to the FLA file and is available
to JavaScript when the file reopens.

Example

The following example adds an integer value of 12 to the current document:

```
fl.getDocumentDOM().addDataToDocument("myData", "integer", 12);
```

The following example returns the value of the data named "myData" and displays the result
in the Output panel:

```
fl.trace(fl.getDocumentDOM().getDataFromDocument("myData"));
```

See also

document.getDataFromDocument(), document.removeDataFromDocument()

document.addDataToSelection()

Availability

Flash MX 2004.

Usage

```
document.addDataToSelection( name, type, data )
```

Parameters

name   A string that specifies the name of the persistent data.

type   Defines the type of data. Acceptable values are "integer", "integerArray",
"double", "doubleArray", "string", and "byteArray".

data   The value to add. Valid types depend on the *type* parameter.

Returns

Nothing.

Description

Method; stores specified data with the selected object(s). Data is written to the FLA file and is available to JavaScript when the file reopens. Only symbols and bitmaps support persistent data.

Example

The following example adds an integer value of 12 to the selected object:

```
fl.getDocumentDOM().addDataToSelection("myData", "integer", 12);
```

See also

`document.removeDataFromSelection()`

document.addFilter()

Availability

Flash 8.

Usage

```
document.addFilter( filterName )
```

Parameters

filterName   A string specifying the filter to be added to the Filter list and enabled for the selected object(s). Acceptable values are `"adjustColorFilter"`, `"bevelFilter"`, `"blurFilter"`, `"dropShadowFilter"`, `"glowFilter"`, `"gradientBevelFilter"`, and `"gradientGlowFilter"`.

Returns

Nothing.

Description

Method; applies a filter to the selected objects and places the filter at the end of the Filter list.

Example

The following example applies a glow filter to the selected object(s):

```
fl.getDocumentDOM().addFilter("glowFilter");
```

See also

`document.changeFilterOrder()`, `document.disableFilter()`, `document.enableFilter()`, `document.getFilters()`, `document.removeFilter()`, `document.setBlendMode()`, `document.setFilterProperty()`

document.addItem()

Availability

Flash MX 2004.

Usage

```
document.addItem( position, item )
```

Parameters

position   A point that specifies the *x* and *y* coordinates of the location at which to add the item. It uses the center of a symbol or the upper-left corner of a bitmap or video.

item   An Item object that specifies the item to add and the library from which to add it (see Item object).

Returns

A Boolean value: `true` if successful; `false` otherwise.

Description

Method; adds an item from any open document or library to the specified Document object.

Example

The following example adds the first item from the library to the first document at the specified location for the selected symbol, bitmap, or video:

```
var item = fl.documents[0].library.items[0];
fl.documents[0].addItem({x:0,y:0}, item);
```

The following example adds the symbol `myMovieClip` from the current document's library to the current document:

```
var itemIndex = fl.getDocumentDOM().library.findItemIndex("myMovieClip");
var theItem = fl.getDocumentDOM().library.items[itemIndex];
fl.getDocumentDOM().addItem({x:0,y:0}, theItem);
```

The following example adds the symbol `myMovieClip` from the second document in the documents array to the third document in the documents array:

```
var itemIndex = fl.documents[1].library.findItemIndex("myMovieClip");
var theItem = fl.documents[1].library.items[itemIndex];
fl.documents[2].addItem({x:0,y:0}, theItem);
```

document.addNewLine()

Availability

Flash MX 2004.

Usage

```
document.addNewLine( startPoint, endpoint )
```

Parameters

startpoint   A pair of floating-point numbers that specify the *x* and *y* coordinates where the line starts.

endpoint   A pair of floating-point numbers that specify the *x* and *y* coordinates where the line ends.

Returns

Nothing.

Description

Method; adds a new path between two points. The method uses the document's current stroke attributes and adds the path on the current frame and current layer. This method works in the same way as clicking on the line tool and drawing a line.

Example

The following example adds a line between the specified starting point and ending point:

```
fl.getDocumentDOM().addNewLine({x:216.7, y:122.3}, {x:366.8, y:165.8});
```

document.addNewOval()

Availability

Flash MX 2004.

Usage

```
document.addNewOval( boundingRectangle [, bSuppressFill [, bSuppressStroke
   ]] )
```

Parameters

boundingRectangle A rectangle that specifies the bounds of the oval to be added. For information on the format of *boundingRectangle*, see `document.addNewRectangle()`.

bSuppressFill A Boolean value that, if set to `true`, causes the method to create the shape without a fill. The default value is `false`. This parameter is optional.

bSuppressStroke A Boolean value that, if set to `true`, causes the method to create the shape without a stroke. The default value is `false`. This parameter is optional.

Returns

Nothing.

Description

Method; adds a new oval in the specified bounding rectangle. This method performs the same operation as the oval tool. The method uses the document's current default stroke and fill attributes and adds the oval on the current frame and layer. If *bSuppressFill* is set to `true`, the oval is drawn without a fill. If *bSuppressStroke* is set to `true`, the oval is drawn without a stroke. If both *bSuppressFill* and *bSuppressStroke* are set to `true`, the method has no effect.

Example

The following example adds a new oval within the specified coordinates; it is 164 pixels in width and 178 pixels in height:

```
flash.getDocumentDOM().addNewOval({left:72,top:50,right:236,bottom:228});
```

The following example draws the oval without a fill:

```
flash.getDocumentDOM().addNewOval({left:72,top:50,right:236,bottom:228},
    true);
```

The following example draws the oval without a stroke:

```
flash.getDocumentDOM().addNewOval({left:72,top:50,right:236,bottom:228},
    false, true);
```

document.addNewPublishProfile()

Availability

Flash MX 2004.

Usage

```
document.addNewPublishProfile( [profileName ] )
```

Parameters

profileName   The unique name of the new profile. If you do not specify a name, a default name is provided. This parameter is optional.

Returns

An integer that is the index of the new profile in the profiles list. Returns -1 if a new profile cannot be created.

Description

Method; adds a new publish profile and makes it the current one.

Example

The following example adds a new publish profile with a default name and then displays the name of the profile in the Output panel:

```
fl.getDocumentDOM().addNewPublishProfile();
fl.outputPanel.trace(fl.getDocumentDOM().currentPublishProfile);
```

The following example adds a new publish profile with the name "my profile":

```
fl.getDocumentDOM().addNewPublishProfile("my profile");
```

See also

```
document.deletePublishProfile()
```

document.addNewRectangle()

Availability

Flash MX 2004.

Usage

```
document.addNewRectangle( boundingRectangle, roundness
  [, bSuppressFill [, bSuppressStroke ] ] )
```

Parameters

boundingRectangle   A rectangle that specifies the bounds within which the new rectangle is added, in the format {left:value1,top:value2,right:value3,bottom:value4}. The left and top values specify the location of the upper-left corner (e.g., left:0,top:0 represents the upper-left of the Stage), and the right and bottom values specify the location of the lower-right corner. Therefore, the width of the rectangle is the difference in value between left and right, and the height of the rectangle is the difference in value between top and bottom.

In other words, the rectangle bounds do not all correspond to the values shown in the Property inspector. The left and top values correspond to the X and Y values in the Property inspector, respectively. However, the right and bottom values don't correspond to the W and H values in the Property inspector. For example, consider a rectangle with the following bounds:

{left:10,top:10,right:50,bottom:100}

This rectangle would display the following values in the Property inspector:

X = 10, Y = 10, W = 40, H = 90

roundness   An integer value from 0 to 999 that specifies the roundness to use for the corners. The value is specified as number of points. The greater the value, the greater the roundness.

bSuppressFill   A Boolean value that, if set to true, causes the method to create the shape without a fill. The default value is false. This parameter is optional.

bSuppressStroke   A Boolean value that, if set to true, causes the method to create the rectangle without a stroke. The default value is false. This parameter is optional.

Returns

Nothing.

Description

Method; adds a new rectangle or rounded rectangle, fitting it into the specified bounds. This method performs the same operation as the rectangle tool. The method uses the document's current default stroke and fill attributes and adds the rectangle on the current frame and layer. If the *bSuppressFill* parameter is set to true, the rectangle is drawn without a fill. If the *bSuppressStroke* parameter is set to true, the rectangle is drawn without a stroke. If both *bSuppressFill* and *bSuppressStroke* are set to true, the method has no effect.

Example

The following example adds a new rectangle with no rounding on the corners within the specified coordinates; it is 100 pixels in width and in height:

```
flash.getDocumentDOM().addNewRectangle({left:0,top:0,right:100,bottom:100},
   0);
```

The following example adds a new rectangle with no rounding on the corners and without a fill; it is 100 pixels in width and 200 in height:

```
flash.getDocumentDOM().addNewRectangle({left:10,top:10,right:110,bottom:210
   },0, true);
```

The following example adds a new rectangle with no rounding on the corners and without a stroke; it is 200 pixels in width and 100 in height:

```
flash.getDocumentDOM().addNewRectangle({left:20,top:20,right:220,bottom:120
   },0, false, true);
```

document.addNewScene()

Availability

Flash MX 2004.

Usage

```
document.addNewScene( [name] )
```

Parameters

name   Specifies the name of the scene. If you do not specify a name, a new scene name is generated.

Returns

A Boolean value: `true` if the scene is added successfully; `false` otherwise.

Description

Method; adds a new scene (`Timeline object`) as the next scene after the currently selected scene and makes the new scene the currently selected scene. If the specified scene name already exists, the scene is not added and the method returns an error.

Example

The following example adds a new scene named `myScene` after the current scene in the current document. The variable `success` will be `true` when the new scene is created; `false` otherwise.

```
var success = flash.getDocumentDOM().addNewScene("myScene");
```

The following example adds a new scene using the default naming convention. If only one scene exists, the newly created scene is named `"Scene 2"`.

```
fl.getDocumentDOM().addNewScene();
```

document.addNewText()

Availability

Flash MX 2004.

Usage

```
document.addNewText( boundingRectangle )
```

Parameters

boundingRectangle   Specifies the size and location of the text field; for information on the format of *boundingRectangle*, see `document.addNewRectangle()`. It should be followed by calling `document.seTextString()` to populate the new text box.

Returns

Nothing.

Description

Method; inserts a new empty text field.

Example

The following example creates a new text field in the upper-left corner of the Stage and then sets the text string to `"Hello World"`:

```
fl.getDocumentDOM().addNewText({left:0, top:0, right:100, bottom:100});
fl.getDocumentDOM().setTextString('Hello World!');
```

See also

```
document.setTextString()
```

document.align()

Availability

Flash MX 2004.

Usage

```
document.align( alignmode [, bUseDocumentBounds ] )
```

Parameters

alignmode   A string that specifies how to align the selection. Acceptable values are `"left"`, `"right"`, `"top"`, `"bottom"`, `"vertical center"`, and `"horizontal center"`.

bUseDocumentBounds   A Boolean value that, if set to `true`, causes the method to align to the bounds of the document. Otherwise, the method uses the bounds of the selected objects. The default is `false`. This parameter is optional.

Returns

Nothing.

Description

Method; aligns the selection.

Example

The following example aligns objects to left and to the Stage. This is equivalent to turning on the To Stage setting in the Align panel and clicking the Align to Left button:

```
fl.getDocumentDOM().align("left", true);
```

See also

```
document.distribute(), document.getAlignToDocument(),
document.setAlignToDocument()
```

document.allowScreens()

Availability

Flash MX 2004.

Usage

```
document.allowScreens()
```

Parameters

None.

Returns

A Boolean value: `true` if `document.screenOutline` can be used safely; `false` otherwise.

Description

Method; use before using the `document.screenOutline` property. If this method returns the value `true`, you can safely access `document.screenOutline`; Flash displays an error if you access `document.screenOutline` in a document without screens.

Example

The following example determines whether `screens` methods can be used in the current document:

```
if(fl.getDocumentDOM().allowScreens()) {
  fl.trace("screen outline is available.");
}
else {
  fl.trace("whoops, no screens.");
}
```

See also

`document.screenOutline`

document.arrange()

Availability

Flash MX 2004.

Usage

`document.arrange( arrangeMode )`

Parameters

arrangeMode   Specifies the direction in which to move the selection. Acceptable values are `"back"`, `"backward"`, `"forward"`, and `"front"`. It provides the same capabilities as these options provide on the Modify >Arrange menu.

Returns

Nothing.

Description

Method; arranges the selection on the Stage. This method applies only to non-shape objects.

Example

The following example moves the current selection to the front:

```
fl.getDocumentDOM().arrange("front");
```

document.autoLabel

Availability

Flash MX 2004.

Usage

```
document.autoLabel
```

Description

Property; a Boolean value that is equivalent to the Auto Label check box in the Accessibility panel. You can use this property to tell Flash to automatically label objects on the Stage with the text associated with them.

Example

The following example gets the value of the `autoLabel` property and displays the result in the Output panel:

```
var isAutoLabel = fl.getDocumentDOM().autoLabel;
fl.trace(isAutoLabel);
```

The following example sets the `autoLabel` property to `true`, telling Flash to automatically label objects on the Stage:

```
fl.getDocumentDOM().autoLabel = true;
```

document.backgroundColor

Availability

Flash MX 2004.

Usage

```
document.backgroundColor
```

Description

Property; the color of the background, in one of the following formats:

- A string in the format "#RRGGBB" or "#RRGGBBAA"
- A hexadecimal number in the format 0xRRGGBB
- An integer that represents the decimal equivalent of a hexadecimal number

Example

The following example sets the background color to black:

```
fl.getDocumentDOM().backgroundColor = '#000000';
```

document.breakApart()

Availability

Flash MX 2004.

Usage

```
document.breakApart()
```

Parameters

None.

Returns

Nothing.

Description

Method; performs a break-apart operation on the current selection.

Example

The following example breaks apart the current selection:

```
fl.getDocumentDOM().breakApart();
```

document.canEditSymbol()

Availability

Flash MX 2004.

Usage

```
document.canEditSymbol()
```

Parameters

None.

Returns

A Boolean value: true if the Edit Symbols menu and functionality are available for use; false otherwise.

Description

Method; indicates whether the Edit Symbols menu and functionality are enabled. This is not related to whether the selection can be edited. This method should not be used to test whether `fl.getDocumentDOM().enterEditMode()` is allowed.

Example

The following example displays in the Output panel the state of the Edit Symbols menu and functionality:

```
fl.trace("fl.getDocumentDOM().canEditSymbol() returns: " +
  fl.getDocumentDOM().canEditSymbol());
```

document.canRevert()

Availability

Flash MX 2004.

Usage

```
document.canRevert()
```

Parameters

None.

Returns

A Boolean value: `true` if you can use the `document.revert()` or `fl.revertDocument()` methods successfully; `false` otherwise.

Description

Method; determines whether you can use the `document.revert()` or `fl.revertDocument()` method successfully.

Example

The following example checks whether the current document can revert to the previously saved version. If so, `fl.getDocumentDOM().revert()` restores the previously saved version.

```
if(fl.getDocumentDOM().canRevert()){
  fl.getDocumentDOM().revert();
}
```

document.canTestMovie()

Availability

Flash MX 2004.

Usage

```
document.canTestMovie()
```

Parameters

None.

Returns

A Boolean value: `true` if you can use the `document.testMovie()` method successfully: `false` otherwise.

Description

Method; determines whether you can use the `document.testMovie()` method successfully.

Example

The following example tests whether `fl.getDocumentDOM().testMovie()` can be used. If so, it calls the method.

```
if(fl.getDocumentDOM().canTestMovie()){
  fl.getDocumentDOM().testMovie();
}
```

See also

`document.canTestScene()`, `document.testScene()`

document.canTestScene()

Availability

Flash MX 2004.

Usage

```
document.canTestScene()
```

Parameters

None.

Returns

A Boolean value: `true` if you can use the `document.testScene()` method successfully; `false` otherwise.

Description

Method; determines whether you can use the `document.testScene()` method successfully.

Example

The following example first tests whether `fl.getDocumentDOM().testScene()` can be used successfully. If so, it calls the method.

```
if(fl.getDocumentDOM().canTestScene()){
   fl.getDocumentDOM().testScene();
}
```

See also

`document.canTestMovie()`, `document.testMovie()`

document.changeFilterOrder()

Availability

Flash 8.

Usage

`document.changeFilterOrder( oldIndex, newIndex )`

Parameters

`oldIndex`   An integer that represents the current zero-based index position of the filter you want to reposition in the Filters list.

`newIndex`   An integer that represents the new index position of the filter in the list.

Returns

Nothing.

Description

Method; changes the index of the filter in the Filter list. Any filters above or below `newIndex` are shifted up or down accordingly. For example, using the filters shown below, if you issue the command `fl.getDocumentDOM().changeFilterOrder(3, 0)`, the filters are rearranged as follows:

Before: `blurFilter, dropShadowFilter, glowFilter, gradientBevelFilter`
After: `gradientBevelFilter, blurFilter, dropShadowFilter, glowFilter`

If you then issue the command `fl.getDocumentDOM().changeFilterOrder(0, 2)`, the filters are rearranged as follows:

> **Before:** `gradientBevelFilter, blurFilter, dropShadowFilter, glowFilter`
> **After:** `blurFilter, dropShadowFilter, gradientBevelFilter, glowFilter`

Example

The following example moves the filter that is currently in the second position in the Filter list to the first position:

```
fl.getDocumentDOM().changeFilterOrder(1,0);
```

See also

`document.addFilter()`, `document.disableFilter()`, `document.enableFilter()`, `document.getFilters()`, `document.removeFilter()`, Filter object

document.clipCopy()

Availability

Flash MX 2004.

Usage

```
document.clipCopy()
```

Parameters

None.

Returns

Nothing.

Description

Method; copies the current selection from the document to the Clipboard.

Example

The following example copies the current selection from the document to the Clipboard:

```
fl.getDocumentDOM().clipCopy();
```

document.clipCut()

Availability

Flash MX 2004.

Usage

```
document.clipCut()
```

Parameters

None.

Returns

Nothing.

Description

Method; cuts the current selection from the document and writes it to the Clipboard.

Example

The following example cuts the current selection from the document and writes it to the Clipboard:

```
fl.getDocumentDOM().clipCut();
```

document.clipPaste()

Availability

Flash MX 2004.

Usage

```
document.clipPaste( [bInPlace] )
```

Parameters

bInPlace A Boolean value that, when set to `true`, causes the method to perform a paste-in-place operation. The default value is `false`, which causes the method to perform a paste operation to the center of the document. This parameter is optional.

Returns

Nothing.

Description

Method; pastes the contents of the Clipboard into the document.

Example

The following examples pastes the Clipboard contents to the center of the document:

```
fl.getDocumentDOM().clipPaste();
```

The following example pastes the Clipboard contents in place in the current document:

```
fl.getDocumentDOM().clipPaste(true);
```

document.close()

Availability

Flash MX 2004.

Usage

```
document.close( [bPromptToSaveChanges] )
```

Parameters

bPromptToSaveChanges   A Boolean value that, when set to `true`, causes the method to prompt the user with a dialog box if there are unsaved changes in the document. If *bPromptToSaveChanges* is set to `false`, the user is not prompted to save any changed documents. The default value is `true`. This parameter is optional.

Returns

Nothing.

Description

Method; closes the specified document.

Example

The following example closes the current document and prompts the user with a dialog box to save changes:

```
fl.getDocumentDOM().close();
```

The following example closes the current document without saving changes:

```
fl.getDocumentDOM().close(false);
```

document.convertLinesToFills()

Availability

Flash MX 2004.

Usage

```
document.convertLinesToFills()
```

Parameters

None.

Returns

Nothing.

Description

Method; converts lines to fills on the selected objects.

Example

The following example converts the current selected lines to fills:

```
fl.getDocumentDOM().convertLinesToFills();
```

document.convertToSymbol()

Availability

Flash MX 2004.

Usage

```
document.convertToSymbol( type, name, registrationPoint )
```

Parameters

type   A string that specifies the type of symbol to create. Acceptable values are "movie clip", "button", and "graphic".

name   A string that specifies the name for the new symbol, which must be unique. You can submit an empty string to have this method create a unique symbol name for you.

registration point   Specifies the point that represents the 0,0 location for the symbol. Acceptable values are: "top left", "top center", "top right", "center left", "center", "center right", "bottom left", "bottom center", and "bottom right".

Returns

An object for the newly created symbol, or null if it cannot create the symbol.

Description

Method; converts the selected Stage item(s) to a new symbol. For information on defining linkage and shared asset properties for a symbol, see Item object.

Example

The following examples create a movie clip symbol with a specified name, a button symbol with a specified name, and a movie clip symbol with a default name:

```
newMc = fl.getDocumentDOM().convertToSymbol("movie clip", "mcSymbolName",
    "top left");
newButton = fl.getDocumentDOM().convertToSymbol("button", "btnSymbolName",
    "bottom right");
newClipWithDefaultName = fl.getDocumentDOM().convertToSymbol("movie clip",
    "", "top left");
```

document.crop()

Availability

Flash 8.

Usage

```
document.crop()
```

Parameters

None.

Returns

A Boolean value: true if successful; false otherwise.

Description

Method; uses the top selected drawing object to crop all selected drawing objects underneath it. This method returns false if there are no drawing objects selected or if any of the selected items are not drawing objects.

Example

The following example crops the currently selected objects:

```
fl.getDocumentDOM().crop();
```

See also

document.deleteEnvelope(), document.intersect(), document.punch(),
document.union(), shape.isDrawingObject

document.currentPublishProfile

Availability

Flash MX 2004.

Usage

```
document.currentPublishProfile
```

Description

Property; a string that specifies the name of the active publish profile for the specified document.

Example

The following example adds a new publish profile with the default name and then displays the name of the profile in the Output panel:

```
fl.getDocumentDOM().addNewPublishProfile();
fl.outputPanel.trace(fl.getDocumentDOM().currentPublishProfile);
```

The following example changes the selected publish profile to "Default":

```
fl.getDocumentDOM().currentPublishProfile = "Default";
```

document.currentTimeline

Availability

Flash MX 2004.

Usage

```
document.currentTimeline
```

Description

Property; an integer that specifies the index of the active timeline. You can set the active timeline by changing the value of this property; the effect is almost equivalent to calling `document.editScene()`. The only difference is that you don't get an error message if the index of the timeline is not valid; the property is simply not set, which causes silent failure.

Example

The following example displays the index of the current timeline.

```
var myCurrentTL = fl.getDocumentDOM().currentTimeline;
fl.trace("The index of the current timeline is: "+ myCurrentTL);
```

The following example changes the active timeline from the main timeline to a scene named "myScene".

```
var i = 0;
var curTimelines = fl.getDocumentDOM().timelines;
while(i < fl.getDocumentDOM().timelines.length){
  if(curTimelines[i].name == "myScene"){
    fl.getDocumentDOM().currentTimeline = i;
  }
  ++i;
}
```

See also

document.getTimeline()

document.deleteEnvelope()

Availability

Flash 8.

Usage

document.deleteEnvelope();

Parameters

None.

Returns

A Boolean value: true if successful; false otherwise.

Description

Method; deletes the envelope (bounding box that contains one or more objects) from the selected objects.

Example

The following example deletes the envelope from the selected objects:

fl.getDocumentDOM().deleteEnvelope();

See also

document.crop(), document.intersect(), document.punch(), document.union(), shape.isDrawingObject

document.deletePublishProfile()

Availability

Flash MX 2004.

Usage

```
document.deletePublishProfile()
```

Parameters

None.

Returns

An integer that is the index of the new current profile. If a new profile is not available, the method leaves the current profile unchanged and returns its index.

Description

Method; deletes the currently active profile, if there is more than one. There must be at least one profile left.

Example

The following example deletes the currently active profile, if there is more than one, and displays the index of the new currently active profile:

```
alert(fl.getDocumentDOM().deletePublishProfile());
```

See also

```
document.addNewPublishProfile()
```

document.deleteScene()

Availability

Flash MX 2004.

Usage

```
document.deleteScene()
```

Parameters

None.

Returns

A Boolean value: true if the scene is successfully deleted; false otherwise.

Description

Method; deletes the current scene (Timeline object) and, if the deleted scene was not the last one, sets the next scene as the current Timeline object. If the deleted scene was the last one, it sets the first object as the current Timeline object. If only one Timeline object (scene) exists, it returns the value `false`.

Example

Assuming there are three scenes (`Scene0`, `Scene1`, and `Scene2`) in the current document, the following example makes `Scene2` the current scene and then deletes it:

```
fl.getDocumentDOM().editScene(2);
var success = fl.getDocumentDOM().deleteScene();
```

document.deleteSelection()

Availability

Flash MX 2004.

Usage

```
document.deleteSelection()
```

Parameters

None.

Returns

Nothing.

Description

Method; deletes the current selection on the Stage. Displays an error message if there is no selection.

Example

The following example deletes the current selection in the document:

```
fl.getDocumentDOM().deleteSelection();
```

document.description

Availability

Flash MX 2004.

Usage

```
document.description
```

Description

Property; a string that is equivalent to the Description field in the Accessibility panel. The description is read by the screen reader.

Example

The following example sets the description of the document:

```
fl.getDocumentDOM().description= "This is the main movie";
```

The following example gets the description of the document and displays it in the Output panel:

```
fl.trace(fl.getDocumentDOM().description);
```

document.disableAllFilters()

Availability

Flash 8.

Usage

```
document.disableAllFilters()
```

Parameters

None.

Returns

Nothing.

Description

Method; disables all filters on the selected objects.

Example

The following example disables all filters on the selected objects:

```
fl.getDocumentDOM().disableAllFilters();
```

See also

document.addFilter(), document.changeFilterOrder(), document.disableFilter(), document.disableOtherFilters(), document.enableAllFilters(), document.getFilters(), document.removeAllFilters(), Filter object

document.disableFilter()

Availability

Flash 8.

Usage

```
document.disableFilter( filterIndex )
```

Parameters

filterIndex   An integer representing the zero-based index of the filter in the Filter list.

Returns

Nothing.

Description

Method; disables the specified filter in the Filters list.

Example

The following example disables the first and third filters (index values of 0 and 2) in the Filters list from the selected object(s):

```
fl.getDocumentDOM().disableFilter(0);
fl.getDocumentDOM().disableFilter(2);
```

See also

document.addFilter(), document.changeFilterOrder(), document.disableAllFilters(), document.disableOtherFilters(), document.enableFilter(), document.getFilters(), document.removeFilter(), Filter object

document.disableOtherFilters()

Availability

Flash 8.

Usage

```
document.disableOtherFilters( enabledFilterIndex )
```

Parameters

enabledFilterIndex   An integer representing the zero-based index of the filter that should remain enabled after other filters are disabled.

Returns

Nothing.

Description

Method; disables all filters except the one at the specified position in the Filters list.

Example

The following example disables all filters except the second filter in the list (index value of 1):

```
fl.getDocumentDom().disableOtherFilters(1);
```

See also

```
document.addFilter(), document.changeFilterOrder(),
document.disableAllFilters(), document.disableFilter(),
document.enableFilter(), document.getFilters(), document.removeFilter(), Filter
object
```

document.distribute()

Availability

Flash MX 2004.

Usage

```
document.distribute( distributemode [, bUseDocumentBounds ] )
```

Parameters

distributemode   A string that specifies where to distribute the selected object. Acceptable values are `"left edge"`, `"horizontal center"`, `"right edge"`, `"top edge"`, `"vertical center"`, and `"bottom edge"`.

bUseDocumentBounds   A Boolean value that, when set to `true`, distributes the selected objects using the bounds of the document. Otherwise, the method uses the bounds of the selected object. The default is `false`.

Returns

Nothing.

Description

Method; distributes the selection.

Example

The following example distributes the selected objects by the top edge:

```
fl.getDocumentDOM().distribute("top edge");
```

The following example distributes the selected objects by top edge and expressly sets the *bUseDcoumentBounds* parameter:

```
fl.getDocumentDOM().distribute("top edge", false);
```

The following example distributes the selected objects by their top edges, using the bounds of the document:

```
fl.getDocumentDOM().distribute("top edge", true);
```

See also

`document.getAlignToDocument()`, `document.setAlignToDocument()`

document.distributeToLayers()

Availability

Flash MX 2004.

Usage

```
document.distributeToLayers()
```

Parameters

None.

Returns

Nothing.

Description

Method; performs a distribute-to-layers operation on the current selection—equivalent to selecting Distribute to Layers. This method displays an error if there is no selection.

Example

The following example distributes the current selection to layers:

```
fl.getDocumentDOM().distributeToLayers();
```

document.documentHasData()

Availability

Flash MX 2004.

Usage

```
document.documentHasData( name )
```

Parameters

name   A string that specifies the name of the data to check.

Returns

A Boolean value: `true` if the document has persistent data; `false` otherwise.

Description

Method; checks the document for persistent data with the specified name.

Example

The following example checks the document for persistent data with the name `"myData"`:

```
var hasData = fl.getDocumentDOM().documentHasData("myData");
```

See also

```
document.addDataToDocument(), document.getDataFromDocument(),
document.removeDataFromDocument()
```

document.duplicatePublishProfile()

Availability

Flash MX 2004.

Usage

```
document.duplicatePublishProfile( [profileName ] )
```

Parameters

profileName   A string that specifies the unique name of the duplicated profile. If you do not specify a name, the method uses the default name. This parameter is optional.

Returns

An integer that is the index of the new profile in the profile list. Returns -1 if the profile cannot be duplicated.

Description

Method; duplicates the currently active profile and gives the duplicate version focus.

Example

The following example duplicates the currently active profile and displays the index of the new profile in the Output panel:

```
fl.trace(fl.getDocumentDOM().duplicatePublishProfile("dup profile"));
```

document.duplicateScene()

Availability

Flash MX 2004.

Usage

```
document.duplicateScene()
```

Parameters

None.

Returns

A Boolean value: `true` if the scene is duplicated successfully; `false` otherwise.

Description

Method; makes a copy of the currently selected scene, giving the new scene a unique name and making it the current scene.

Example

The following example duplicates the second scene in the current document:

```
fl.getDocumentDOM().editScene(1); //set the middle scene to current scene
var success = fl.getDocumentDOM().duplicateScene();
```

document.duplicateSelection()

Availability

Flash MX 2004.

Usage

```
document.duplicateSelection()
```

Parameters

None.

Returns

Nothing.

Description

Method; duplicates the selection on the Stage.

Example

The following example duplicates the current selection, which is similar to Alt-clicking and then dragging an item:

```
fl.getDocumentDOM().duplicateSelection();
```

document.editScene()

Availability

Flash MX 2004.

Usage

```
document.editScene( index )
```

Parameters

index   A zero-based integer that specifies which scene to edit.

Returns

Nothing.

Description

Method; makes the specified scene the currently selected scene for editing.

Example

Assuming that there are three scenes (Scene0, Scene1, and Scene2) in the current document, the following example makes Scene2 the current scene and then deletes it:

```
fl.getDocumentDOM().editScene(2);
fl.getDocumentDOM().deleteScene();
```

document.enableAllFilters()

Availability

Flash 8.

Usage

```
document.enableAllFilters()
```

Parameters

None.

Returns

Nothing.

Description

Method; enables all the filters on the Filters list for the selected object(s).

Example

The following example enables all the filters on the Filters list for the selected object(s):

```
fl.getDocumentDOM().enableAllFilters()
```

See also

document.addFilter(), document.changeFilterOrder(), document.disableAllFilters(), document.enableFilter(), document.getFilters(), document.removeAllFilters(), Filter object

document.enableFilter()

Availability

Flash 8.

Usage

```
document.enableFilter( filterIndex )
```

Parameters

filterIndex   An integer specifying the zero-based index of the filter in the Filters list to enable.

Returns

Nothing.

Description

Method; enables the specified filter for the selected object(s).

Example

The following example enables the second filter of the selected object(s):

```
fl.getDocumentDOM().enableFilter(1);
```

See also

document.addFilter(), document.changeFilterOrder(), document.disableFilter(), document.enableAllFilters(), document.getFilters(), document.removeFilter(), Filter object

document.enterEditMode()

Availability

Flash MX 2004.

Usage

```
document.enterEditMode( [editMode] )
```

Parameters

editMode   A string that specifies the editing mode. Acceptable values are "inPlace" or "newWindow". If no parameter is specified, the default is symbol-editing mode. This parameter is optional.

Returns

Nothing.

Description

Method; switches the authoring tool into the editing mode specified by the parameter. If no parameter is specified, the method defaults to symbol-editing mode, which has the same result as right-clicking the symbol to invoke the context menu and selecting Edit.

Example

The following example puts Flash in edit-in-place mode for the currently selected symbol:

```
fl.getDocumentDOM().enterEditMode('inPlace');
```

The following example puts Flash in edit-in-new-window mode for the currently selected symbol:

```
fl.getDocumentDOM().enterEditMode('newWindow');
```

See also

```
document.exitEditMode()
```

document.exitEditMode()

Availability

Flash MX 2004.

Usage

```
document.exitEditMode()
```

Parameters

None.

Returns

Nothing.

Description

Method; exits from symbol-editing mode and returns focus to the next level up from the editing mode. For example, if you are editing a symbol inside another symbol, this method takes you up a level from the symbol you are editing, into the parent symbol.

Example

The following example exits symbol-editing mode:

```
fl.getDocumentDOM().exitEditMode();
```

See also

```
document.enterEditMode()
```

document.exportPNG()

Availability

Flash 8.

Usage

```
document.exportPNG([fileURI [, bCurrentPNGSettings [, bCurrentFrame]]])
```

Parameters

fileURI   A string, expressed as a file:/// URI, that specifies the filename for the exported file. If *fileURI* is an empty string or is not specified, Flash displays the Export Movie dialog box.

bCurrentPNGSettings   A Boolean value that specifies whether to use the current PNG publish settings (true) or to display the Export PNG dialog box (false). This parameter is optional. The default value is false.

bCurrentFrame   A Boolean value that specifies whether to export only the current frame (true) or to export all frames, with each frame a separate PNG file (false). This parameter is optional. The default value is false.

Returns

A Boolean value of true if the file is successfully exported as a PNG file; false otherwise.

Description

Method; exports the document as one or more PNG files. If *fileURI* is specified and the file already exists, it is overwritten without warning.

Example

The following example exports the current frame in the current document to myFile.png, using the current PNG publish settings:

```
fl.getDocumentDOM().exportPNG("file:///C|/myProject/myFile.png", true,
  true);
```

document.exportPublishProfile()

Availability

Flash MX 2004.

Usage

```
document.exportPublishProfile( fileURI )
```

Parameters

fileURI   A string, expressed as a file:/// URI, that specifies the path of the XML file to which the profile is exported.

Returns

Nothing.

Description

Method; exports the currently active profile to an XML file.

Example

The following example exports the currently active profile to the file named profile.xml in the folder /Documents and Settings/username/Desktop on the C drive:

```
fl.getDocumentDOM().exportPublishProfile('file:///C|/Documents and
    Settings/username/Desktop/profile.xml');
```

document.exportSWF()

Availability

Flash MX 2004.

Usage

```
document.exportSWF( [ fileURI [, bCurrentSettings ] ] )
```

Parameters

fileURI   A string, expressed as a file:/// URI, that specifies the name of the exported file. If *fileURI* is empty or not specified, Flash displays the Export Movie dialog box. This parameter is optional.

bCurrentSettings   A Boolean value that, when set to true, causes Flash to use current SWF publish settings. Otherwise, Flash displays the Export Flash Player dialog box. The default is false. This parameter is optional.

Returns

Nothing.

Description

Method; exports the document in the Flash SWF format.

Example

The following example exports the document to the specified file location with the current publish settings:

```
fl.getDocumentDOM().exportSWF("file:///C|/Documents and Settings/joe_user/
    Desktop/qwerty.swf");
```

The following example displays the Export Movie dialog box and the Export Flash Player dialog box and then exports the document based on the specified settings:

```
fl.getDocumentDOM().exportSWF("", true);
```

The following example displays the Export Movie dialog box and then exports the document based on the specified settings:

```
fl.getDocumentDOM().exportSWF();
```

document.forceSimple

Availability

Flash MX 2004.

Usage

```
document.forceSimple
```

Description

Property; a Boolean value that specifies whether the children of the specified object are accessible. This is equivalent to the inverse logic of the Make Child Objects Accessible setting in the Accessibility panel. That is, if forceSimple is true, it is the same as the Make Child Object Accessible option being unchecked. If forceSimple is false, it is the same as the Make Child Object Accessible option being checked.

Example

The following example sets the `areChildrenAccessible` variable to the value of the `forceSimple` property; a value of `false` means the children are accessible:

```
var areChildrenAccessible = fl.getDocumentDOM().forceSimple;
```

The following example sets the `forceSimple` property to allow the children of the document to be accessible:

```
fl.getDocumentDOM().forceSimple = false;
```

document.frameRate

Availability

Flash MX 2004.

Usage

```
document.frameRate
```

Description

Property; a float value that specifies the number of frames displayed per second when the SWF file plays; the default is 12. Setting this property is the same as setting the default frame rate in the Document Properties dialog box (Modify > Document) in the FLA file.

Example

The following example sets the frame rate to 25.5 frames per second:

```
fl.getDocumentDOM().frameRate = 25.5;
```

document.getAlignToDocument()

Availability

Flash MX 2004.

Usage

```
document.getAlignToDocument()
```

Parameters

None.

Returns

A Boolean value: `true` if the preference is set to align the objects to the Stage; `false` otherwise.

Description

Method; identical to retrieving the value of the To Stage button in the Align panel. Gets the preference that can be used for `document.align()`, `document.distribute()`, `document.match()`, and `document.space()` methods on the document.

Example

The following example retrieves the value of the To Stage button in the Align panel. If the return value is `true`, the To Stage button is active; otherwise, it is not.

```
var isAlignToDoc = fl.getDocumentDOM().getAlignToDocument();
fl.getDocumentDOM().align("left", isAlignToDoc);
```

See also

```
document.setAlignToDocument()
```

document.getBlendMode()

Availability

Flash 8.

Usage

```
document.getBlendMode()
```

Parameters

None.

Returns

A string that specifies the blend mode for the selected object(s). If more than one object is selected and they have different blend modes, the string reflects the blend mode of the object with the highest depth.

 The return value is unpredictable if the selection contains objects that don't support blend modes, or that have a blend mode value of `"normal"`.

Description

Method; returns a string that specifies the blend mode for the selected object(s).

Example

The following example displays the name of the blend mode in the Output panel:

```
fl.trace(fl.getDocumentDom().getBlendMode());
```

document.getCustomFill()

Availability

Flash MX 2004.

Usage

```
document.getCustomFill( [ objectToFill ] )
```

Parameters

objectToFill A string that specifies the location of the fill object. The following values are valid:

- "toolbar" returns the fill object of the Tools panel and Property inspector.
- "selection" returns the fill object of the selection.

If you omit this parameter, the default value is "selection". If there is no selection, the method returns undefined. This parameter is optional.

Returns

The Fill object specified by the *objectToFill* parameter, if successful; otherwise, it returns undefined.

Description

Method; retrieves the fill object of the selected shape or, if specified, of the Tools panel and Property inspector.

Example

The following example gets the fill object of the selection and then changes the selection's color to white:

```
var fill = fl.getDocumentDOM().getCustomFill();
fill.color = '#FFFFFF';
fill.style = "solid";
fl.getDocumentDOM().setCustomFill(fill);
```

The following example returns the fill object of the Tools panel and Property inspector and then changes the color swatch to a linear gradient:

```
var fill = fl.getDocumentDOM().getCustomFill("toolbar");
fill.style = "linearGradient";
fill.colorArray = [ 0x00ff00, 0xff0000, 0x0000ff ];
fill.posArray = [0, 100, 200];
fl.getDocumentDOM().setCustomFill( fill );
```

See also

```
document.setCustomFill()
```

---

document.getCustomStroke()

Availability

Flash MX 2004.

Usage

```
document.getCustomStroke( [locationOfStroke] )
```

Parameters

locationOfStroke   A string that specifies the location of the stroke object. The following values are valid:

- "toolbar", if set, returns the stroke object of the Tools panel and Property inspector.
- "selection", if set, returns the stroke object of the selection.

If you omit this parameter, it defaults to "selection". If there is no selection, it returns undefined. This parameter is optional.

Returns

The Stroke object specified by the *locationOfStroke* parameter, if successful; otherwise, it returns undefined.

Description

Returns the stroke object of the selected shape or, if specified, of the Tools panel and Property inspector.

Example

The following example returns the current stroke settings of the selection and changes the stroke thickness to 2:

```
var stroke = fl.getDocumentDOM().getCustomStroke("selection");
stroke.thickness = 2;
fl.getDocumentDOM().setCustomStroke(stroke);
```

The following example returns the current stroke settings of the Tools panel and Property inspector and sets the stroke color to red:

```
var stroke = fl.getDocumentDOM().getCustomStroke("toolbar");
stroke.color = "#FF0000";
fl.getDocumentDOM().setCustomStroke(stroke);
```

See also

```
document.setCustomStroke()
```

document.getDataFromDocument()

Availability

Flash MX 2004.

Usage

```
document.getDataFromDocument( name )
```

Parameters

name   A string that specifies the name of the data to return.

Returns

The specified data.

Description

Method; retrieves the value of the specified data. The type returned depends on the type of data that was stored.

Example

The following example adds an integer value of 12 to the current document and uses this method to display the value in the Output panel:

```
fl.getDocumentDOM().addDataToDocument("myData", "integer", 12);
fl.trace(fl.getDocumentDOM().getDataFromDocument("myData"));
```

See also

```
document.addDataToDocument(), document.documentHasData(),
document.removeDataFromDocument()
```

document.getElementProperty()

Availability

Flash MX 2004.

Usage

```
document.getElementProperty( propertyName )
```

Parameters

propertyName   A string that specifies the name of the Element property for which to retrieve the value.

Returns

The value of the specified property. Returns `null` if the property is an indeterminate state, as when multiple elements are selected with different property values. Returns `undefined` if the property is not a valid property of the selected element.

Description

Method; gets the specified `Element` property for the current selection. For a list of acceptable values, see "Property summary for the Element object" on page 193.

Example

The following example gets the `name` of the Element property for the current selection:

```
// elementName = the instance name of the selected object.
var elementName = fl.getDocumentDOM().getElementProperty("name");
```

See also

`document.setElementProperty()`

document.getElementTextAttr()

Availability

Flash MX 2004.

Usage

```
document.getElementTextAttr( attrName [, startIndex [, endIndex]] )
```

Parameters

attrName   A string that specifies the name of the `TextAttrs` property to be returned. For a list of property names and expected values, see "Property summary for the TextAttrs object" on page 457.

startIndex   An integer that specifies the index of first character, with 0 (zero) specifying the first position. This parameter is optional.

endIndex   An integer that specifies the index of last character. This parameter is optional.

Returns

If one text field is selected, the property is returned if there is only one value used within the text. Returns undefined if there are several values used inside the text field. If several text fields are selected, and all the text alignment values are equal, the method returns this value. If several text fields are selected, but all the text alignment values are not equal, the method returns undefined. If the optional arguments are not passed, these rules apply to the range of text currently selected or the whole text field if the text is not currently being edited. If only *startIndex* is passed, the property of the character to the right of the index is returned, if all the selected text objects match values. If *startIndex* and *endIndex* are passed, the value returned reflects the entire range of characters from *startIndex* up to, but not including, *endIndex*.

Description

Method; gets a specific TextAttrs property of the selected text objects. Selected objects that are not text fields are ignored. For a list of property names and expected values, see "Property summary for the TextAttrs object" on page 457. See also document.setElementTextAttr().

Example

The following example gets the size of the selected text fields:

```
fl.getDocumentDOM().getElementTextAttr("size");
```

The following example gets the color of the character at index 3 in the selected text fields:

```
fl.getDocumentDOM().getElementTextAttr("fillColor", 3);
```

The following example gets the font name of the text from index 2 up to, but not including, index 10 of the selected text fields:

```
fl.getDocumentDOM().getElementTextAttr("face", 2, 10);
```

document.getFilters()

Availability

Flash 8.

Usage

```
document.getFilters()
```

Parameters

None.

Returns

An array that contains a list of filters applied to the currently selected object(s).

Description

Method; returns an array that contains the list of filters applied to the currently selected object(s). If multiple objects are selected and they don't have identical filters, this method returns the list of filters applied to the first selected object.

Example

See `document.setFilters()`.

See also

`document.addFilter()`, `document.changeFilterOrder()`, `document.setFilters()`, Filter object

document.getMetadata()

Availability

Flash 8.

Usage

`document.getMetadata()`

Parameters

None.

Returns

A string containing the XML metadata associated with the document, or an empty string if there is no metadata.

Description

Method; returns a string containing the XML metadata associated with the document, or an empty string if there is no metadata.

Example

The following example displays XML metadata from the current document in the Output panel:

`fl.trace("XML Metadata is :" + fl.getDocumentDOM().getMetadata());`

See also

`document.setMetadata()`

document.getSelectionRect()

Availability

Flash MX 2004.

Usage

```
document.getSelectionRect()
```

Parameters

None.

Returns

The bounding rectangle of the current selection, or 0 if nothing is selected. For information on the format of the return value, see `document.addNewRectangle()`.

Description

Method; gets the bounding rectangle of the current selection. If a selection is non-rectangular, the smallest rectangle encompassing the entire selection is returned. The rectangle is based on the document space or, when in edit mode, the registration point of the symbol being edited.

Example

The following example gets the bounding rectangle for the current selection and then displays its properties:

```
var newRect = fl.getDocumentDOM().getSelectionRect();
var outputStr = "left: " + newRect.left + " top: " + newRect.top + " right:
  " + newRect.right + " bottom: " + newRect.bottom;
alert(outputStr);
```

See also

`document.selection`, `document.setSelectionRect()`

document.getTextString()

Availability

Flash MX 2004.

Usage

```
document.getTextString( [startIndex [, endIndex]] )
```

Parameters

startIndex   An integer that is an index of first character to get. This parameter is optional.

endIndex   An integer that is an index of last character to get. This parameter is optional.

Returns

A string that contains the selected text.

Description

Method; gets the currently selected text. If the optional parameters are not passed, the current text selection is used. If text is not currently opened for editing, the whole text string is returned. If only *startIndex* is passed, the string starting at that index and ending at the end of the field is returned. If *startIndex* and *endIndex* are passed, the string starting from *startIndex* up to, but not including, *endIndex* is returned.

If there are several text fields selected, the concatenation of all the strings is returned.

Example

The following example gets the string in the selected text fields:

```
fl.getDocumentDOM().getTextString();
```

The following example gets the string at character index 5 in the selected text fields:

```
fl.getDocumentDOM().getTextString(5);
```

The following example gets the string from character index 2 up to, but not including, character index 10:

```
fl.getDocumentDOM().getTextString(2, 10);
```

See also

```
document.setTextString()
```

document.getTimeline()

Availability

Flash MX 2004.

Usage

```
document.getTimeline()
```

Parameters

None.

Returns

The current Timeline object.

Description

Method; retrieves the current Timeline object in the document. The current timeline can be the current scene, the current symbol being edited, or the current screen.

Example

The following example gets the Timeline object and returns the number of frames in the longest layer:

```
var longestLayer = fl.getDocumentDOM().getTimeline().frameCount;
fl.trace("The longest layer has" + longestLayer + "frames");
```

The following example enters edit-in-place mode for the selected symbol on the Stage and inserts a frame on the symbol's timeline.

```
fl.getDocumentDOM().enterEditMode("inPlace");
fl.getDocumentDOM().getTimeline().insertFrames();
```

The following example gets the Timeline object and displays its name:

```
var timeline = fl.getDocumentDOM().getTimeline();
alert(timeline.name);
```

See also

```
document.currentTimeline, document.timelines, symbolItem.timeline
```

document.getTransformationPoint()

Availability

Flash MX 2004.

Usage

```
document.getTransformationPoint()
```

Parameters

None.

Returns

The location of the transformation point.

Description

Method; gets the location of the transformation point of the current selection. You can use the transformation point for commutations such as rotate and skew.

Example

The following example gets the transformation point for the current selection. The
`transPoint.x` property gives the *x* coordinate of the transformation point. The
`transPoint.y` property gives the *y* coordinate of the transformation point:

```
var transPoint = fl.getDocumentDOM().getTransformationPoint();
```

See also

`document.setTransformationPoint()`

document.group()

Availability

Flash MX 2004.

Usage

```
document.group()
```

Parameters

None.

Returns

Nothing.

Description

Method; converts the current selection to a group.

Example

The following example converts the objects in the current selection to a group:

```
fl.getDocumentDOM().group();
```

See also

`document.unGroup()`

document.height

Availability

Flash MX 2004.

Usage

```
document.height
```

Description

Property; an integer that specifies the height of the document (Stage) in pixels.

Example

The following example sets the height of the Stage to 400 pixels:

```
fl.getDocumentDOM().height = 400;
```

See also

```
document.width
```

document.importFile()

Availability

Flash 8.

Usage

```
document.importFile(fileURI [, importToLibrary])
```

Parameters

fileURI   A string, expressed as a file:/// URI, that specifies the path of the file to import.

importToLibrary   A Boolean value that specifies whether to import the file only into the document's library (true) or to also place a copy on the Stage (false). The default value is false.

Returns

A Boolean value that indicates whether the file was successfully imported.

Description

Method; imports a file into a document. This method performs the same operation as the Import to Library or Import to Stage menu command. To import a publish profile, use document.importPublishProfile().

Example

The following example lets the user browse for a file to import onto the Stage.

```
var dom = fl.getDocumentDOM();
var URI = fl.browseForFileURL("select", "Import File");
dom.importFile(URI);
```

See also

```
document.importSWF(), fl.browseForFileURL()
```

document.importPublishProfile()

Availability

Flash MX 2004.

Usage

```
document.importPublishProfile( fileURI )
```

Parameters

fileURI   A string, expressed as a file:/// URI, that specifies the path of the XML file defining the profile to import.

Returns

An integer that is the index of the imported profile in the profiles list. Returns -1 if the profile cannot be imported.

Description

Method; imports a profile from a file.

Example

The following example imports the profile contained in the profile.xml file and displays its index in the profiles list:

```
alert(fl.getDocumentDOM().importPublishProfile('file:///C|/Documents and
    Settings/janeUser/Desktop/profile.xml'));
```

document.importSWF()

Availability

Flash MX 2004.

Usage

```
document.importSWF( fileURI )
```

Parameters

fileURI   A string, expressed as a file:/// URI, that specifies the file for the SWF file to import.

Returns

Nothing.

Description

Method; imports a SWF file into the document. This method performs the same operation as using the Import menu command to specify a SWF file. In Flash 8 and later, you can also use `document.importFile()` to import a SWF file (as well as other types of files).

Example

The following example imports the `"mySwf.swf"` file from the Flash Configuration folder:

```
fl.getDocumentDOM().importSWF(fl.configURI+"mySwf.swf");
```

See also

`document.importFile()`

document.intersect()

Availability

Flash 8.

Usage

```
document.intersect();
```

Parameters

None.

Returns

A Boolean value: `true` if successful; `false` otherwise.

Description

Method; creates an intersection drawing object from all selected drawing objects. This method returns `false` if there are no drawing objects selected, or if any of the selected items are not drawing objects.

Example

The following example creates an intersection drawing object from all selected drawing objects.

```
fl.getDocumentDOM().intersect();
```

See also

`document.crop()`, `document.deleteEnvelope()`, `document.punch()`, `document.union()`, `shape.isDrawingObject`

document.library

Availability

Flash MX 2004.

Usage

```
document.library
```

Description

Read-only property; the library object for a document.

Example

The following example gets the library for the currently focused document:

```
var myCurrentLib = fl.getDocumentDOM().library;
```

Assuming the currently focused document is not `fl.documents[1]`, the following example gets the library for a non-focused library or for a library you opened using File > Open as external library:

```
var externalLib = fl.documents[1].library;
```

document.livePreview

Availability

Flash MX 2004.

Usage

```
document.livePreview
```

Description

Property; a Boolean value that specifies if Live Preview is enabled. If set to `true`, components appear on the Stage as they will appear in the published Flash content, including their approximate size. If set to `false`, components appear only as outlines. The default value is `true`.

Example

The following example sets Live Preview to `false`:

```
fl.getDocumentDOM().livePreview = false;
```

document.match()

Availability

Flash MX 2004.

Usage

```
document.match( bWidth, bHeight [, bUseDocumentBounds] )
```

Parameters

bWidth   A Boolean value that, when set to `true`, causes the method to make the widths of the selected items the same.

bHeight   A Boolean value that, when set to `true`, causes the method to make the heights of the selected items the same.

bUseDocumentBounds   A Boolean value that, when set to `true`, causes the method to match the size of the objects to the bounds of the document. Otherwise, the method uses the bounds of the largest object. The default is `false`. This parameter is optional.

Returns

Nothing.

Description

Method; makes the size of the selected objects the same.

Example

The following example matches the width of the selected objects only:

```
fl.getDocumentDOM().match(true,false);
```

The following example matches the height only:

```
fl.getDocumentDOM().match(false,true);
```

The following example matches the width only to the bounds of the document:

```
fl.getDocumentDOM().match(true,false,true);
```

See also

`document.getAlignToDocument()`, `document.setAlignToDocument()`

document.mouseClick()

Availability

Flash MX 2004.

Usage

```
document.mouseClick( position, bToggleSel, bShiftSel )
```

Parameters

position   A pair of floating-point values that specify the *x* and *y* coordinates of the click in pixels.

bToggleSel   A Boolean value that specifies the state of the Shift key: `true` for pressed; `false` for not pressed.

bShiftSel   A Boolean value that specifies the state of the application preference Shift select: `true` for on; `false` for off.

Returns

Nothing.

Description

Method; performs a mouse click from the arrow tool.

Example

The following example performs a mouse click at the specified location:

```
fl.getDocumentDOM().mouseClick({x:300, y:200}, false);
```

See also

```
document.mouseDblClk()
```

document.mouseDblClk()

Availability

Flash MX 2004.

Usage

```
document.mouseDblClk( position, bAltDown, bShiftDown, bShiftSelect )
```

Parameters

position   A pair of floating-point values that specify the *x* and *y* coordinates of the click in pixels.

bAltdown   A Boolean value that records whether the Alt key is down at the time of the event: `true` for pressed; `false` for not pressed.

bShiftDown   A Boolean value that records whether the Shift key was down when the event occurred: `true` for pressed; `false` for not pressed.

bShiftSelect   A Boolean value that indicates the state of the application preference Shift select: `true` for on; `false` for off.

Returns

Nothing.

Description

Method; performs a double mouse click from the arrow tool.

Example

The following example performs a double mouse click at the specified location:

```
fl.getDocumentDOM().mouseDblClk({x:392.9, y:73}, false, false, true);
```

See also

```
document.mouseClick()
```

document.moveSelectedBezierPointsBy()

Availability

Flash MX 2004.

Usage

```
document.moveSelectedBezierPointsBy( delta )
```

Parameters

delta   A pair of floating-point values that specify the *x* and *y* coordinates in pixels by which the selected Bézier points are moved. For example, passing ({x:1,y:2}) specifies a location that is to the right by one pixel and down by two pixels from the current location.

Returns

Nothing.

Description

Method; if the selection contains at least one path with at least one Bézier point selected, moves all selected Bézier points on all selected paths by the specified amount.

Example

The following example moves the selected Bézier points 10 pixels to the right and 5 pixels down:

```
fl.getDocumentDOM().moveSelectedBezierPointsBy({x:10, y:5});
```

document.moveSelectionBy()

Availability

Flash MX 2004.

Usage

```
document.moveSelectionBy( distanceToMove )
```

Parameters

distanceToMove   A pair of floating-point values that specify the *x* and *y* coordinate values by which the method moves the selection. For example, passing ({x:1,y:2}) specifies a location one pixel to the right and two pixels down from the current location.

Returns

Nothing.

Description

Method; moves selected objects by a specified distance.

 NOTE When using arrow keys to move the item, the History panel combines all presses of the arrow key as one move step. When the user presses the arrow keys repeatedly, rather than taking multiple steps in the History panel, the method performs one step, and the arguments are updated to reflect the repeated arrow keys.

For information on making a selection, see `document.setSelectionRect()`, `document.mouseClick()`, `document.mouseDblClk()`, and the Element object.

Example

The following example moves the selected item 62 pixels to the right and 84 pixels down:

```
flash.getDocumentDOM().moveSelectionBy({x:62, y:84});
```

document.name

Availability

Flash MX 2004.

Usage

```
document.name
```

Description

Read-only property; a string that represents the name of a document (FLA file).

Example

The following example sets the variable `fileName` to the filename of the first document in the documents array:

```
var fileName = flash.documents[0].name;
```

The following example displays the names of all the open documents in the Output panel:

```
var openDocs = fl.documents;
for(var i=0;i < opendocs.length; i++){
  fl.trace(i + " " + opendocs[i].name +"\n");
}
```

document.optimizeCurves()

Availability

Flash MX 2004.

Usage

```
document.optimizeCurves( smoothing, bUseMultiplePasses )
```

Parameters

smoothing   An integer in the range from 0 to 100, with 0 specifying no smoothing, and 100 specifying maximum smoothing.

bUseMultiplePasses   A Boolean value that, when set to `true`, indicates that the method should use multiple passes, which is slower but produces a better result. This parameter has the same effect as clicking the Use multiple passes button in the Optimize Curves dialog box.

Returns

Nothing.

Description

Method; optimizes smoothing for the current selection, allowing multiple passes, if specified, for optimal smoothing. This method is equivalent to selecting Modify > Shape > Optimize.

Example

The following example optimizes the curve of the current selection to 50° of smoothing with multiple passes:

```
fl.getDocumentDOM().optimizeCurves(50, true);
```

document.path

Availability

Flash MX 2004.

Usage

```
document.path
```

Description

Read-only property; a string that represents the path of the document in a platform-specific format. If the document has never been saved, this property is `undefined`.

Example

The following example displays the path of the first document in the documents array in the Output panel:

```
var filePath = flash.documents[0].path;
fl.trace(filePath);
```

document.publish()

Availability

Flash MX 2004.

Usage

```
document.publish()
```

Parameters

None.

Returns

Nothing.

Description

Method; publishes the document according to the active Publish Settings (File > Publish Settings). This method is equivalent to selecting File > Publish.

Example

The following example publishes the current document:

```
fl.getDocumentDOM().publish();
```

document.publishProfiles

Availability

Flash MX 2004.

Usage

```
document.publishProfiles
```

Description

Read-only property; an array of the publish profile names for the document.

Example

The following example displays the names of the publish profiles for the document:

```
var myPubProfiles = fl.getDocumentDOM().publishProfiles;
for (var i=0; i < myPubProfiles.length; i++){
  fl.trace(myPubProfiles[i]);
}
```

document.punch()

Availability

Flash 8.

Usage

```
document.punch()
```

Parameters

None.

Returns

A Boolean value: `true` if successful; `false` otherwise.

Description

Method; uses top selected drawing object to punch through all selected drawing objects underneath it. This method returns `false` if there are no drawing objects selected, or if any of the selected items are not drawing objects.

Example

The following example punches through drawing objects underneath the selected drawing object:

```
fl.getDocumentDOM().punch();
```

See also

`document.crop()`, `document.deleteEnvelope()`, `document.intersect()`, `document.union()`, `shape.isDrawingObject`

document.removeDataFromDocument()

Availability

Flash MX 2004.

Usage

```
document.removeDataFromDocument( name )
```

Parameters

name   A string that specifies the name of the data to remove.

Returns

Nothing.

Description

Method; removes persistent data with the specified name that has been attached to the document.

Example

The following example removes from the document the persistent data named `"myData"`:

```
fl.getDocumentDOM().removeDataFromDocument("myData");
```

See also

`document.addDataToDocument()`, `document.documentHasData()`, `document.getDataFromDocument()`

document.removeDataFromSelection()

Availability

Flash MX 2004.

Usage

```
document.removeDataFromSelection( name )
```

Parameters

name   A string that specifies the name of the persistent data to remove.

Returns

Nothing.

Description

Method; removes persistent data with the specified name that has been attached to the selection.

Example

The following example removes from the selection the persistent data named "myData":

```
fl.getDocumentDOM().removeDataFromSelection("myData");
```

See also

```
document.addDataToSelection()
```

document.removeAllFilters()

Availability

Flash 8.

Usage

```
document.removeAllFilters()
```

Parameters

None.

Returns

Nothing.

Description

Method; removes all filters from the selected object(s).

Example

The following example removes all filters from the selected object(s):

```
fl.getDocumentDOM().removeAllFilters();
```

See also

`document.addFilter()`, `document.changeFilterOrder()`,
`document.disableAllFilters()`, `document.getFilters()`, `document.removeFilter()`,
Filter object

document.removeFilter()

Availability

Flash 8.

Usage

```
document.removeFilter( filterIndex )
```

Parameters

filterIndex An integer specifying the zero-based index of the filter to remove from the
selected object(s).

Returns

Nothing.

Description

Method; removes the specified filter from the Filters list of the selected object(s).

Example

The following example removes the first filter (index value 0) from the Filters list of
the selected object(s):

```
fl.getDocumentDOM().removeFilter(0);
```

See also

`document.addFilter()`, `document.changeFilterOrder()`, `document.disableFilter()`,
`document.getFilters()`, `document.removeAllFilters()`, Filter object

document.renamePublishProfile()

Availability

Flash MX 2004.

Usage

```
document.renamePublishProfile( [profileNewName ] )
```

Parameters

profileNewName   An optional parameter that specifies the new name for the profile. The new name must be unique. If the name is not specified, a default name is provided.

Returns

A Boolean value: true if the name is changed successfully; false otherwise.

Description

Method; renames the current profile.

Example

The following example renames the current profile to a default name and displays it:

```
alert(fl.getDocumentDOM().renamePublishProfile());
```

document.renameScene()

Availability

Flash MX 2004.

Usage

```
document.renameScene( name )
```

Parameters

name   A string that specifies the new name of the scene.

Returns

A Boolean value: true if the name is changed successfully; false otherwise. If the new name is not unique, for example, the method returns false.

Description

Method; renames the currently selected scene in the Scenes panel. The new name for the selected scene must be unique.

Example

The following example renames the current scene to `"new name"`:

```
var success = fl.getDocumentDOM().renameScene("new name");
```

document.reorderScene()

Availability

Flash MX 2004.

Usage

```
document.reorderScene( sceneToMove, sceneToPutItBefore )
```

Parameters

sceneToMove   An integer that specifies which scene to move, with 0 (zero) being the first scene.

sceneToPutItBefore   An integer that specifies the scene before which you want to move the scene specified by *sceneToMove*. Specify 0 (zero) for the first scene. For example, if you specify 1 for *sceneToMove* and 0 for *sceneToPutItBefore*, the second scene is placed before the first scene. Specify -1 to move the scene to the end.

Returns

Nothing.

Description

Method; moves the specified scene before another specified scene.

Example

The following example moves the second scene to before the first scene:

```
fl.getDocumentDOM().reorderScene(1, 0);
```

document.resetTransformation()

Availability

Flash MX 2004.

Usage

```
document.resetTransformation()
```

Parameters

None.

Returns

Nothing.

Description

Method; resets the transformation matrix. This method is equivalent to selecting Modify > Transform > Remove transform.

Example

The following example resets the transformation matrix for the current selection:

```
fl.getDocumentDOM().resetTransformation();
```

document.revert()

Availability

Flash MX 2004.

Usage

```
document.revert()
```

Parameters

None.

Returns

Nothing.

Description

Method; reverts the specified document to its previously saved version. This method is equivalent to selecting File > Revert.

Example

The following example reverts the current document to the previously saved version:

```
fl.getDocumentDOM().revert();
```

See also

`document.canRevert()`, `fl.revertDocument()`

document.rotateSelection()

Availability

Flash MX 2004.

Usage

```
document.rotateSelection( angle [, rotationPoint] )
```

Parameters

angle A floating-point value that specifies the angle of the rotation.

rotationPoint A string that specifies which side of the bounding box to rotate. Acceptable values are `"top right"`, `"top left"`, `"bottom right"`, `"bottom left"`, `"top center"`, `"right center"`, `"bottom center"`, and `"left center"`. If unspecified, the method uses the transformation point. This parameter is optional.

Returns

Nothing.

Description

Method; rotates the selection by a specified number of degrees. The effect is the same as using the Free Transform tool to rotate the object.

Example

The following example rotates the selection by 45° around the transformation point:

```
flash.getDocumentDOM().rotateSelection(45);
```

The following example rotates the selection by 45° around the lower left corner:

```
fl.getDocumentDOM().rotateSelection(45, "bottom left");
```

document.save()

Availability

Flash MX 2004.

Usage

```
document.save( [ bOkToSaveAs ] )
```

Parameters

bOkToSaveAs   An optional parameter that specifies whether to open the Save As dialog box.

Returns

A Boolean value: `true` if the save operation completes successfully; `false` otherwise.

Description

Method; saves the document in its default location. This method is equivalent to selecting File > Save.

> If the file has never been saved, or has not been modified since the last time it was saved, the file isn't saved and false is returned. To allow an unsaved or unmodified file to be saved, use `fl.saveDocumentAs()`.

Example

The following example saves the current document in its default location:

```
fl.getDocumentDOM().save();
```

See also

`document.saveAndCompact()`, `fl.saveAll()`, `fl.saveDocument()`, `fl.saveDocumentAs()`

document.saveAndCompact()

Availability

Flash MX 2004.

Usage

```
document.saveAndCompact( [ bOkToSaveAs ] )
```

Parameters

bOkToSaveAs An optional parameter that, if `true` or omitted and the file was never saved, opens the Save As dialog box. If `false` and the file was never saved, the file is not saved. The default value is `true`.

Returns

A Boolean value: `true` if the save-and-compact operation completes successfully; `false` otherwise.

Description

Method; saves and compacts the file. This method is equivalent to selecting File > Save and Compact.

 If the file has never been saved, this method returns true even if the user cancels the Save As dialog box. To allow an unsaved file to be saved, use `fl.saveDocumentAs()`.

Example

The following example saves and compacts the current document:

```
fl.getDocumentDOM().saveAndCompact();
```

See also

`document.save()`, `fl.saveDocumentAs()`, `fl.saveDocument()`, `fl.saveAll()`

document.scaleSelection()

Availability

Flash MX 2004.

Usage

```
document.scaleSelection( xScale, yScale [, whichCorner] )
```

Parameters

xScale A floating-point value that specifies the amount of *x* by which to scale.

yScale A floating-point value that specifies the amount of *y* by which to scale.

whichCorner A string value that specifies the edge about which the transformation occurs. If omitted, scaling occurs about the transformation point. Acceptable values are: `"bottom left"`, `"bottom right"`, `"top right"`, `"top left"`, `"top center"`, `"right center"`, `"bottom center"`, and `"left center"`. This parameter is optional.

Returns

Nothing.

Description

Method; scales the selection by a specified amount. This method is equivalent to using the Free Transform tool to scale the object.

Example

The following example expands the width of the current selection to double the original width and shrinks the height to half:

```
flash.getDocumentDOM().scaleSelection(2.0, 0.5);
```

The following example flips the selection vertically:

```
fl.getDocumentDOM().scaleSelection(1, -1);
```

The following example flips the selection horizontally:

```
fl.getDocumentDOM().scaleSelection(-1, 1);
```

The following example scales the selection vertically by 1.9 from the top center:

```
fl.getDocumentDOM().scaleSelection(1, 1.90, 'top center');
```

document.screenOutline

Availability

Flash MX 2004.

Usage

```
document.screenOutline
```

Description

Read-only property; the current ScreenOutline object for the document. Before accessing the object for the first time, make sure to use document.allowScreens() to determine whether the property exists.

Example

The following example displays the array of values in the screenOutline property:

```
var myArray = new Array();
for(var i in fl.getDocumentDOM().screenOutline) {
  myArray.push(" "+i+" : "+fl.getDocumentDOM().screenOutline[i]) ;
}
fl.trace("Here is the property dump for screenOutline: "+myArray);
```

document.allowScreens(), ScreenOutline object

document.selectAll()

Availability

Flash MX 2004.

Usage

document.selectAll()

Parameters

None.

Returns

Nothing.

Description

Method; selects all items on the Stage. This method is equivalent to pressing Control+A (Windows) or Command+A (Macintosh) or selecting Edit > Select All.

Example

The following example selects everything that is currently visible to the user:

fl.getDocumentDOM().selectAll();

See also

document.selection, document.selectNone()

document.selection

Availability

Flash MX 2004.

Usage

document.selection

Description

Property; an array of the selected objects in the document. If nothing is selected, returns an array of length zero. If no document is open, returns null.

To add objects to the array, you must first select them in one of the following ways:

- Manually select object(s) on the Stage.
- Use one of the selection methods, such as `document.setSelectionRect()`, `document.setSelectionBounds()`, `document.mouseClick()`, `document.mouseDblClk()`, or `document.selectAll()`.
- Manually select a frame or frames.
- Use one of the methods of the Timeline object to select a frame or frames, such as `timeline.getSelectedFrames()`, `timeline.setSelectedFrames()`, or `timeline.selectAllFrames()`.
- Specify a particular element in a particular frame. For example, the following code specifies and selects an element:

```
fl.getDocumentDOM().selection =
    fl.getDocumentDOM().getTimeline().layers[0].frames[0].elements[0];
```

Example

The following example assigns all elements on Frame 11 to the current selection (remember that index values are different from frame number values):

```
fl.getDocumentDOM().getTimeline().currentFrame = 10;
fl.getDocumentDOM().selection =
    fl.getDocumentDOM().getTimeline().layers[0].frames[10].elements;
```

The following example creates a rectangle in the upper-left corner of the Stage and a text string underneath the rectangle. Then it selects both objects using `document.setSelectionRect()` and adds them to the `document.selection` array. Finally, it displays the contents of `document.selection` in the Output panel.

```
fl.getDocumentDOM().addNewRectangle({left:0, top:0, right:99, bottom:99},
    0);
fl.getDocumentDOM().addNewText({left:-1, top:117.3, right:9.2,
    bottom:134.6});
fl.getDocumentDOM().setTextString('Hello World');
fl.getDocumentDOM().setSelectionRect({left:-28, top:-22, right:156.0,
    bottom:163});

var theSelectionArray = fl.getDocumentDOM().selection;

for(var i=0;i<theSelectionArray.length;i++){
    fl.trace("fl.getDocumentDOM().selection["+i+"] = " +
        theSelectionArray[i]);
}
```

The following example is an advanced example. It shows how to loop through the layer array and elements array to locate instances of a particular symbol and select them. You could extend this example to include loops for multiple frames or scenes. This example assigns all instances of the movie clip `myMovieClip` in the first frame to the current selection:

```
// Assigns the layers array to the variable "theLayers".
var theLayers = fl.getDocumentDOM().getTimeline().layers;
// Creates an array to hold all the elements
// that are instances of "myMovieClip".
var myArray = new Array();
// Counter variable
var x = 0;
// Begin loop through all the layers.
for (var i = 0; i < theLayers.length; i++) {
  // Gets the array of elements in Frame 1
  // and assigns it to the array "theElems".
  var theElems = theLayers[i].frames[0].elements;
  // Begin loop through the elements on a layer.
  for (var c = 0; c < theElems.length; c++) {
    // Checks to see if the element is of type "instance".
    if (theElems[c].elementType == "instance") {
      // If the element is an instance, it checks
      // if it is an instance of "myMovieClip".
      if (theElems[c].libraryItem.name == "myMovieClip") {
        // Assigns elements that are instances of "myMovieClip" to
"myArray".
        myArray[x] = theElems[c];
        // Increments counter variable.
        x++;
      }
    }
  }
}
// Now that you have assigned all the instances of "myMovieClip"
// to "myArray", you then set the document.selection array
// equal to myArray. This selects the objects on the Stage.
fl.getDocumentDOM().selection = myArray;
```

document.selectNone()

Availability

Flash MX 2004.

Usage

```
document.selectNone()
```

Parameters

None.

Returns

Nothing.

Description

Method; deselects any selected items.

Example

The following example deselects any items that are selected:

```
fl.getDocumentDOM().selectNone();
```

See also

document.selectAll(), document.selection

document.setAlignToDocument()

Availability

Flash MX 2004.

Usage

```
document.setAlignToDocument( bToStage )
```

Parameters

bToStage A Boolean value that, if set to `true`, aligns objects to the Stage. If set to `false`, it does not.

Returns

Nothing.

Description

Method; sets the preferences for document.align(), document.distribute(), document.match(), and document.space() to act on the document. This method is equivalent to enabling the To Stage button in the Align panel.

Example

The following example enables the To Stage button in the Align panel to align objects with the Stage:

```
fl.getDocumentDOM().setAlignToDocument(true);
```

See also

```
document.getAlignToDocument()
```

document.setBlendMode()

Availability

Flash 8.

Usage

```
document.setBlendMode( mode )
```

Parameters

mode   A string that represents the desired blend mode for the selected objects. Acceptable values are `"normal"`, `"layer"`, `"multiply"`, `"screen"`, `"overlay"`, `"hardlight"`, `"lighten"`, `"darken"`, `"difference"`, `"add"`, `"subtract"`, `"invert"`, `"alpha"`, and `"erase"`.

Returns

Nothing.

Description

Method; sets the blend mode for the selected objects.

Example

The following example sets the blend mode for the selected object to `"add"`.

```
fl.getDocumentDOM().setBlendMode("add");
```

See also

```
document.addFilter(), document.setFilterProperty(), symbolInstance.blendMode
```

document.setCustomFill()

Availability

Flash MX 2004.

Usage

```
document.setCustomFill( fill )
```

Parameters

fill   A Fill object that specifies the fill settings to be used. See Fill object.

Returns

Nothing.

Description

Method; sets the fill settings for the Tools panel, Property inspector, and any selected shapes. This allows a script to set the fill settings before drawing the object, rather than drawing the object, selecting it, and changing the fill settings. It also lets a script change the Tools panel and Property inspector fill settings.

Example

The following example changes the color of the fill color swatch in the Tools panel, Property inspector, and any selected shapes to white:

```
var fill = fl.getDocumentDOM().getCustomFill();
fill.color = '#FFFFFF';
fill.style = "solid";
fl.getDocumentDOM().setCustomFill(fill);
```

See also

```
document.getCustomFill()
```

document.setCustomStroke()

Availability

Flash MX 2004.

Usage

```
document.setCustomStroke( stroke )
```

Parameters

stroke   A Stroke object.

Returns

Nothing.

Description

Method; sets the stroke settings for the Tools panel, Property inspector, and any selected shapes. This allows a script to set the stroke settings before drawing the object, rather than drawing the object, selecting it, and changing the stroke settings. It also lets a script change the Tools panel and Property inspector stroke settings.

Example

The following example changes the stroke thickness setting in the Tools panel, Property inspector, and any selected shapes:

```
var stroke = fl.getDocumentDOM().getCustomStroke();
stroke.thickness += 2;
fl.getDocumentDOM().setCustomStroke(stroke);
```

See also

document.getCustomStroke()

document.setElementProperty()

Availability

Flash MX 2004.

Usage

document.setElementProperty(*property*, *value*)

Parameters

property   A string that specifies the name of the Element property to set. For a complete list of properties and values, see "Property summary for the Element object" on page 193.

 You can't use this method to set values for read-only properties, such as element.elementType, element.top, and element.left.

value   An integer that specifies the value to set in the specified Element property.

Returns

Nothing.

Description

Method; sets the specified `Element` property on selected object(s) in the document. This method does nothing if there is no selection.

Example

The following example sets the width of all selected objects to 100 and the height to 50:

```
fl.getDocumentDOM().setElementProperty("width", 100);
fl.getDocumentDOM().setElementProperty("height", 50);
```

document.setElementTextAttr()

Availability

Flash MX 2004.

Usage

```
document.setElementTextAttr( attrName, attrValue [, startIndex [,
   endIndex]] )
```

Parameters

attrName   A string that specifies the name of the `TextAttrs` property to change.

attrValue   The value to which to set the `TextAttrs` property. For a list of property names and expected values, see "Property summary for the TextAttrs object" on page 457.

startIndex   An integer value that specifies the index of the first character that is affected. This parameter is optional.

endIndex   An integer value that specifies the index of the last character that is affected. This parameter is optional.

Returns

A Boolean value: `true` if at least one text attribute property is changed; `false` otherwise.

Description

Method; sets the specified `textAttrs` property of the selected text items to the specified value. For a list of property names and allowable values, see "Property summary for the TextAttrs object" on page 457. If the optional parameters are not passed, the method sets the style of the currently selected text range, or the whole text field if no text is selected. If only *startIndex* is passed, the method sets that character's attributes. If *startIndex* and *endIndex* are passed, the method sets the attributes on the characters starting from *startIndex* up to, but not including, *endIndex*. If paragraph styles are specified, all the paragraphs that fall within the range are affected.

Example

The following examples set the `fillColor`, `italic`, and `bold` text attributes for the selected text items:

```
var success = fl.getDocumentDOM().setElementTextAttr("fillColor",
  "#00ff00");
var pass = fl.getDocumentDOM().setElementTextAttr("italic", true, 10);
var ok = fl.getDocumentDOM().setElementTextAttr("bold", true, 5, 15);
```

document.setFillColor()

Availability

Flash MX 2004.

Usage

```
document.setFillColor( color )
```

Parameters

`color`   The color of the fill, in one of the following formats:

- A string in the format "#RRGGBB" or "#RRGGBBAA"
- A hexadecimal number in the format 0xRRGGBB
- An integer that represents the decimal equivalent of a hexadecimal number

If set to `null`, no fill color is set, which is the same as setting the Fill color swatch in the user interface to no fill.

Returns

Nothing.

Description

Method; changes the fill color of the selection to the specified color. For information on changing the fill color in the Tools panel and Property inspector, see `document.setCustomFill()`.

Example

The first three statements in the following example set the fill color using each of the different formats for specifying color. The fourth statement sets the fill to no fill.

```
flash.getDocumentDOM().setFillColor("#cc00cc");
flash.getDocumentDOM().setFillColor(0xcc00cc);
flash.getDocumentDOM().setFillColor(120000);
flash.getDocumentDOM().setFillColor(null);
```

document.setFilterProperty()

Availability

Flash 8.

Usage

```
document.setFilterProperty( property, filterIndex, value )
```

Parameters

property   A string specifying the property to be set. Acceptable values are `"blurX"`, `"blurY"`, `"quality"`, `angle"`, `"distance"`, `"strength"`, `"knockout"`, `"inner"`, `"bevelType"`, `"color"`, `"shadowColor"`, and `"highlightColor"`.

filterIndex   An integer specifying the zero-based index of the filter in the Filters list.

value   A number or string specifying the value to be set for the specified filter property. Acceptable values depend on the property and the filter being set.

Returns

Nothing.

Description

Method; sets a specified filter property for the currently selected object(s) that support the filter property.

Example

The following example sets the `quality` property to 2 for the second filter (index value of 1) in the Filters list of the selected objects, and then sets the `shadowColor` property of the first filter in the Filters list on the selected object(s):

```
fl.getDocumentDOM().setFilterProperty("quality", 1, 2);
fl.getDocumentDOM().setFilterProperty("shadowColor", 0, "#FF00FF");
```

See also

document.addFilter(), document.getFilters(), document.setBlendMode(), document.setFilters(), Filter object

document.setFilters()

Availability

Flash 8.

Usage

```
document.setFilters( filterArray )
```

Parameters

filterArray   The array of filters currently specified.

Returns

Nothing.

Description

Method; applies filters to the selected objects. Use this method after calling `document.getFilters()` and making any desired changes to the filters.

Example

The following example gets the filters on the selected object and sets the `blurX` property for all Blur filters to 50:

```
var myFilters = fl.getDocumentDOM().getFilters();
for (i=0; i < myFilters.length; i++) {
  if (myFilters[i].name == "blurFilter"){
    myFilters[i].blurX = 50;
  }
}
fl.getDocumentDOM().setFilters(myFilters);
```

See also

`document.addFilter()`, `document.getFilters()`, `document.setFilterProperty()`, Filter object

document.setInstanceAlpha()

Availability

Flash MX 2004.

Usage

```
document.setInstanceAlpha( opacity )
```

Parameters

opacity An integer between 0 (transparent) and 100 (completely saturated) that adjusts the transparency of the instance.

Returns

Nothing.

Description

Methods; sets the opacity of the instance.

Example

The following example sets the opacity of the tint to a value of 50:

```
fl.getDocumentDOM().setInstanceAlpha(50);
```

document.setInstanceBrightness()

Availability

Flash MX 2004.

Usage

```
document.setInstanceBrightness( brightness )
```

Parameters

brightness An integer that specifies brightness as a value from -100 (black) to 100 (white).

Returns

Nothing.

Description

Method; sets the brightness for the instance.

Example

The following example sets the brightness for the instance to a value of 50:

```
fl.getDocumentDOM().setInstanceBrightness(50);
```

document.setInstanceTint()

Availability

Flash MX 2004.

Usage

```
document.setInstanceTint( color, strength )
```

Parameters

color   The color of the tint, in one of the following formats:

- A string in the format "#RRGGBB" or "#RRGGBBAA"
- A hexadecimal number in the format 0xRRGGBB
- An integer that represents the decimal equivalent of a hexadecimal number

This parameter is equivalent to picking the Color: Tint value for a symbol in the Property Inspector.

strength   An integer between 0 and 100 that specifies the opacity of the tint.

Returns

Nothing.

Description

Method; sets the tint for the instance.

Example

The following example sets the tint for the selected instance to red with an opacity value of 50:

```
fl.getDocumentDOM().setInstanceTint(0xff0000, 50);
```

document.setMetadata()

Availability

Flash 8.

Usage

```
document.setMetadata( strMetadata )
```

Parameters

strMetadata   A string containing the XML metadata to be associated with the document. For more information, see the following description.

Returns

A Boolean value: `true` if successful; `false` otherwise.

Description

Method; sets the XML metadata for the specified document, overwriting any existing metadata. The XML passed as *strMetadata* is validated and may be rewritten before being stored. If it cannot be validated as legal XML or violates specific rules, then the XML metadata is not set and `false` is returned. (If `false` is returned, there is no way to get more detailed error information.)

 NOTE Even if true is returned, the XML that is set may not be exactly the same string that you passed in. To get the exact value to which the XML was set, use `document.getMetadata()`.

The format of the metadata is RDF that is compliant with the XMP specification. For more information about RDF and XMP, see the following sources:

- The RDF Primer at www.w3.org/TR/rdf-primer/
- The RDF specification at www.w3.org/TR/1999/REC-rdf-syntax-19990222/
- The XMP home page at www.adobe.com/products/xmp/

Example

The following examples show several different legal ways to represent the same data. In all of these cases but the second one, if the data were sent to `Document.setMetadata()`, it would not be rewritten (aside from removing line breaks).

In the first example, metadata is in tags, with different schemas placed in separate `rdf:Description` tags:

```
<rdf:RDF xmlns:rdf='http://www.w3.org/1999/02/22-rdf-syntax-ns#'>
  <rdf:Description rdf:about='' xmlns:dc='http://purl.org/dc/1.1/'>
    <dc:title>Simple title</dc:title>
    <dc:description>Simple description</dc:description>
  </rdf:Description>
  <rdf:Description rdf:about='' xmlns:xmp='http://ns.adobe.com/xap/1.0/'>
    <xmp:CreateDate>2004-10-12T10:29-07:00</xmp:CreateDate>
    <xmp:CreatorTool>Flash Authoring WIN 8,0,0,215</xmp:CreatorTool>
  </rdf:Description>
</rdf:RDF>
```

In the second example, metadata is in tags, but with different schemas all in one rdf:Description tag. This example also includes comments, which will be ignored and discarded by the Document.setMetadata():

```
<rdf:RDF xmlns:rdf='http://www.w3.org/1999/02/22-rdf-syntax-ns#'>
  <!-- This is before the first rdf:Description tag -->
  <rdf:Description rdf:about='' xmlns:dc='http://purl.org/dc/1.1/'>
    <dc:title>Simple title</dc:title>
    <dc:description>Simple description</dc:description>
  </rdf:Description>
  <!-- This is between the two rdf:Description tags -->
  <rdf:Description rdf:about='' xmlns:xmp='http://ns.adobe.com/xap/1.0/'>
    <xmp:CreateDate>2004-10-12T10:29-07:00</xmp:CreateDate>
    <xmp:CreatorTool>Flash Authoring WIN 8,0,0,215</xmp:CreatorTool>
  </rdf:Description>
  <!-- This is after the second rdf:Description tag -->
</rdf:RDF>
```

In the third example, metadata is in attributes, and different schemas are all in one rdf:Description tag:

```
<rdf:RDF xmlns:rdf='http://www.w3.org/1999/02/22-rdf-syntax-ns#'>
  <rdf:Description rdf:about='' xmlns:dc='http://purl.org/dc/1.1/'
  dc:title='Simple title'
dc:description='Simple description' />
  <rdf:Description rdf:about='' xmlns:xmp='http://ns.adobe.com/xap/1.0/'
xmp:CreateDate='2004-10-12T10:29-07:00' xmp:CreatorTool='Flash Authoring
  WIN 8,0,0,215' />
</rdf:RDF>
```

See also

document.getMetadata()

document.setSelectionBounds()

Availability

Flash MX 2004; *bContactSensitiveSelection* parameter added in Flash 8.

Usage

```
document.setSelectionBounds(boundingRectangle [,
  bContactSensitiveSelection])
```

Parameters

boundingRectangle   A rectangle that specifies the new location and size of the selection. For information on the format of *boundingRectangle*, see `document.addNewRectangle()`.

bContactSensitiveSelection   A Boolean value that specifies whether the Contact Sensitive selection mode is enabled (`true`) or disabled (`false`) during object selection. The default value is `false`.

Returns

Nothing.

Description

Method; moves and resizes the selection in a single operation.

If you pass a value for *bContactSensitiveSelection*, it is valid only for this method, and doesn't affect the Contact Sensitive selection mode for the document (see `fl.contactSensitiveSelection`).

Example

The following example moves the current selection to 10, 20 and resizes it to 100, 200:

```
var l = 10;
var t = 20;
fl.getDocumentDOM().setSelectionBounds({left:l, top:t, right:(100+l),
  bottom:(200+t)});
```

See also

`document.selection`, `document.setSelectionRect()`

document.setSelectionRect()

Availability

Flash MX 2004; *bContactSensitiveSelection* parameter added in Flash 8.

Usage

```
document.setSelectionRect(rect [, bReplaceCurrentSelection
  [, bContactSensitiveSelection]])
```

Parameters

rect   A rectangle object to set as selected. For information on the format of *rect*, see `document.addNewRectangle()`.

bReplaceCurrentSelection   A Boolean value that specifies whether the method replaces the current selection (`true`) or adds to the current selection (`false`). The default value is `true`.

bContactSensitiveSelection   A Boolean value that specifies whether the Contact Sensitive selection mode is enabled (`true`) or disabled (`false`) during object selection. The default value is `false`.

Returns

Nothing.

Description

Method; draws a rectangular selection marquee relative to the Stage, using the specified coordinates. This is unlike `document.getSelectionRect()`, in which the rectangle is relative to the object being edited.

This method is equivalent to dragging a rectangle with the arrow tool. An instance must be fully enclosed by the rectangle to be selected.

If you pass a value for *bContactSensitiveSelection*, it is valid only for this method, and doesn't affect the Contact Sensitive selection mode for the document (see `fl.contactSensitiveSelection`).

 NOTE Repeating `setSelectionRect()` using the History panel or menu item repeats the step previous to the `setSelectionRect()` operation.

Example

In the following example, the second selection replaces the first one:

```
fl.getDocumentDOM().setSelectionRect({left:1, top:1, right:200,
    bottom:200});
fl.getDocumentDOM().setSelectionRect({left:364.0, top:203.0, right:508.0,
    bottom:434.0}, true);
```

In the following example, the second selection is added to the first selection. This is the same as the manual operation of holding down Shift and selecting a second object.

```
fl.getDocumentDOM().setSelectionRect({left:1, top:1, right:200,
    bottom:200});
fl.getDocumentDOM().setSelectionRect({left:364.0, top:203.0, right:508.0,
    bottom:434.0}, false);
```

See also

`document.getSelectionRect()`, `document.selection`, `document.setSelectionBounds()`

document.setStroke()

Availability

Flash MX 2004.

Usage

```
document.setStroke( color, size, strokeType )
```

Parameters

color   The color of the stroke, in one of the following formats:

- A string in the format "#RRGGBB" or "#RRGGBBAA"
- A hexadecimal number in the format 0xRRGGBB
- An integer that represents the decimal equivalent of a hexadecimal number

size   A floating-point value that specifies the new stroke size for the selection.

strokeType   A string that specifies the new type of stroke for the selection.
Acceptable values are "hairline", "solid", "dashed", "dotted", "ragged", "stipple", and "hatched".

Returns

Nothing.

Description

Method; sets the color, width, and style of the selected strokes. For information on changing the stroke in the Tools panel and Property inspector, see `document.setCustomStroke()`.

Example

The following example sets the color of the stroke to red, the size to 3.25, and the type to dashed:

```
fl.getDocumentDOM().setStroke("#ff0000", 3.25, "dashed");
```

document.setStrokeColor()

Availability

Flash MX 2004.

Usage

```
document.setStrokeColor( color )
```

Parameters

color The color of the stroke, in one of the following formats:

- A string in the format "#RRGGBB" or "#RRGGBBAA"
- A hexadecimal number in the format 0xRRGGBB
- An integer that represents the decimal equivalent of a hexadecimal number

Returns

Nothing.

Description

Method; changes the stroke color of the selection to the specified color. For information on changing the stroke in the Tools panel and Property inspector, see `document.setCustomStroke()`.

Example

The three statements in the following example set the stroke color using each of the different formats for specifying color:

```
flash.getDocumentDOM().setStrokeColor("#cc00cc");
flash.getDocumentDOM().setStrokeColor(0xcc00cc);
flash.getDocumentDOM().setStrokeColor(120000);
```

document.setStrokeSize()

Availability

Flash MX 2004.

Usage

```
document.setStrokeSize( size )
```

Parameters

size A floating-point value from 0.25 to 10 that specifies the stroke size. The method ignores precision greater than two decimal places.

Returns

Nothing.

Description

Method; changes the stroke size of the selection to the specified size. For information on changing the stroke in the Tools panel and Property inspector, see `document.setCustomStroke()`.

Example

The following example changes the stroke size for the selection to 5:

```
fl.getDocumentDOM().setStrokeSize(5);
```

document.setStrokeStyle()

Availability

Flash MX 2004.

Usage

```
document.setStrokeStyle( strokeType )
```

Parameters

strokeType   A string that specifies the stroke style for the current selection. Acceptable values are `"hairline"`, `"solid"`, `"dashed"`, `"dotted"`, `"ragged"`, `"stipple"`, and `"hatched"`.

Returns

Nothing.

Description

Method; changes the stroke style of the selection to the specified style. For information on changing the stroke in the Tools panel and Property inspector, see `document.setCustomStroke()`.

Example

The following example changes the stroke style for the selection to `"dashed"`:

```
fl.getDocumentDOM().setStrokeStyle("dashed");
```

document.setTextRectangle()

Availability

Flash MX 2004.

Usage

```
document.setTextRectangle( boundingRectangle )
```

Parameters

boundingRectangle   A text rectangle object that specifies the new size within which the text item should flow. For information on the format of *boundingRectangle*, see `document.addNewRectangle()`.

Returns

A Boolean value: `true` if the size of at least one text field is changed; `false` otherwise.

Description

Method; changes the bounding rectangle for the selected text item to the specified size. This method causes the text to reflow inside the new rectangle; the text item is not scaled or transformed. The values passed in *boundingRectangle* are used as follows:

- If the text is horizontal and static, the method takes into account only the width value passed in *boundingRectangle*; the height is automatically computed to fit all the text.
- If the text is vertical (and therefore static), the method takes into account only the height value passed in *boundingRectangle*; the width is automatically computed to fit all the text.
- If the text is dynamic or input, the method takes into account both the width and height values passed in *boundingRectangle*, and the resulting rectangle might be larger than needed to fit all the text. However, if the parameters specify a rectangle size that is too small to fit all the text, the method takes into account only the width value passed in *boundingRectangle* (the height is automatically computed to fit all the text).

Example

The following example changes the size of the bounding text rectangle to the specified dimensions:

```
fl.getDocumentDOM().setTextRectangle({left:0, top:0, right:50, bottom:200})
```

document.setTextSelection()

Availability

Flash MX 2004.

Usage

```
document.setTextSelection( startIndex, endIndex )
```

Parameters

startIndex   An integer that specifies the position of the first character to select. The first character position is 0 (zero).

endIndex   An integer that specifies the end position of the selection up to, but not including, *endIndex*. The first character position is 0 (zero).

Returns

A Boolean value: true if the method can successfully set the text selection; false otherwise.

Description

Method; sets the text selection of the currently selected text field to the values specified by the *startIndex* and *endIndex* values. Text editing is activated, if it isn't already.

Example

The following example selects the text from the 6th character through the 25th character:

```
fl.document.setTextSelection(5, 25);
```

document.setTextString()

Availability

Flash MX 2004.

Usage

```
document.setTextString( text [, startIndex [, endIndex]] )
```

Parameters

text   A string of the characters to insert in the text field.

startIndex   An integer that specifies first character to replace. The first character position is 0 (zero). This parameter is optional.

endIndex   An integer that specifies the last character to replace. The first character position is 0 (zero). This parameter is optional.

Returns

A Boolean value: true if the text of at least one text string is set; false otherwise.

Description

Method; inserts a string of text. If the optional parameters are not passed, the existing text selection is replaced; if the text object isn't currently being edited, the whole text string is replaced. If only *startIndex* is passed, the string passed is inserted at this position. If *startIndex* and *endIndex* are passed, the string passed replaces the segment of text starting from *startIndex* up to, but not including, *endIndex*.

Example

The following example replaces the current text selection with "Hello World":

```
var success = fl.getDocumentDOM().setTextString("Hello World!");
```

The following example inserts "hello" at position 6 of the current text selection:

```
var pass = fl.getDocumentDOM().setTextString("hello", 6);
```

The following example inserts "Howdy" starting at position 2 and up to, but not including, position 7 of the current text selection:

```
var ok = fl.getDocumentDOM().setTextString("Howdy", 2, 7);
```

See also

```
document.getTextString()
```

document.setTransformationPoint()

Availability

Flash MX 2004.

Usage

```
document.setTransformationPoint( transformationPoint )
```

Parameters

transformationPoint   A pair of floating-point numbers that specifies values for each of the following elements:

- Shapes: *transformationPoint* is set relative to document. 0,0 is the same as the Stage (upper-left corner).
- Symbols: *transformationPoint* is set relative to the symbol's registration point. 0,0 is located at the registration point.

- Text: *transformationPoint* is set relative to the text field. 0,0 is the upper-eft corner of text field.

- Bitmaps/videos: *transformationPoint* is set relative to bitmap/video. 0,0 is the upper-left corner of the bitmap or video.

- Groups: *transformationPoint* is set relative to document. 0,0 is the same as the Stage (upper-left corner).

Returns

Nothing.

Description

Method; moves the transformation point of the current selection.

Example

The following example sets the transformation point of the current selection to 100, 200:

```
fl.getDocumentDOM().setTransformationPoint({x:100, y:200});
```

See also

```
document.getTransformationPoint()
```

document.silent

Availability

Flash MX 2004.

Usage

```
document.silent
```

Description

Property; a Boolean value that specifies whether the object is accessible. This is equivalent to the inverse logic of the Make Movie Accessible setting in the Accessibility panel. That is, if document.silent is true, it is the same as the Make Movie Accessible option being unchecked. If it is false, it is the same as the Make Movie Accessible option being checked.

Example

The following example sets the isSilent variable to the value of the silent property:

```
var isSilent = fl.getDocumentDOM().silent;
```

The following example sets the silent property to false, indicating that the document is accessible:

```
fl.getDocumentDOM().silent = false;
```

document.skewSelection()

Availability

Flash MX 2004.

Usage

```
document.skewSelection( xSkew, ySkew [, whichEdge] )
```

Parameters

xSkew   A floating-point number that specifies the amount of *x* by which to skew, measured in degrees.

ySkew   A floating-point number that specifies the amount of *y* by which to skew, measured in degrees.

whichEdge   A string that specifies the edge where the transformation occurs; if omitted, skew occurs at the transformation point. Acceptable values are "top center", "right center", "bottom center", and "left center". This parameter is optional.

Returns

Nothing.

Description

Method; skews the selection by a specified amount. The effect is the same as using the Free Transform tool to skew the object.

Example

The following examples skew the selected object by 2.0 vertically and 1.5 horizontally. The second example transforms the object at the top center edge:

```
flash.getDocumentDOM().skewSelection(2.0, 1.5);
flash.getDocumentDOM().skewSelection(2.0, 1.5, "top center");
```

document.smoothSelection()

Availability

Flash MX 2004.

Usage

```
document.smoothSelection()
```

Parameters

None.

Returns

Nothing.

Description

Method; smooths the curve of each selected fill outline or curved line. This method performs the same action as the Smooth button in the Tools panel.

Example

The following example smooths the curve of the current selection:

```
fl.getDocumentDOM().smoothSelection();
```

document.space()

Availability

Flash MX 2004.

Usage

```
document.space( direction [, bUseDocumentBounds] )
```

Parameters

direction   A string that specifies the direction in which to space the objects in the selection. Acceptable values are `"horizontal"` or `"vertical"`.

bUseDocumentBounds   A Boolean value that, when set to `true`, spaces the objects to the document bounds. Otherwise, the method uses the bounds of the selected objects. The default is `false`. This parameter is optional.

Returns

Nothing.

Description

Method; spaces the objects in the selection evenly.

Example

The following example spaces the objects horizontally, relative to the Stage:

```
fl.getDocumentDOM().space("horizontal",true);
```

The following example spaces the objects horizontally, relative to each other:

```
fl.getDocumentDOM().space("horizontal");
```

The following example spaces the objects horizontally, relative to each other, with *bUseDcoumentBounds* expressly set to `false`:

```
fl.getDocumentDOM().space("horizontal",false);
```

See also

`document.getAlignToDocument()`, `document.setAlignToDocument()`

document.straightenSelection()

Availability

Flash MX 2004.

Usage

```
document.straightenSelection()
```

Parameters

None.

Returns

Nothing.

Description

Method; straightens the currently selected strokes. This method is equivalent to using the Straighten button in the Tools panel.

Example

The following example straightens the curve of the current selection:

```
fl.getDocumentDOM().straightenSelection();
```

document.swapElement()

Availability

Flash MX 2004.

Usage

```
document.swapElement( name )
```

Parameters

name   A string that specifies the name of the library item to use.

Returns

Nothing.

Description

Method; swaps the current selection with the specified one. The selection must contain a graphic, button, movie clip, video, or bitmap. This method displays an error message if no object is selected or the given object could not be found.

Example

The following example swaps the current selection with Symbol 1 from the library:

```
fl.getDocumentDOM().swapElement('Symbol 1');
```

document.swapStrokeAndFill()

Availability

Flash 8.

Usage

```
document.swapStrokeAndFill();
```

Parameters

None.

Returns

Nothing.

Description

Method; swaps the Stroke and Fill colors.

Example

The following example swaps the Stroke and Fill colors in the current document:

```
fl.getDocumentDOM().swapStrokeAndFill();
```

document.testMovie()

Availability

Flash MX 2004.

Usage

```
document.testMovie()
```

Parameters

None.

Returns

Nothing.

Description

Method; executes a Test Movie operation on the document.

Example

The following example tests the movie for the current document:

```
fl.getDocumentDOM().testMovie();
```

See also

```
document.canTestMovie(), document.testScene()
```

document.testScene()

Availability

Flash MX 2004.

Usage

```
document.testScene()
```

Parameters

None.

Returns

Nothing.

Description

Method; executes a Test Scene operation on the current scene of the document.

Example

The following example tests the current scene in the document:

```
fl.getDocumentDOM().testScene();
```

See also

`document.canTestScene()`, `document.testMovie()`

document.timelines

Availability

Flash MX 2004.

Usage

```
document.timelines
```

Description

Read-only property; an array of Timeline objects (see Timeline object).

Example

The following example gets the array of current timelines in the active document and displays their names in the Output panel:

```
var i = 0;
var curTimelines = fl.getDocumentDOM().timelines;
while(i < fl.getDocumentDOM().timelines.length){
  alert(curTimelines[i].name);
  ++i;
}
```

See also

`document.currentTimeline`, `document.getTimeline()`

document.traceBitmap()

Availability

Flash MX 2004.

Usage

```
document.traceBitmap( threshold, minimumArea, curveFit, cornerThreshold )
```

Parameters

threshold   An integer that controls the number of colors in your traced bitmap. Acceptable values are integers between 0 and 500.

minimumArea   An integer that specifies the radius measured in pixels. Acceptable values are integers between 1 and 1000.

curveFit   A string that specifies how smoothly outlines are drawn. Acceptable values are "pixels", "very tight", "tight", "normal", "smooth", and "very smooth".

cornerThreshold   A string that is similar to *curveFit*, but it pertains to the corners of the bitmap image. Acceptable values are "many corners", "normal", and "few corners".

Returns

Nothing.

Description

Method; performs a trace bitmap on the current selection. This method is equivalent to selecting Modify > Bitmap > Trace Bitmap.

Example

The following example traces the selected bitmap, using the specified parameters:

```
fl.getDocumentDOM().traceBitmap(0, 500, 'normal', 'normal');
```

document.transformSelection()

Availability

Flash MX 2004.

Usage

```
document.transformSelection( a, b, c, d)
```

Parameters

a   A floating-point number that specifies the (0,0) element of the transformation matrix.

b   A floating-point number that specifies the (0,1) element of the transformation matrix.

c   A floating-point number that specifies the (1,0) element of the transformation matrix.

d   A floating-point number that specifies the (1,1) element of the transformation matrix.

Returns

Nothing.

Description

Method; performs a general transformation on the current selection by applying the matrix specified in the arguments. For more information, see the `element.matrix` property.

Example

The following example stretches the selection by a factor of 2 in the x direction:

```
fl.getDocumentDOM().transformSelection(2.0, 0.0, 0.0, 1.0);
```

document.unGroup()

Availability

Flash MX 2004.

Usage

```
document.unGroup()
```

Parameters

None.

Returns

Nothing.

Description

Method; ungroups the current selection.

Example

The following example ungroups the elements in the current selection:

```
fl.getDocumentDOM().unGroup();
```

See also

```
document.group()
```

document.union()

Availability

Flash 8.

Usage

```
document.union()
```

Parameters

None.

Returns

A Boolean value: `true` if successful; `false` otherwise.

Description

Method; combines all selected shapes into a drawing object.

Example

The following example combines all selected shapes into a drawing object:

```
fl.getDocumentDOM().union();
```

See also

`document.crop()`, `document.deleteEnvelope()`, `document.intersect()`, `document.punch()`, `shape.isDrawingObject`

document.unlockAllElements()

Availability

Flash MX 2004.

Usage

```
document.unlockAllElements()
```

Parameters

None.

Returns

Nothing.

Description

Method; unlocks all locked elements on the currently selected frame.

Example

The following example unlocks all locked objects in the current frame:

```
fl.getDocumentDOM().unlockAllElements();
```

See also

`element.locked`

document.viewMatrix

Availability

Flash MX 2004.

Usage

```
document.viewMatrix
```

Description

Read-only property; a Matrix object. The `viewMatrix` is used to transform from object space to document space when the document is in edit mode. The mouse location, as a tool receives it, is relative to the object that is currently being edited. See Matrix object.

For example, if you create a symbol, double-click to edit it, and draw with the PolyStar tool, the point (0,0) will be at the registration point of the symbol. However, the drawingLayer object expects values in document space, so if you draw a line from (0,0) using the drawingLayer, it will start at the upper-left corner of the Stage. The `viewMatrix` provides a way to transform from the space of the object being edited to document space.

Example

The following example gets the value of the `viewMatrix` property:

```
var mat = fl.getDocumentDOM().viewMatrix;
```

document.width

Availability

Flash MX 2004.

Usage

```
document.width
```

Description

Property; an integer that specifies the width of the document (Stage) in pixels.

Example

The following example sets the width of the Stage to 400 pixels.

```
fl.getDocumentDOM().width= 400;
```

See also

```
document.height
```

document.xmlPanel()

Availability

Flash MX 2004.

Usage

```
document.xmlPanel( fileURI )
```

Parameters

fileURI   A string, expressed as a file:/// URI, that specifies the path to the XML file defining the controls in the panel. The full path is required.

Returns

An object that has properties defined for all controls defined in the XML file. All properties are returned as strings. The returned object will have one predefined property named "dismiss" that will have the string value "accept" or "cancel".

Description

Method; posts an XMLUI dialog box. See `fl.xmlui`.

Example

The following example loads the Test.xml file and displays each property contained within it:

```
var obj = fl.getDocumentDOM().xmlPanel(fl.configURI + "Commands/Test.xml");
for (var prop in obj) {
  fl.trace("property " + prop + " = " + obj[prop]);
}
```

document.zoomFactor

Availability

Flash 8.

Usage

```
document.zoomFactor
```

Description

Property; specifies the zoom percent of the Stage at author time. A value of 1 equals 100% zoom, 8 equals 800%, .5 equals 50%, and so on.

Example

The following example sets the zoom factor of the Stage to 200%.

```
fl.getDocumentDOM().zoomFactor = 2;
```

drawingLayer object

Availability

Flash MX 2004.

Description

The drawingLayer object is accessible from JavaScript as a child of the flash object. The drawingLayer object is used for extensible tools when the user wants to temporarily draw while dragging—for example, when creating a selection marquee. You should call drawingLayer.beginFrame() before you call any other drawingLayer methods.

Method summary for the drawingLayer object

The following methods are available for the drawingLayer object:

Methods	Description
drawingLayer.beginDraw()	Puts Flash in drawing mode.
drawingLayer.beginFrame()	Erases what was previously drawn using the drawingLayer and prepares for more drawing commands.
drawingLayer.cubicCurveTo()	Draws a cubic curve from the current pen location using the parameters as the coordinates of the cubic segment.
drawingLayer.curveTo()	Draws a quadratic curve segment starting at the current drawing position and ending at a specified point.
drawingLayer.drawPath()	Draws the specified path.
drawingLayer.endDraw()	Exits drawing mode.
drawingLayer.endFrame()	Signals the end of a group of drawing commands.
drawingLayer.lineTo()	Draws a line from the current drawing position to the point (x,y).
drawingLayer.moveTo()	Sets the current drawing position.
drawingLayer.newPath()	Returns a new Path object.
drawingLayer.setColor()	Sets the color of subsequently drawn data.

drawingLayer.beginDraw()

Availability

Flash MX 2004.

Usage

```
drawingLayer.beginDraw([persistentDraw])
```

Parameters

persistentDraw   A Boolean value (optional). If set to `true`, it indicates that the drawing in the last frame remains on the Stage until a new `beginDraw()` or `beginFrame()` call is made. (In this context, *frame* refers to where you start and end drawing; it does not refer to timeline frames.) For example, when users draw a rectangle, they can preview the outline of the shape while dragging the mouse. If you want that preview shape to remain after the user releases the mouse button, set *persistentDraw* to `true`.

Returns

Nothing.

Description

Method; puts Flash in drawing mode. Drawing mode is used for temporary drawing while the mouse button is pressed. You typically use this method only when creating extensible tools.

Example

The following example puts Flash in drawing mode:

```
fl.drawingLayer.beginDraw();
```

drawingLayer.beginFrame()

Availability

Flash MX 2004.

Usage

```
drawingLayer.beginFrame()
```

Parameters

None.

Returns

Nothing.

Description

Method; erases what was previously drawn using the drawingLayer and prepares for more drawing commands. Should be called after `drawingLayer.beginDraw()`. Everything drawn between `drawingLayer.beginFrame()` and an `drawingLayer.endFrame()` remains on the Stage until you call the next `beginFrame()` and `endFrame()`. (In this context, *frame* refers to where you start and end drawing; it does not refer to timeline frames.) You typically use this method only when creating extensible tools. See `drawingLayer.beginDraw()`.

drawingLayer.cubicCurveTo()

Availability

Flash MX 2004.

Usage

```
drawingLayer.cubicCurveTo(x1Ctrl, y1Ctrl, x2Ctl, y2Ctl, xEnd, yEnd)
```

Parameters

x1Ctl   A floating-point value that is the *x* location of the first control point.

y1Ctl   A floating-point value that is the *y* location of the first control point.

x2Ctl   A floating-point value that is the *x* position of the middle control point.

y2Ctl   A floating-point value that is the *y* position of the middle control point.

xEnd   A floating-point value that is the *x* position of the end control point.

yEnd   A floating-point value that is the *y* position of the end control point.

Returns

Nothing.

Description

Method; draws a cubic curve from the current pen location using the parameters as the coordinates of the cubic segment. You typically use this method only when creating extensible tools.

Example

The following example draws a cubic curve using the specified control points:

```
fl.drawingLayer.cubicCurveTo(0, 0, 1, 1, 2, 0);
```

drawingLayer.curveTo()

Availability

Flash MX 2004.

Usage

```
drawingLayer.curveTo(xCtl, yCtl, xEnd, yEnd)
```

Parameters

xCtl   A floating-point value that is the *x* position of the control point.

yCtl   A floating-point value that is the *y* position of the control point.

xEnd   A floating-point value that is the *x* position of the end control point.

yEnd   A floating-point value that is the *y* position of the end control point.

Returns

Nothing.

Description

Method; draws a quadratic curve segment starting at the current drawing position and ending at a specified point. You typically use this method only when creating extensible tools.

Example

The following example draws a quadratic curve using the specified control points:

```
fl.drawingLayer.curveTo(0, 0, 2, 0);
```

drawingLayer.drawPath()

Availability

Flash MX 2004.

Usage

```
drawingLayer.drawPath(path)
```

Parameters

path   A Path object to draw.

Returns

Nothing.

Description

Method; draws the path specified by the *path* parameter. You typically use this method only when creating extensible tools.

Example

The following example draws a path specified by the Path object named `gamePath`:

```
fl.drawingLayer.drawPath(gamePath);
```

drawingLayer.endDraw()

Availability

Flash MX 2004.

Usage

```
drawingLayer.endDraw()
```

Parameters

None.

Returns

Nothing.

Description

Method; exits drawing mode. Drawing mode is used when you want to temporarily draw while the mouse button is pressed. You typically use this method only when creating extensible tools.

Example

The following example exits drawing mode:

```
fl.drawingLayer.endDraw();
```

drawingLayer.endFrame()

Availability

Flash MX 2004.

Usage

```
drawingLayer.endFrame()
```

Parameters

None.

Returns

Nothing.

Description

Method; signals the end of a group of drawing commands. A group of drawing commands refers to everything drawn between `drawingLayer.beginFrame()` and `drawingLayer.endFrame()`. The next call to `drawingLayer.beginFrame()` will erase whatever was drawn in this group of drawing commands. You typically use this method only when creating extensible tools.

drawingLayer.lineTo()

Availability

Flash MX 2004.

Usage

```
drawingLayer.lineTo(x, y)
```

Parameters

x   A floating-point value that is the *x* coordinate of the end point of the line to draw.

y   A floating-point value that is the *y* coordinate of the end point of the line to draw.

Returns

Nothing.

Description

Method; draws a line from the current drawing position to the point (*x,y*). You typically use this method only when creating extensible tools.

Example

The following example draws a line from the current drawing position to the point (20,30):

```
fl.drawingLayer.lineTo(20, 30);
```

drawingLayer.moveTo()

Availability

Flash MX 2004.

Usage

```
drawingLayer.moveTo(x, y)
```

Parameters

x   A floating-point value that specifies the *x* coordinate of the position at which to start drawing.

y   A floating-point value that specifies the *y* coordinate of the position at which to start drawing.

Returns

Nothing.

Description

Method; sets the current drawing position. You typically use this method only when creating extensible tools.

Example

The following example sets the current drawing position at the point (10,15):

```
fl.drawingLayer.moveTo(10, 15);
```

drawingLayer.newPath()

Availability

Flash MX 2004.

Usage

```
drawingLayer.newPath()
```

Parameters

None.

Returns

A Path object.

Description

Method; returns a new Path object. You typically use this method only when creating extensible tools. See Path object.

Example

The following example returns a new Path object:

```
fl.drawingLayer.newPath();
```

drawingLayer.setColor()

Availability

Flash MX 2004.

Usage

```
drawingLayer.setColor(color)
```

Parameters

color   The color of subsequently drawn data, in one of the following formats:

- A string in the format "#RRGGBB" or "#RRGGBBAA"
- A hexadecimal number in the format 0xRRGGBB
- An integer that represents the decimal equivalent of a hexadecimal number

Returns

Nothing.

Description

Method; sets the color of subsequently drawn data. Applies only to persistent data. To use this method, the parameter passed to `drawingLayer.beginDraw()` must be set to `true`. You typically use this method only when creating extensible tools. See `drawingLayer.beginDraw()`.

Example

The following example draws a red line on the Stage:

```
fl.drawingLayer.beginDraw( true );
fl.drawingLayer.beginFrame();
fl.drawingLayer.setColor( "#ff0000" );
fl.drawingLayer.moveTo(0,0);
fl.drawingLayer.lineTo(100,100);
fl.drawingLayer.endFrame();
fl.drawingLayer.endDraw();
```

Edge object

Availability

Flash MX 2004.

Description

The Edge object represents an edge of a shape on the Stage.

Method summary for the Edge object

The following methods are available for the Edge object:

Method	Description
edge.getControl()	Gets a point object set to the location of the specified control point of the edge.
edge.getHalfEdge()	Returns a HalfEdge object.
edge.setControl()	Sets the position of the control point of the edge.
edge.splitEdge()	Splits the edge into two pieces.

Property summary for the Edge object

The following properties are available for the Edge object:

Property	Description
edge.id	Read-only; an integer that represents a unique identifier for the edge.
edge.isLine	Read-only; an integer with a value of 0 or 1.

edge.getControl()

Availability

Flash MX 2004.

Usage

edge.getControl(*i*)

Parameters

i An integer that specifies which control point of the edge to return. Specify 0 for the first control point, 1 for the middle control point, or 2 for the end control point. If the edge.isLine property is true, the middle control point is set to the midpoint of the segment joining the beginning and ending control points.

Returns

The specified control point.

Description

Method; gets a point object set to the location of the specified control point of the edge.

Example

The following example stores the first control point of the specified shape in the pt variable:

```
var shape = fl.getDocumentDOM().selection[0];
var pt = shape.edges[0].getControl(0);
```

edge.getHalfEdge()

Availability

Flash MX 2004.

Usage

```
edge.getHalfEdge(index)
```

Parameters

index An integer that specifies which half edge to return. The value of *index* must be either 0 for the first half edge or 1 for the second half edge.

Returns

A HalfEdge object.

Description

Method; returns a HalfEdge object.

Example

The following example stores the half edges of the specified edge in the `hEdge0` and `hEdge1` variables:

```
var shape = fl.getDocumentDOM().selection[0];
var edge = shape.edges[0];
var hEdge0 = edge.getHalfEdge(0);
var hEdge1 = edge.getHalfEdge(1);
```

edge.id

Availability

Flash MX 2004.

Usage

```
edge.id
```

Description

Read-only property; an integer that represents a unique identifier for the edge.

Example

The following example stores a unique identifier for the specified edge in the `my_shape_id` variable:

```
var shape = fl.getDocumentDOM().selection[0];
var my_shape_id = shape.edges[0].id;
```

edge.isLine

Availability

Flash MX 2004.

Usage

```
edge.isLine
```

Description

Read-only property; an integer with a value of 0 or 1. A value of 1 indicates that the edge is a straight line. In that case, the middle control point bisects the line joining the two end points.

Example

The following example determines whether the specified edge is a straight line, and shows a value of 1 (it is a straight line) or 0 (it isn't a straight line) in the Output panel:

```
var shape = fl.getDocumentDOM().selection[0];
fl.trace(shape.edges[0].isLine);
```

edge.setControl()

Availability

Flash MX 2004.

Usage

```
edge.setControl( index, x, y )
```

Parameters

index   An integer that specifies which control point to set. Use values 0, 1, or 2 to specify the beginning, middle, and end control points, respectively.

x   A floating-point value that specifies the horizontal location of the control point. If the Stage is in Edit or Edit-in-place mode, the point coordinate is relative to the edited object. Otherwise, the point coordinate is relative to the Stage.

y   A floating-point value that specifies the vertical location of the control point. If the Stage is in Edit or Edit-in-place mode, the point coordinate is relative to the edited object. Otherwise, the point coordinate is relative to the Stage.

Returns

Nothing.

Description

Method; sets the position of the control point of the edge. You must call `shape.beginEdit()` before using this method. See `shape.beginEdit()`.

Example

The following example sets the beginning control point of the specified edge to the (0, 1) coordinates:

```
x = 0; y = 1;
var shape = fl.getDocumentDOM().selection[0];
shape.beginEdit();
shape.edges[0].setControl(0, x, y);
shape.endEdit();
```

edge.splitEdge()

Availability

Flash MX 2004.

Usage

```
edge.splitEdge( t )
```

Parameters

t   A floating-point value between 0 and 1 that specifies where to split the edge. A value of 0 represents one end point, and 1 the other. For example, passing a value of 0.5 splits the edge in the middle, which, for a line is exactly in the center. If the edge represents a curve, 0.5 represents the parametric middle of the curve.

Returns

Nothing.

Description

Method; splits the edge into two pieces. You must call `shape.beginEdit()` before using this method.

Example

The following example splits the specified edge in half:

```
var shape = fl.getDocumentDOM().selection[0];
shape.beginEdit()
shape.edges[0].splitEdge( 0.5 );
shape.endEdit()
```

Effect object

Availability

Flash MX 2004.

Description

This is a single effect descriptor object. The `fl.activeEffect` and the `fl.effects` properties contain this type of object. The Effect object represents an instance of a timeline effect. See `fl.activeEffect` and `fl.effects`.

Property summary for the Effect object

In addition to the properties listed in the following table, Effect objects can also have user-defined parameters, which must be specified in the same XML file that specifies the `effect.effectName` and `effect.sourceFile` properties. These parameters specify which user interface elements should be created (such as edit fields, check boxes, and list boxes), which is controlled by the type of effect you are creating. You can specify labels that will appear with the control in addition to default values.

Property	Description
effect.effectName	Read-only; a string that appears in the Context menu for effects.
effect.groupName	Read-only; a string that represents the name of the effect group used for the hierarchical Context menu for effects.
effect.sourceFile	Read-only; a string that specifies the name of JSFL source file for the specified effect.
effect.symbolType	Read-only; a string that specifies the type of symbol to create during the initial application of the effect.
effect.useXMLToUI	A Boolean value that lets you override the default behavior of using XMLUI to construct a dialog box that consists of one or more controls.

effect.effectName

Availability

Flash MX 2004.

Usage

`effect.effectName`

Description

Read-only property; a string that appears in the Context menu for effects. Each effect must be uniquely named.

Example

The following example stores the name of the current effect in the `efName` variable:

```
var efName = fl.activeEffect.effectName;
```

effect.groupName

Availability

Flash MX 2004.

Usage

```
effect.groupName
```

Description

Read-only property; a string that represents the name of the effect group used for the hierarchical Context menu for effects. If this value is an empty string, the effect appears ungrouped at the top level of the Context menu. The group name and effect name are specified in the XML file for the effect.

Example

The following example stores the group name of the current effect in the `efGroupName` variable:

```
var efGroupName = fl.activeEffect.groupName;
```

effect.sourceFile

Availability

Flash MX 2004.

Usage

```
effect.sourceFile
```

Description

Read-only property; a string that specifies the name of JSFL source file for the specified effect. This string is used to bind an XML parameter file to its JSFL effect implementation. You must include this XML parameter in the XML file for the effect.

Example

The following example stores the name of the JSFL effect source file in the `efSourceFile` variable:

```
var efSourceFile = fl.activeEffect.sourceFile;
```

effect.symbolType

Availability

Flash MX 2004.

Usage

```
effect.symbolType
```

Description

Read-only property; a string that specifies the type of symbol to create during the initial application of the effect. The supported types are: `"graphic"`, `"movie clip"`, and `"button"`. If a symbol type was not specified when the effect was created, the default value is `"graphic"`.

Example

The following example stores the symbol type for the current effect in the `efType` variable:

```
var efType = fl.activeEffect.symbolType;
```

effect.useXMLToUI

Availability

Flash MX 2004.

Usage

```
effect.useXMLToUI
```

Description

Property; a Boolean value that lets you override the default behavior of using XMLUI to construct a dialog box that consists of one or more controls. The default value is `true`. If set to `false`, the standard XMLUI dialog box will not be posted and you are responsible for posting a UI.

Example

The following example specifies that the effect posts its own UI:

```
function configureEffect() {
  fl.activeEffect.useXMLToUI = false;
}
```

Element object

Availability

Flash MX 2004.

Description

Everything that appears on the Stage is of the type Element. The following code example lets you select an element:

```
fl.getDocumentDOM().getTimeline().layers[0].frames[0].elements[0];
```

Method summary for the Element object

The following methods are available for the Element object:

Method	Description
element.getPersistentData()	Retrieves the value of the data specified by the *name* parameter.
element.hasPersistentData()	Determines whether the specified data has been attached to the specified element.
element.removePersistentData()	Removes any persistent data with the specified name that has been attached to the object.
element.setPersistentData()	Stores data with an element.

Property summary for the Element object

The following properties are available for the Element object:

Property	Description
element.depth	Read-only; an integer that has a value greater than 0 for the depth of the object in the view.
element.elementType	Read-only; a string that represents the type of the specified element.
element.height	A float value that specifies the height of the element in pixels.
element.layer	Read-only; represents the Layer object on which the element is located.
element.left	Read-only; a float value that represents the left side of the element.

Property	Description
element.locked	A Boolean value: `true` if the element is locked; `false` otherwise.
element.matrix	A Matrix object. The `matrix` has properties `a, b, c, d, tx,` and `ty. a, b, c, d` are floating-point values; `tx` and `ty` are coordinates.
element.name	A string that specifies the name of the element, normally referred to as the Instance name.
element.selected	A Boolean value that specifies whether the element is selected or not.
element.top	Read-only; top side of the element.
element.width	A float value that specifies the width of the element in pixels.

element.depth

Availability

Flash MX 2004.

Usage

`element.depth`

Description

Read-only property; an integer that has a value greater than 0 for the depth of the object in the view. The drawing order of objects on the Stage specifies which one is on top of the others. Object order can also be managed with the Modify > Arrange menu item.

Example

The following example displays the depth of the specified element in the Output panel:

```
// Select an object and run this script.
fl.trace("Depth of selected object: " +
    fl.getDocumentDOM().selection[0].depth);
```

See the example for `element.elementType`.

element.elementType

Availability

Flash MX 2004.

Usage

```
element.elementType
```

Description

Read-only property; a string that represents the type of the specified element. The value
is one of the following: `"shape"`, `"text"`, `"instance"`, or `"shapeObj"`. A `"shapeObj"` is
created with an extensible tool.

Example

The following example stores the type of the first element in the eType variable:

```
// In a new file, place a movie clip on first frame top layer, and
// then run this line of script.
var eType =
    fl.getDocumentDOM().getTimeline().layers[0].frames[0].elements[0].elemen
    tType; // eType = instance
```

The following example displays several properties for all the elements in the current layer
or frame:

```
var tl = fl.getDocumentDOM().getTimeline()
var elts = tl.layers[tl.currentLayer].frames[tl.currentFrame].elements;
for (var x = 0; x < elts.length; x++) {
    var elt = elts[x];
    fl.trace("Element "+ x +" Name = " + elt.name + " Type = " +
    elt.elementType + " location = " + elt.left + "," + elt.top + " Depth = "
    + elt.depth);
}
```

element.getPersistentData()

Availability

Flash MX 2004.

Usage

```
element.getPersistentData( name )
```

Parameters

name   A string that identifies the data to be returned.

Returns

The data specified by the *name* parameter, or 0 if the data doesn't exist.

Description

Method; retrieves the value of the data specified by the *name* parameter. The type of data depends on the type of the data that was stored (see element.setPersistentData()). Only symbols and bitmaps support persistent data.

Example

The following example sets and gets data for the specified element, shows its value in the Output panel, and then removes the data:

```
// At least one symbol or bitmap is selected in the first layer, first
   frame.
var elt =
   fl.getDocumentDOM().getTimeline().layers[0].frames[0].elements[0];
elt.setPersistentData("myData","integer", 12);
if (elt.hasPersistentData("myData")){

   fl.trace("myData = "+ elt.getPersistentData("myData"));
   elt.removePersistentData( "myData" );
   fl.trace("myData = "+ elt.getPersistentData("myData"));

}
```

element.hasPersistentData()

Availability

Flash MX 2004.

Usage

element.hasPersistentData(*name*)

Parameters

name   A string that specifies the name of the data item to test.

Returns

A Boolean value: true if the specified data is attached to the object; false otherwise.

Description

Method; determines whether the specified data has been attached to the specified element. Only symbols and bitmaps support persistent data.

Example

See `element.getPersistentData()`.

element.height

Availability

Flash MX 2004.

Usage

`element.height`

Description

Property; a float value that specifies the height of the element in pixels.

 Do not use this property to resize a text field. Instead, select the text field and use `document.setTextRectangle()`. Using this property with a text field scales the text.

Example

The following example sets the height of the specified element to 100:

```
fl.getDocumentDOM().getTimeline().layers[0].frames[0].elements[0].height =
    100;
```

element.layer

Availability

Flash 8.

Usage

`element.layer`

Description

Read-only property; represents the Layer object on which the element is located.

Example

The following example stores the Layer object that contains the element in the `theLayer` variable:

```
var theLayer = element.layer;
```

element.left

Availability

Flash MX 2004.

Usage

```
element.left
```

Description

Read-only property; a float value that represents the left side of the element. The value of element.left is relative to the upper left of the Stage for elements that are in a scene, and is relative to the symbol's registration point if the element is stored within a symbol. Use document.setSelectionBounds() or document.moveSelectionBy() to set this property.

Example

The following example illustrates how the value of this property changes when an element is moved:

```
// Select an element on the Stage and then run this script.
var sel = fl.getDocumentDOM().selection[0];
fl.trace("Left (before) = " + sel.left);
fl.getDocumentDOM().moveSelectionBy({x:100, y:0});
fl.trace("Left (after) = " + sel.left);
```

See the element.elementType example.

element.locked

Availability

Flash MX 2004.

Usage

```
element.locked
```

Description

Property; a Boolean value: true if the element is locked; false otherwise. If the value of element.elementType is "shape", this property is ignored.

Example

The following example locks the first element in the first frame, top layer:

```
// Similar to Modify > Arrange > Lock:
fl.getDocumentDOM().getTimeline().layers[0].frames[0].elements[0].locked =
    true;
```

element.matrix

Availability

Flash MX 2004.

Usage

```
element.matrix
```

Description

Property; a Matrix object. A matrix has properties a, b, c, d, tx, and ty. The a, b, c, and d properties are floating-point values; the tx and ty properties are coordinates. See Matrix object.

Example

The following example moves the specified element by 10 pixels in *x* and 20 pixels in *y*:

```
var mat =
    fl.getDocumentDOM().getTimeline().layers[0].frames[0].elements[0].matrix
    ;
mat.tx += 10;
mat.ty += 20;
fl.getDocumentDOM().getTimeline().layers[0].frames[0].elements[0].matrix =
    mat;
```

element.name

Availability

Flash MX 2004.

Usage

```
element.name
```

Description

Property; a string that specifies the name of the element, normally referred to as the Instance name. If the value of element.elementType is "shape", this property is ignored. See element.elementType.

Example

The following example sets the Instance name of the first element in Frame 1, top layer to "clip_mc":

```
fl.getDocumentDOM().getTimeline().layers[0].frames[0].elements[0].name =
    "clip_mc";
```

See the element.elementType example.

element.removePersistentData()

Availability

Flash MX 2004.

Usage

```
element.removePersistentData( name )
```

Parameters

name A string that specifies the name of the data to remove.

Returns

Nothing.

Description

Method; removes any persistent data with the specified name that has been attached to the object. Only symbols and bitmaps support persistent data.

Example

See element.getPersistentData().

element.selected

Availability

Flash 8.

Usage

```
element.selected
```

Description

Property; a Boolean value that specifies whether the element is selected (true) or not (false).

Example

The following example selects the element:

```
element.selected = true;
```

element.setPersistentData()

Availability

Flash MX 2004.

Usage

```
element.setPersistentData( name, type, value )
```

Parameters

name   A string that specifies the name to associate with the data. This name is used to retrieve the data.

type   A string that defines the type of the data. The allowable values are `"integer"`, `"integerArray"`, `"double"`, `"doubleArray"`, `"string"`, and `"byteArray"`.

value   Specifies the value to associate with the object. The data type of *value* depends on the value of the *type* parameter. The specified value should be appropriate to the data type specified by the *type* parameter.

Returns

Nothing.

Description

Method; stores data with an element. The data is available when the FLA file containing the element is reopened. Only symbols and bitmaps support persistent data.

Example

See `element.getPersistentData()`.

element.top

Availability

Flash MX 2004.

Usage

```
element.top
```

Description

Read-only property; top side of the element. The value of `element.top` is relative to the upper left of the Stage for elements that are in a scene, and is relative to the symbol's registration point if the element is stored within a symbol. Use `document.setSelectionBounds()` or `document.moveSelectionBy()` to set this property.

Example

The following example shows how the value of this property changes when an element is moved:

```
// Select an element on the Stage and then run this script.
var sel = fl.getDocumentDOM().selection[0];
fl.trace("Top (before) = " + sel.top);
fl.getDocumentDOM().moveSelectionBy({x:0, y:100});
fl.trace("Top (after) = " + sel.top);
```

See the `element.elementType` example.

element.width

Availability

Flash MX 2004.

Usage

`element.width`

Description

Property; a float value that specifies the width of the element in pixels.

 Do not use this property to resize a text field. Instead, select the text field and use `document.setTextRectangle()`. Using this property with a text field scales the text.

Example

The following example sets the width of the specified element to 100:

```
fl.getDocumentDOM().getTimeline().layers[0].frames[0].elements[0].width=
    100;
```

Fill object

Availability

Flash MX 2004.

Description

This object contains all the properties of the Fill color setting of the Tools panel or of a selected shape. To retrieve a Fill object, use `document.getCustomFill()`.

Property summary for the Fill object

The following properties are available for the Fill object:

Property	Description
`fill.color`	A string, hexadecimal value, or integer that represents the fill color.
`fill.colorArray`	An array of colors in gradient.
`fill.focalPoint`	An integer that specifies the gradient focal point horizontal offset from the transformation point.
`fill.linearRGB`	A Boolean value that specifies whether to render the fill as a linear or radial RGB gradient.
`fill.matrix`	A Matrix object that defines the placement, orientation, and scales for gradient fills.
`fill.overflow`	A string that specifies the behavior of a gradient's overflow.
`fill.posArray`	An array of integers, each in the range 0 ... 255, indicating the position of the corresponding color.
`fill.style`	A string that specifies the fill style.

fill.color

Availability

Flash MX 2004.

Usage

```
fill.color
```

Description

Property; the color of the fill, in one of the following formats:

- A string in the format "#RRGGBB" or "#RRGGBBAA"
- A hexadecimal number in the format 0xRRGGBB
- An integer that represents the decimal equivalent of a hexadecimal number

Example

The following example sets the fill color of the current selection:

```
var fill = fl.getDocumentDOM().getCustomFill();
fill.color = '#FFFFFF';
fl.getDocumentDOM().setCustomFill( fill );
```

fill.colorArray

Availability

Flash MX 2004.

Usage

```
fill.colorArray
```

Description

Property; an array of colors in the gradient, expressed as integers. This property is available only if the value of the fill.style property is either "radialGradient" or "linearGradient". See fill.style

Example

The following example displays the color array of the current selection, if appropriate, in the Output panel:

```
var fill = fl.getDocumentDOM().getCustomFill();
if(fill.style == "linearGradient" || fill.style == "radialGradient")
    alert(fill.colorArray);
```

fill.focalPoint

Availability

Flash 8.

Usage

```
fill.focalPoin
```

Description

Property; an integer that specifies the gradient focal point horizontal offset from the transformation point. A value of 10, for example, would place the focal point at 10/255 of the distance from the transformation point to the edge of the gradient. A value of -255 would place the focal point at the left boundary of the gradient. The default value is 0.

This property is available only if the value of the `fill.style` property is `"radialGradient"`.

Example

The following example sets the focal point of a radial gradient to 10 pixels to the right of the shape's center.

```
var fill = fl.getDocumentDOM().getCustomFill();
fill.focalPoint = 10;
fl.getDocumentDOM().setCustomFill(fill);
```

fill.linearRGB

Availability

Flash 8.

Usage

```
fill.linearRGB
```

Description

Property; a Boolean value that specifies whether to render the fill as a linear or radial RGB gradient. Set this property to `true` to specify a linear interpolation of a gradient; set it to `false` to specify a radial interpolation of a gradient. The default value is `false`.

Example

The following example specifies that the gradient should be rendered with a linear RGB.

```
var fill = fl.getDocumentDOM().getCustomFill();
fill.linearRGB = true;
fl.getDocumentDOM().setCustomFill(fill);
```

fill.matrix

Availability

Flash MX 2004.

Usage

```
fill.matrix
```

Description

Property; a Matrix object that defines the placement, orientation, and scales for gradient fills.

fill.overflow

Availability

Flash 8.

Usage

```
fill.overflow
```

Description

Property; a string that specifies the behavior of a gradient's overflow. Acceptable values are `"extend"`, `"repeat"`, and `"reflect"`; the strings are not case-sensitive. The default value is `"extend"`.

Example

The following example specifies that the behavior of the overflow should be `"extend"`.

```
var fill = fl.getDocumentDOM().getCustomFill();
fill.overflow = "extend";
fl.getDocumentDOM().setCustomFill(fill);
```

fill.posArray

Availability

Flash MX 2004.

Usage

```
fill.posArray
```

Description

Property; an array of integers, each in the range 0 ... 255, indicating the position of the corresponding color. This property is available only if the value of the `fill.style` property is either `"radialGradient"` or `"linearGradient"`.

Example

The following example specifies the colors to use in a linear gradient for the current selection:

```
var fill = fl.getDocumentDOM().getCustomFill();
fill.style - "linearGradient";
fill.colorArray = [ 0x00ff00, 0xff0000, 0x0000ff ];
fill.posArray  = [0,  100, 200];
fl.getDocumentDOM().setCustomFill( fill );
```

fill.style

Availability

Flash MX 2004.

Usage

`fill.style`

Description

Property; a string that specifies the fill style. Acceptable values are `"solid"`, `"linearGradient"`, `"radialGradient"`, and `"noFill"`. If an object has no fill, this property has a value of `"noFill"`.

If this value is `"linearGradient"` or `"radialGradient"`, the properties `fill.colorArray` and `fill.posArray` are also available.

Example

The following example specifies the colors to use in a linear gradient for the current selection:

```
var fill = fl.getDocumentDOM().getCustomFill();
fill.style= "linearGradient";
fill.colorArray = [ 0x00ff00, 0xff0000, 0x0000ff ];
fill.posArray  = [0,  100, 200];
fl.getDocumentDOM().setCustomFill( fill );
```

Filter object

Availability

Flash 8.

Description

This object contains all the properties for all filters. The filter.name property specifies the type of filter, and determines which properties are applicable to each filter. See filter.name.

To return the filter list for an object or objects, use document.getFilters(). To apply filters to an object or objects, use document.setFilters(). See document.getFilters() and document.setFilters().

Property summary for the Filter object

The following properties can be used with the Filter object.

Property	Description
filter.angle	A float value that specifies the angle of the shadow or highlight color, in degrees.
filter.blurX	A float value that specifies the amount to blur in the x direction, in pixels.
filter.blurY	A float value that specifies the amount to blur in the y direction.
filter.brightness	A float value that specifies the brightness of the filter.
filter.color	A string, hexadecimal value, or integer that represents the filter color.
filter.contrast	A float value that specifies the contrast value of the filter.
filter.distance	A float value that specifies the distance between the filter's effect and an object, in pixels.
filter.hideObject	A Boolean value that specifies whether the source image is hidden (true) or displayed (false).
filter.highlightColor	A string, hexadecimal value, or integer that represents the highlight color.
filter.hue	A float value that specifies the hue of the filter.
filter.inner	A Boolean value that specifies whether the shadow is an inner shadow (true) or not (false).

Property	Description
filter.knockout	A Boolean value that specifies whether the filter is a knockout filter (`true`) or not (`false`).
filter.name	A string that specifies the type of filter (read-only property).
filter.quality	A string that specifies the blur quality.
filter.saturation	A float value that specifies the saturation value of the filter.
filter.shadowColor	A string, hexadecimal value, or integer that represents the shadow color.
filter.strength	An integer that specifies the percentage strength of the filter.
filter.type	A string that specifies the type of bevel or glow.

filter.angle

Availability

Flash 8.

Usage

```
filter.angle
```

Description

Property; a float value that specifies the angle of the shadow or highlight color, in degrees. Acceptable values are between 0 and 360. This property is defined for Filter objects with a value of `"bevelFilter"`, `"dropShadowFilter"`, `"gradientBevelFilter"`, or `"gradientGlowFilter"` for the `filter.name` property.

Example

The following example sets the angle to 120 for the Bevel filters on the selected object(s):

```
var myFilters = fl.getDocumentDOM().getFilters();
for(i=0; i < myFilters.length; i++) {
  if(myFilters[i].name == 'bevelFilter'){
    myFilters[i].angle = 120;
  }
}
fl.getDocumentDOM().setFilters(myFilters);
```

See also

```
document.setFilterProperty()
```

filter.blurX

Availability

Flash 8.

Usage

```
filter.blurX
```

Description

Property; a float value that specifies the amount to blur in the *x* direction, in pixels. Acceptable values are between 0 and 255. This property is defined for Filter objects with a value of `"bevelFilter"`, `"blurFilter"`, `"dropShadowFilter"`, `"glowFilter"`, `"gradientBevelFilter"`, or `"gradientGlowFilter"` for the `filter.name` property.

Example

The following example sets the `blurX` value to 30 and the `blurY` value to 20 for the Blur filters on the selected object(s):

```
var myFilters = fl.getDocumentDOM().getFilters();
for(i=0; i < myFilters.length; i++){
   if(myFilters[i].name == 'blurFilter'){
      myFilters[i].blurX = 30;
      myFilters[i].blurY = 20;
   }
}
fl.getDocumentDOM().setFilters(myFilters);
```

See also

`document.setFilterProperty()`, `filter.blurY`

filter.blurY

Availability

Flash 8.

Usage

```
filter.blurY
```

Description

Property; a float value that specifies the amount to blur in the *y* direction, in pixels. Acceptable values are between 0 and 255. This property is defined for Filter objects with a value of `"bevelFilter"`, `"blurFilter"`, `"dropShadowFilter"`, `"glowFilter"`, `"gradientBevelFilter"`, or `"gradientGlowFilter"` for the `filter.name` property.

Example

See `filter.blurX`.

See also

`document.setFilterProperty()`, `filter.blurX`

filter.brightness

Availability

Flash 8.

Usage

`filter.brightness`

Description

Property; a float value that specifies the brightness of the filter. Acceptable values are between -100 and 100. This property is defined for Filter objects with a value of `"adjustColorFilter"` for the `filter.name` property.

Example

The following example sets the brightness to 30.5 for the Adjust Color filters on the selected object(s):

```
var myFilters = fl.getDocumentDOM().getFilters();
for(i=0; i < myFilters.length; i++){
  if(myFilters[i].name == 'adjustColorFilter'){
    myFilters[i].brightness = 30.5;
  }
}
fl.getDocumentDOM().setFilters(myFilters);
```

filter.color

Availability

Flash 8.

Usage

`filter.color`

Description

Property; the color of the filter, in one of the following formats:

- A string in the format "#RRGGBB" or "#RRGGBBAA"
- A hexadecimal number in the format 0xRRGGBB
- An integer that represents the decimal equivalent of a hexadecimal number

This property is defined for Filter objects with a value of "dropShadowFilter" or "glowFilter" for the filter.name property.

Example

The following example sets the color to "#ff00003e" for the Drop Shadow filters on the selected object(s):

```
var myFilters = fl.getDocumentDOM().getFilters();
for(i=0; i < myFilters.length; i++){
   if(myFilters[i].name == 'dropShadowFilter'){
     myFilters[i].color = '#ff00003e';
   }
}
fl.getDocumentDOM().setFilters(myFilters);
```

See also

document.setFilterProperty()

filter.contrast

Availability

Flash 8.

Usage

filter.contrast

Description

Property; a float value that specifies the contrast value of the filter. Acceptable values are between -100 and 100. This property is defined for Filter objects with a value of "adjustColorFilter" for the filter.name property.

Example

The following example sets the contrast value to -15.5 for the Adjust Color filters on the selected object(s):

```
var myFilters = fl.getDocumentDOM().getFilters();
for(i=0; i < myFilters.length; i++){
  if(myFilters[i].name == 'adjustColorFilter'){
    myFilters[i].contrast = -15.5;
  }
}
fl.getDocumentDOM().setFilters(myFilters);
```

filter.distance

Availability

Flash 8.

Usage

```
filter.distance
```

Description

Property; a float value that specifies the distance between the filter's effect and an object, in pixels. Acceptable values are from -255 to 255. This property is defined for Filter objects with a value of "bevelFilter", "dropShadowFilter", "gradientBevelFilter", or "gradientGlowFilter" for the filter.name property.

Example

The following example sets the distance to 10 pixels for the Drop Shadow filters on the selected object(s):

```
var myFilters = fl.getDocumentDOM().getFilters();
for(i=0; i < myFilters.length; i++){
  if(myFilters[i].name == 'dropShadowFilter'){
    myFilters[i].distance = 10;
  }
}
fl.getDocumentDOM().setFilters(myFilters);
```

See also

```
document.setFilterProperty()
```

filter.hideObject

Availability

Flash 8.

Usage

```
filter.hideObject
```

Description

Property; a Boolean value that specifies whether the source image is hidden (`true`) or displayed (`false`). This property is defined for Filter objects with a value of `"dropShadowFilter"` for the `filter.name` property.

Example

The following example sets the `hideObject` value to `true` for the Drop Shadow filters on the selected object(s):

```
var myFilters = fl.getDocumentDOM().getFilters();
for(i=0; i < myFilters.length; i++){
   if(myFilters[i].name == 'dropShadowFilter'){
      myFilters[i].hideObject = true;
   }
}
fl.getDocumentDOM().setFilters(myFilters);
```

filter.highlightColor

Availability

Flash 8.

Usage

```
filter.highlightColor
```

Description

Property; the color of the highlight, in one of the following formats:

- A string in the format `"#RRGGBB"` or `"#RRGGBBAA"`
- A hexadecimal number in the format `0xRRGGBB`
- An integer that represents the decimal equivalent of a hexadecimal number

This property is defined for Filter objects with a value of `"bevelFilter"` for the `filter.name` property.

Example

The following example sets the highlight color to "#ff00003e" for the Bevel filters on the selected object(s):

```
var myFilters = fl.getDocumentDOM().getFilters();
for(i=0; i < myFilters.length; i++){
  if(myFilters[i].name == 'bevelFilter'){
    myFilters[i].highlightColor = '#ff00003e';
  }
}
fl.getDocumentDOM().setFilters(myFilters);
```

filter.hue

Availability

Flash 8.

Usage

```
filter.hue
```

Description

Property; a float value that specifies the hue of the filter. Acceptable values are between -180 and 180. This property is defined for Filter objects with a value of "adjustColorFilter" for the filter.name property.

Example

The following example sets the hue to 120 for the Adjust Color filters on the selected object(s):

```
var myFilters = fl.getDocumentDOM().getFilters();
for(i=0; i < myFilters.length; i++){
  if(myFilters[i].name == 'adjustColorFilter'){
    myFilters[i].hue = 120;
  }
}
fl.getDocumentDOM().setFilters(myFilters);
```

filter.inner

Availability

Flash 8.

Usage

```
filter.inner
```

Description

Property; a Boolean value that specifies whether the shadow is an inner shadow (`true`) or not (`false`). This property is defined for Filter objects with a value of `"dropShadowFilter"` or `"glowFilter"` for the `filter.name` property.

Example

The following example sets the value of the `inner` property to `true` for the Glow filters on the selected object(s):

```
var myFilters = fl.getDocumentDOM().getFilters();
for(i=0; i < myFilters.length; i++){
  if(myFilters[i].name == 'glowFilter'){
    myFilters[i].inner = true;
  }
}
fl.getDocumentDOM().setFilters(myFilters);
```

See also

```
document.setFilterProperty()
```

filter.knockout

Availability

Flash 8.

Usage

```
filter.knockout
```

Description

Property; a Boolean value that specifies whether the filter is a knockout filter (`true`) or not (`false`). This property is defined for Filter objects with a value of `"bevelFilter"`, `"dropShadowFilter"`, `"glowFilter"`, `"gradientBevelFilter"`, or `"gradientGlowFilter"` for the `filter.name` property.

Example

The following example sets the knockout property to true for the Glow filters on the selected object(s):

```
var myFilters = fl.getDocumentDOM().getFilters();
for(i=0; i < myFilters.length; i++){
   if(myFilters[i].name == 'glowFilter'){
     myFilters[i].knockout = true;
   }
}
fl.getDocumentDOM().setFilters(myFilters);
```

See also

```
document.setFilterProperty()
```

filter.name

Availability

Flash 8.

Usage

```
filter.name
```

Description

Read-only property; a string that specifies the type of filter. The value of this property determines which other properties of the Filter object are available. The value is one of the following: "adjustColorFilter", "bevelFilter", "blurFilter", "dropShadowFilter", "glowFilter", "gradientBevelFilter", or "gradientGlowFilter".

Example

The following example displays the filter names and index positions in the Output panel:

```
var myFilters = fl.getDocumentDOM().getFilters();
var traceStr = "";
for(i=0; i < myFilters.length; i++){
   traceStr = traceStr + " At index " + i + ": " + myFilters[i].name;
}
fl.trace(traceStr);
```

See also

```
document.getFilters(), document.setFilterProperty()
```

filter.quality

Availability

Flash 8.

Usage

```
filter.quality
```

Description

Property; a string that specifies the blur quality. Acceptable values are `"low"`, `"medium"`, and `"high"` (`"high"` is similar to a Gaussian blur). This property is defined for Filter objects with a value of `"bevelFilter"`, `"blurFilter"`, `"dropShadowFilter"`, "`glowFilter`", `"gradientGlowFilter"`, or `"gradientBevelFilter"` for the `filter.name` property.

Example

The following example sets the blur quality to `"medium"` for the Glow filters on the selected object(s):

```
var myFilters = fl.getDocumentDOM().getFilters();
for(i=0; i < myFilters.length; i++){
   if(myFilters[i].name == 'glowFilter'){
     myFilters[i].quality = 'medium';
   }
}
fl.getDocumentDOM().setFilters(myFilters);
```

See also

```
document.setFilterProperty()
```

filter.saturation

Availability

Flash 8.

Usage

```
filter.saturation
```

Description

Property; a float value that specifies the saturation value of the filter. Acceptable values are from -100 to 100. This property is defined for Filter objects with a value of `"adjustColorFilter"` for the `filter.name` property.

Example

The following example sets the saturation value to 0 (grayscale) for the Adjust Color filters on the selected object(s):

```
var myFilters = fl.getDocumentDOM().getFilters();
for(i=0; i < myFilters.length; i++){
  if(myFilters[i].name == 'adjustColorFilter'){
    myFilters[i].saturation = 0;
  }
}
fl.getDocumentDOM().setFilters(myFilters);
```

See also

document.setFilterProperty()

filter.shadowColor

Availability

Flash 8.

Usage

filter.shadowColor

Description

Property; the color of the shadow, in one of the following formats:

- A string in the format "#RRGGBB" or "#RRGGBBAA"
- A hexadecimal number in the format 0xRRGGBB
- An integer that represents the decimal equivalent of a hexadecimal number

This property is defined for Filter objects with a value of "bevelFilter" for the filter.name property.

Example

The following example sets the shadow color to "#ff00003e" for the Bevel filters on the selected object(s):

```
var myFilters = fl.getDocumentDOM().getFilters();
for(i=0; i < myFilters.length; i++){
  if(myFilters[i].name == 'bevelFilter'){
    myFilters[i].shadowColor = '#ff00003e';
  }
}
fl.getDocumentDOM().setFilters(myFilters);
```

See also

document.setFilterProperty()

filter.strength

Availability

Flash 8.

Usage

filter.strength

Description

Property; an integer that specifies the percentage strength of the filter. Acceptable values are between 0 and 25,500. This property is defined for Filter objects with a value of "bevelFilter", "dropShadowFilter", "glowFilter", "gradientGlowFilter", or "gradientBevelFilter" for the filter.name property.

Example

The following example sets the strength to 50 for the Glow filters on the selected object(s):

```
var myFilters = fl.getDocumentDOM().getFilters();
for(i=0; i < myFilters.length; i++){
  if(myFilters[i].name == 'glowFilter'){
    myFilters[i].strength = 50;
  }
}
fl.getDocumentDOM().setFilters(myFilters);
```

See also

document.setFilterProperty()

filter.type

Availability

Flash 8.

Usage

```
filter.type
```

Description

Property; a string that specifies the type of bevel or glow. Acceptable values are `"inner"`, `"outer"`, and `"full"`. This property is defined for Filter objects with a value of `"bevelFilter"`, `"gradientGlowFilter"`, or `"gradientBevelFilter"` for the `filter.name` property.

Example

The following example sets the type to `"full"` for all Bevel filters on the selected object(s):

```
var myFilters = fl.getDocumentDOM().getFilters();
for(i=0; i < myFilters.length; i++){
  if(myFilters[i].name == 'bevelFilter'){
    myFilters[i].type = 'full';
  }
}
fl.getDocumentDOM().setFilters(myFilters);
```

See also

```
document.setFilterProperty()
```

flash object (fl)

Availability

Flash MX 2004.

Description

The flash object represents the Flash application. You can use `flash` or `fl` to refer to this object. This documentation uses `fl` throughout.

Method summary for the flash object

The following methods can be used with the flash object.

Method	Description
`fl.browseForFileURL()`	Opens a File Open or File Save system dialog box and lets the user specify a file to be opened or saved.
`fl.browseForFolderURL()`	Displays a Browse for Folder dialog box and lets the user select a folder.
`fl.closeAll()`	Closes all open documents, displaying the Save As dialog box for any documents that were not previously saved.
`fl.closeDocument()`	Closes the specified document.
`fl.closeProject()`	Closes the Flash Project (FLP) file that is currently open.
`fl.createDocument()`	Opens a new document and selects it.
`fl.createProject()`	Creates a Flash Project (FLP) file with the specified name.
`fl.enableImmediateUpdates()`	Lets the script developer enable immediate visual updates of the timeline when executing effects.
`fl.fileExists()`	Checks whether a file already exists on disk.
`fl.findDocumentIndex()`	Returns an array of integers that represent the position of a document in the `fl.documents` array.
`fl.getAppMemoryInfo()`	Returns an integer that represents the number of bytes being used in a specified area of Flash.exe memory.
`fl.getDocumentDOM()`	Retrieves the DOM (Document object) of the currently active document.
`fl.getProject()`	Returns a Project object that represents the currently open project.
`fl.mapPlayerURL()`	Maps an escaped Unicode URL to a UTF-8 or MBCS URL.

Method	Description
fl.openDocument()	Opens a Flash (FLA) document for editing in a new Flash Document window and gives it the focus.
fl.openProject()	Opens a Flash Project (FLP) file in the Flash authoring tool for editing.
fl.openScript()	Opens a script (JSFL, AS, ASC) or other file (XML, TXT) in the Flash text editor.
fl.quit()	Quits Flash, prompting the user to save any changed documents.
fl.reloadEffects()	Reloads all effects descriptors defined in the user's Configuration Effects folder.
fl.reloadTools()	Rebuilds the Tools panel from the toolconfig.xml file. Used only when creating extensible tools.
fl.revertDocument()	Reverts the specified FLA document to its last saved version.
fl.runScript()	Executes a JavaScript file.
fl.saveAll()	Saves all open documents, displaying the Save As dialog box for any documents that were not previously saved.
fl.saveDocument()	Saves the specified document as a FLA document.
fl.saveDocumentAs()	Displays the Save As dialog box for the specified document.
fl.setActiveWindow()	Sets the active window to be the specified document.
fl.showIdleMessage()	Lets you disable the warning about a script running too long .
fl.trace()	Sends a text string to the Output panel.

Property summary for the flash object

The following properties can be used with the flash object.

Properties	Description
fl.activeEffect	Read-only; the Effect object for the current effect being applied.
fl.componentsPanel	Read-only; a componentsPanel object, which represents the Components panel.
fl.configDirectory	Read-only; a string that specifies the full path for the local user's Configuration folder as a platform-specific path.
fl.configURI	Read-only; a string that specifies the full path for the local user's Configuration directory as a file:/// URI.

Properties	Description
fl.contactSensitiveSelection	A Boolean value that specifies whether Contact Sensitive selection mode is enabled.
fl.createNewDocList	Read-only; an array of strings that represent the various types of documents that can be created.
fl.createNewDocListType	Read-only; an array of strings that represent the file extensions of the types of documents that can be created.
fl.createNewTemplateList	Read-only; an array of strings that represent the various types of templates that can be created.
fl.documents	Read-only; an array of Document objects (see Document object) that represent the documents (FLA files) that are currently open for editing.
fl.drawingLayer	Read-only; the drawingLayer object that an extensible tool should use when the user wants to temporarily draw while dragging.
fl.effects	Read-only; an array of Effect objects (see Effect object), based on XML parameter file.
fl.Math	Read-only; the Math object, which provides methods for matrix and point operations.
fl.mruRecentFileList	Read-only; an array of the complete filenames in the Most Recently Used (MRU) list that the Flash authoring tool manages.
fl.mruRecentFileListType	Read-only; an array of the file types in the MRU list that the Flash authoring tool manages.
fl.objectDrawingMode	A Boolean value that specifies whether the object drawing model is enabled.
fl.outputPanel	Read-only; reference to the outputPanel object.
fl.tools	Read-only; an array of Tools objects.
fl.version	Read-only; the long string version of the Flash authoring tool, including platform.
fl.xmlui	Read-only; an XMLUI object.

fl.activeEffect

Availability

Flash MX 2004.

Usage

```
fl.activeEffect
```

Description

Read-only property; the Effect object for the current effect being applied. For a list of properties available to `fl.activeEffect`, see "Property summary for the Effect object" on page 190.

Example

The following example stores an object that represents the current effect in the `ef` variable.

```
var ef = fl.activeEffect;
```

fl.browseForFileURL()

Availability

Flash MX 2004.

Usage

```
fl.browseForFileURL( browseType [, title [, previewArea ] ])
```

Parameters

browseType A string that specifies the type of file browse operation. Acceptable values are `"open"`, `"select"` or `"save"`. The values `"open"` and `"select"` open the system File Open dialog box. Each value is provided for compatibility with Dreamweaver. The value `"save"` opens a system File Save dialog box.

title A string that specifies the title for the File Open or File Save dialog box. If this parameter is omitted, a default value is used. This parameter is optional.

previewArea An optional parameter that is ignored by Flash and Fireworks and is present only for compatibility with Dreamweaver.

Returns

The URL of the file, expressed as a file:/// URI; returns `null` if the user cancels out of the dialog box.

Description

Method; opens a File Open or File Save system dialog box and lets the user specify a file to be opened or saved.

Example

The following example lets the user choose a FLA file to open and then opens the file. (The `fl.browseForFileURL()` method can browse for any type of file, but `fl.openDocument()` can open only FLA files.)

```
var fileURL = fl.browseForFileURL("open", "Select file");
var doc = fl.openDocument(fileURL);
```

See also

`fl.browseForFolderURL()`

fl.browseForFolderURL()

Availability

Flash 8.

Usage

`fl.browseForFolderURL( [ description ] )`

Parameters

description   An optional string that specifies the description of the Browse For Folder dialog box. If this parameter is omitted, nothing is shown in the description area.

Returns

The URL of the folder, expressed as a file:/// URI; returns `null` if the user cancels out of the dialog box.

Description

Method; displays a Browse for Folder dialog box and lets the user select a folder.

> **NOTE**
>
> The title of the dialog box is always "Browse for Folder." Use the description parameter to add more detail in the description area under the title, such as "Select a folder" or "Select the path that contains the profile you want to import."

Example

The following example lets the user select a folder and then displays a list of files in that folder.

```
var folderURI = fl.browseForFolderURL("Select a folder.");
var folderContents = FLfile.listFolder(folderURI);
```

See also

`fl.browseForFileURL()`, FLfile object

fl.closeAll()

Availability

Flash MX 2004.

Usage

```
fl.closeAll()
```

Parameters

None.

Returns

Nothing.

Description

Method; closes all open documents, displaying the Save As dialog box for any documents that were not previously saved. The method prompts the user, if necessary, but does not terminate the application. See also `fl.closeDocument()`.

Example

The following code closes all open documents.

```
fl.closeAll();
```

fl.closeDocument()

Availability

Flash MX 2004.

Usage

```
fl.closeDocument( documentObject [, bPromptToSaveChanges] )
```

Parameters

documentObject, [*bPromptToSaveChanges*]

documentObject   A Document object. If *documentObject* refers to the active document, the Document window might not close until the script that calls this method finishes executing.

bPromptToSaveChanges   A Boolean value. If it is `false`, the user is not prompted if the document contains unsaved changes; that is, the file is closed and the changes are discarded. If the value is `true`, and if the document contains unsaved changes, the user is prompted with the standard yes-or-no dialog box. The default value is `true`. This parameter is optional.

Returns

A Boolean value: `true` if successful; `false` otherwise.

Description

Method; closes the specified document. See also `fl.closeAll()`.

Example

The following example illustrates two ways of closing a document.

```
// Closes the specified document and prompts to save changes.
fl.closeDocument(fl.documents[0]);
fl.closeDocument(fl.documents[0] , true); // Use of true is optional.
// Closes the specified document without prompting to save changes.
fl.closeDocument(fl.documents[0], false);
```

fl.closeProject()

Availability

Flash 8.

Usage

```
fl.closeProject()
```

Parameters

None.

Returns

A Boolean value of `true` if the project was successfully closed; `false` if there is no project file open.

Description

Method; closes the Flash Project (FLP) file that is currently open.

The following example attempts to close a project file, and displays a message indicating whether the file was successfully closed.

```
fl.trace("The project was" + (fl.closeProject() ? "closed" : "not
    closed"));
```

See also

`fl.getProject()`, `fl.openProject()`, Project object

fl.componentsPanel

Availability

Flash MX 2004.

Usage

`fl.componentsPanel`

Description

Read-only property; a componentsPanel object, which represents the Components panel.

Example

The following example stores a componentsPanel object in the `comPanel` variable.

```
var comPanel = fl.componentsPanel;
```

fl.configDirectory

Availability

Flash MX 2004.

Usage

`fl.configDirectory`

Description

Read-only property; a string that specifies the full path for the local user's Configuration directory in a platform-specific format. To specify this path as a file:/// URI, which is not platform-specific, use `fl.configURI`.

Example

The following example displays the Configuration directory in the Output panel.

```
fl.trace( "My local configuration directory is " + fl.configDirectory );
```

fl.configURI

Availability

Flash MX 2004.

Usage

```
fl.configURI
```

Description

Read-only property; a string that specifies the full path for the local user's Configuration directory as a file:/// URI. See also `fl.configDirectory`.

Example

The following example runs a specified script. Using `fl.configURI` lets you specify the location of the script without knowing which platform the script is running on.

```
// To run a command in your commands menu, change "Test.Jsfl"
// to the command you want to run in the line below.
fl.runScript( fl.configURI + "Commands/Test.jsfl" );
```

fl.contactSensitiveSelection

Availability

Flash 8.

Usage

```
fl.contactSensitiveSelection
```

Description

A Boolean value that specifies whether Contact Sensitive selection mode is enabled (`true`) or not (`false`).

Example

The following example shows how to disable Contact Sensitive selection mode before making a selection, and then how to reset it to its original value after making the selection.

```
var contact = fl.contactSensitiveSelection;
fl.contactSensitiveSelection = false;
// Insert selection code here.
fl.contactSensitiveSelection = contact;
```

fl.createDocument()

Availability

Flash MX 2004.

Usage

```
fl.createDocument( [docType] )
```

Parameters

docType   A string that specifies the type of document to create. Acceptable values are "timeline", "presentation", and "application". The default value is "timeline". This parameter is optional.

Returns

The Document object for the newly created document, if the method is successful. If an error occurs, the value is undefined.

Description

Method; opens a new document and selects it. Values for size, resolution, and color are the same as the current defaults.

Example

The following example creates different types of documents.

```
// Create a timeline-based Flash document.
fl.createDocument();
fl.createDocument("timeline");
// Create a Slide Presentation document.
fl.createDocument("presentation");
// Create a Form Application document.
fl.createDocument("application");
```

fl.createNewDocList

Availability

Flash MX 2004.

Usage

```
fl.createNewDocList
```

Description

Read-only property; an array of strings that represent the various types of documents that can be created.

Example

The following example displays the types of documents that can be created in the Output panel.

```
fl.trace("Number of choices " + fl.createNewDocList.length);
for (i = 0; i < fl.createNewDocList.length; i++)
  fl.trace("choice: " + fl.createNewDocList[i]);
```

fl.createNewDocListType

Availability

Flash MX 2004.

Usage

```
fl.createNewDocListType
```

Description

Read-only property; an array of strings that represent the file extensions of the types of documents that can be created. The entries in the array correspond directly (by index) to the entries in the `fl.createNewDocList` array.

Example

The following example displays the extensions of the types of documents that can be created in the Output panel.

```
fl.trace("Number of types " + fl.createNewDocListType.length);
for (i = 0; i < fl.createNewDocListType.length; i++) fl.trace("type: " +
  fl.createNewDocListType[i]);
```

fl.createNewTemplateList

Availability

Flash MX 2004.

Usage

```
fl.createNewTemplateList
```

Description

Read-only property; an array of strings that represent the various types of templates that can be created.

Example

The following example displays the types of templates that can be created in the Output panel.

```
fl.trace("Number of template types: " + fl.createNewTemplateList.length);
  for (i = 0; i < fl.createNewTemplateList.length; i++) fl.trace("type: " +
  fl.createNewTemplateList[i]);
```

fl.createProject()

Availability

Flash 8.

Usage

```
fl.createProject( fileURI [ , name ] )
```

Parameters

fileURI   A string, expressed as a file:/// URI, that specifies the name of the Flash Project (FLP) file to be created.

name   An optional string that is displayed as the project name in the Project panel. If *name* is omitted, the name of the FLP file (excluding path or extension) is displayed in the Project panel.

Returns

A Project object if the method is successful; undefined if the file can't be created (for example, *fileURI* contains a directory that doesn't exist).

Description

Method; creates a Flash Project (FLP) file with the specified name. If the file can't be created, an informational dialog box is displayed. If the file already exists, a dialog box is displayed asking whether to overwrite the file.

Example

The following example creates a project file in the specified directory (if it exists) and specifies a name to display in the Project panel.

```
var myProject = fl.createProject("file:///C|/Projects/
  MasterProject_2005.flp", "Master Project");
```

See also

fl.getProject(), fl.openProject(), Project object

fl.documents

Availability

Flash MX 2004.

Usage

```
fl.documents
```

Description

Read-only property; an array of Document objects (see Document object) that represent the documents (FLA files) that are currently open for editing.

Example

The following example stores an array of open documents in the docs variable.

```
var docs = fl.documents;
```

The following example displays the names of currently open documents in the Output panel.

```
for (doc in fl.documents) {
  fl.trace(fl.documents[doc].name);
}
```

fl.drawingLayer

Availability

Flash MX 2004.

Usage

```
fl.drawingLayer
```

Description

Read-only property; the drawingLayer object that an extensible tool should use when the user wants to temporarily draw while dragging (for example, when creating a selection marquee).

Example

See `drawingLayer.setColor()`.

fl.effects

Availability

Flash MX 2004.

Usage

```
fl.effects
```

Description

Read-only property; an array of Effect objects (see Effect object), based on XML parameter file. These are not effects, but a description of effects. The array length corresponds to the number of effects (based on the XML parameter definition files, not the number of JSFL implementation files) registered when the program opens.

Example

The following example returns the first registered effect:

```
ef = fl.effects[0]
```

fl.enableImmediateUpdates()

Availability

Flash MX 2004.

Usage

```
fl.enableImmediateUpdates(bEnableUpdates)
```

Parameters

bEnableUpdates   A Boolean value that specifies whether to enable (true) or disable
(false) immediate visual updates of the timeline when executing effects.

Returns

Nothing.

Description

Method; lets the script developer enable immediate visual updates of the timeline when
executing effects. Immediate updates are normally suppressed so the user does not see
intermediate steps that can be visually distracting and can make the effect appear to take
longer than necessary. This method is purely for debugging purposes and should not be used
in effects that are deployed in the field. After the effect completes, the internal state is reset to
suppress immediate updates.

Example

The following example enables immediate updates.

```
fl.enableImmediateUpdates(true) ;
fl.trace("Immediate updates are enabled");
```

fl.fileExists()

Availability

Flash MX 2004.

Usage

```
fl.fileExists( fileURI )
```

Parameters

fileURI   A string, expressed as a file:/// URI, that contains the path to the file.

Returns

A Boolean value: true if the file exists on disk; false otherwise.

Description

Method; checks whether a file already exists on disk.

Example

The following example displays `true` or `false` in the Output panel for each specified file, depending on whether the file exists.

```
alert(fl.fileExists("file:///C|/example.fla"));
alert(fl.fileExists("file:///C|/example.jsfl"));
alert(fl.fileExists(""));
```

fl.findDocumentIndex()

Availability

Flash MX 2004.

Usage

```
fl.findDocumentIndex( name )
```

Parameters

name   The document name for which you want to find the index. The document must be open.

Returns

An array of integers that represent the position of the document *name* in the `fl.documents` array.

Description

Method; returns an array of integers that represent the position of the document *name* in the `fl.documents` array. More than one document with the same name can be open (if the documents are located in different folders).

Example

The following example displays information about the index position of any open files named test.fla in the Output panel:

```
var filename = "test.fla"
var docIndex = fl.findDocumentIndex(filename);
for (var index in docIndex)
  fl.trace(filename + " is open at index " + docIndex[index]);
```

See also

`fl.documents`

fl.getAppMemoryInfo()

Availability

Flash 8 (Windows only).

Usage

```
fl.getAppMemoryInfo( memType )
```

Parameters

memType   An integer that specifies the memory utilization area to be queried. For a list of acceptable values, see the following description.

Returns

An integer that represents the number of bytes being used in a specified area of Flash.exe memory.

Description

Method (Windows only); returns an integer that represents the number of bytes being used in a specified area of Flash.exe memory. Use the following table to determine which value you want to pass as *memType*.

memType	Resource data
0	PAGEFAULTCOUNT
1	PEAKWORKINGSETSIZE
2	WORKINGSETSIZE
3	QUOTAPEAKPAGEDPOOLUSAGE
4	QUOTAPAGEDPOOLUSAGE
5	QUOTAPEAKNONPAGEDPOOLUSAGE
6	QUOTANONPAGEDPOOLUSAGE
7	PAGEFILEUSAGE
8	PEAKPAGEFILEUSAGE

Example

The following example displays the current working memory consumption.

```
var memsize = fl.getAppMemoryInfo(2);
fl.trace("Flash current memory consumption is " + memsize + " bytes or " +
  memsize/1024 + " KB");
```

fl.getDocumentDOM()

Availability

Flash MX 2004.

Usage

```
fl.getDocumentDOM()
```

Parameters

None.

Returns

A Document object, or null if no documents are open.

Description

Method; retrieves the DOM (Document object) of the currently active document (FLA file). If one or more documents are open but a document does not currently have focus (for example, if a JSFL file has focus), retrieves the DOM of the most recently active document.

Example

The following example displays the name of the current or most recently active document in the Output panel:

```
var currentDoc = fl.getDocumentDOM();
fl.trace(currentDoc.name);
```

fl.getProject()

Availability

Flash 8.

Usage

```
fl.getProject()
```

Parameters

None.

Returns

A Project object that represents the currently open project. If no project is currently open, returns undefined.

Description

Method; returns a Project object that represents the currently open project.

Example

The following example displays the name of the currently open project in the Output panel.

```
fl.trace("Current project: " + fl.getProject().name);
```

See also

`fl.createProject()`, `fl.openProject()`, Project object

fl.mapPlayerURL()

Availability

Flash MX 2004.

Usage

```
fl.mapPlayerURL( URI [, returnMBCS] )
```

Parameters

URI   A string that contains the escaped Unicode URL to map.

returnMBCS   A Boolean value that you must set to `true` if you want an escaped MBCS path returned. Otherwise, the method returns UTF-8. The default value is `false`. This parameter is optional.

Returns

A string that is the converted URL.

Description

Method; maps an escaped Unicode URL to a UTF-8 or MBCS URL. Use this method when the string will be used in ActionScript to access an external resource. You must use this method if you need to handle multibyte characters.

Example

The following example converts a URL to UTF-8 so the player can load it.

```
var url = MMExecute( "fl.mapPlayerURL(" + myURL + ", false);" );
mc.loadMovie( url);
```

fl.Math

Availability

Flash MX 2004.

Usage

```
fl.Math
```

Description

Read-only property; the Math object provides methods for matrix and point operations.

Example

The following shows the transformation matrix of the selected object, and its inverse.

```
// Select an element on the Stage and then run this script.
var mat =fl.getDocumentDOM().selection[0].matrix;
for(var prop in mat){
  fl.trace("mat."+prop+" = " + mat[prop]);
}
var invMat = fl.Math.invertMatrix( mat );
for(var prop in invMat) {
fl.trace("invMat."+prop+" = " + invMat[prop]);
}
```

fl.mruRecentFileList

Availability

Flash MX 2004.

Usage

```
fl.mruRecentFileList
```

Description

Read-only property; an array of the complete filenames in the Most Recently Used (MRU) list that the Flash authoring tool manages.

Example

The following example displays the number of recently opened files, and the name of each file, in the Output panel.

```
fl.trace("Number of recently opened files: " +
  fl.mruRecentFileList.length);
for (i = 0; i < fl.mruRecentFileList.length; i++) fl.trace("file: " +
  fl.mruRecentFileList[i]);
```

fl.mruRecentFileListType

Availability

Flash MX 2004.

Usage

```
fl.mruRecentFileListType
```

Description

Read-only property; an array of the file types in the MRU list that the Flash authoring tool manages. This array corresponds to the array in the `fl.mruRecentFileList` property.

Example

The following example displays the number of recently opened files, and the type of each file, in the Output panel.

```
fl.trace("Number of recently opened files: " +
  fl.mruRecentFileListType.length);
for (i = 0; i < fl.mruRecentFileListType.length; i++) fl.trace("type: " +
  fl.mruRecentFileListType[i]);
```

fl.objectDrawingMode

Availability

Flash 8.

Usage

```
fl.objectDrawingMode
```

Description

Property; a Boolean value that specifies whether the object drawing mode is enabled (`true`) or the merge drawing mode is enabled (`false`).

Example

The following example toggles the state of the object drawing mode:

```
var toggleMode = fl.objectDrawingMode;
if (toggleMode) {
  fl.objectDrawingMode = false;
} else {
  fl.objectDrawingMode = true;
}
```

fl.openDocument()

Availability

Flash MX 2004.

Usage

```
fl.openDocument( fileURI )
```

Parameters

fileURI A string, expressed as a file:/// URI, that specifies the name of the file to be opened.

Returns

The Document object for the newly opened document, if the method is successful. If the file is not found, or is not a valid FLA file, an error is reported and the script is cancelled.

Description

Method; opens a Flash document (FLA file) for editing in a new Flash Document window and gives it the focus. For a user, the effect is the same as selecting File > Open and then selecting a file. If the specified file is already open, the window that contains the document comes to the front. The window that contains the specified file becomes the currently selected document.

Example

The following example opens a file named Document.fla that is stored in the root directory on the C drive, stores a Document object representing that document in the doc variable, and sets the document to be the currently selected document. That is, until focus is changed, `fl.getDocumentDOM()` refers to this document.

```
var doc = fl.openDocument("file:///c|/Document.fla");
```

fl.openProject()

Availability

Flash MX 2004; return value changed in Flash 8.

Usage

```
fl.openProject( fileURI )
```

Parameters

fileURI   A string, expressed as a file:/// URI, that specifies the path of the Flash Project (FLP) file to open.

Returns

Nothing in Flash MX 2004; a Project object in Flash 8.

Description

Method; opens a Flash Project (FLP) file in the Flash authoring tool for editing.

Example

The following example opens a project file named myProjectFile.flp that is stored in the root directory on the C drive.

```
fl.openProject("file:///c|/myProjectFile.flp");
```

See also

fl.closeProject(), fl.createProject(), fl.getProject(), Project object

fl.openScript()

Availability

Flash MX 2004.

Usage

```
fl.openScript( fileURI )
```

Parameters

fileURI   A string, expressed as a file:/// URI, that specifies the path of the JSFL, AS, ASC, XML, TXT or other file that should be loaded into the Flash text editor.

Returns

Nothing.

Description

Method; opens a script (JSFL, AS, ASC) or other file (XML, TXT) in the Flash text editor.

Example

The following example opens a file named my_test.jsfl that is stored in the /temp directory on the C drive.

```
fl.openScript("file:///c|/temp/my_test.jsfl");
```

fl.outputPanel

Availability

Flash MX 2004.

Usage

```
fl.outputPanel
```

Description

Read-only property; reference to the outputPanel object.

Example

See outputPanel object.

fl.quit()

Availability

Flash MX 2004.

Usage

```
fl.quit( [bPromptIfNeeded] )
```

Parameters

bPromptIfNeeded   A Boolean value that is `true` (default) if you want the user to be prompted to save any modified documents. Set this parameter to `false` if you do not want the user to be prompted to save modified documents. In the latter case, any modifications in open documents will be discarded and the application will exit immediately. Although it is useful for batch processing, use this method with caution. This parameter is optional.

Returns

Nothing.

Description

Method; quits Flash, prompting the user to save any changed documents.

Example

The following example illustrates quitting with and without asking to save modified documents.

```
// Quit with prompt to save any modified documents.
fl.quit();
fl.quit(true); // True is optional.
// Quit without saving any files.
fl.quit(false);
```

fl.reloadEffects()

Availability

Flash MX 2004.

Usage

```
fl.reloadEffects()
```

Parameters

None.

Returns

Nothing.

Description

Method; reloads all effects descriptors defined in the user's Configuration Effects folder. This permits you to rapidly change the scripts during development, and it provides a mechanism to improve the effects without relaunching the application. This method works best if used in a command placed in the Commands folder.

Example

The following example is a one-line script that you can place in the Commands folder. When you need to reload effects, go to the Commands menu and execute the script.

```
fl.reloadEffects();
```

fl.reloadTools()

Availability

Flash MX 2004.

Usage

```
fl.reloadTools()
```

Parameters

None.

Returns

Nothing.

Description

Method; rebuilds the Tools panel from the toolconfig.xml file. This method is used only when creating extensible tools. Use this method when you need to reload the Tools panel, for example, after modifying the JSFL file that defines a tool that is already present in the panel.

Example

The following example is a one-line script that you can place in the Commands folder. When you need to reload the Tools panel, run the script from the Commands menu.

```
fl.reloadTools();
```

fl.revertDocument()

Availability

Flash MX 2004.

Usage

```
fl.revertDocument( documentObject )
```

Parameters

documentObject   A Document object. If *documentObject* refers to the active document, the Document window might not revert until the script that calls this method finishes executing.

Returns

A Boolean value: true if the Revert operation completes successfully; false otherwise.

Description

Method; reverts the specified FLA document to its last saved version. Unlike the File > Revert menu option, this method does not display a warning window that asks the user to confirm the operation. See also document.revert() and document.canRevert().

Example

The following example reverts the current FLA document to its last saved version; any changes made since the last save are lost.

```
fl.revertDocument(fl.getDocumentDOM());
```

fl.runScript()

Availability

Flash MX 2004.

Usage

```
fl.runScript( fileURI [, funcName [, arg1, arg2, ...] ])
```

Parameters

fileURI   A string, expressed as a file:/// URI, that specifies the name of the script file to execute.

funcName   A string that identifies a function to execute in the JSFL file that is specified in *fileURI*. This parameter is optional.

arg   An optional parameter that specifies one or more arguments to be passed to *funcname*.

Returns

The function's result as a string, if *funcName* is specified; otherwise, nothing.

Description

Method; executes a JavaScript file. If a function is specified as one of the arguments, it runs the function and also any code in the script that is not within the function. The rest of the code in the script runs before the function is run.

Example

Suppose there is a script file named testScript.jsfl in the root directory on the C drive, and its contents are as follows:

```
function testFunct(num, minNum) {
   fl.trace("in testFunct: 1st arg: " + num + " 2nd arg: " + minNum);
}
for (i=0; i<2; i++) {
   fl.trace("in for loop i=" + i);
}
fl.trace("end of for loop");
// End of testScript.jsfl
```

If you issue the following command:

```
fl.runScript("file:///C|/testScript.jsfl", "testFunct", 10, 1);
```

The following information appears in the Output panel:

```
in for loop i=0
in for loop i=1
end of for loop
in testFunct: 1st arg: 10 2nd arg: 1
```

You can also just call testScript.jsfl without executing a function:

```
fl.runScript("file:///C|/testScript.jsfl");
```

which produces the following in the Output panel:

```
in for loop i=0
in for loop i=1
end of for loop
```

fl.saveAll()

Availability

Flash MX 2004.

Usage

```
fl.saveAll()
```

Parameters

None.

Returns

Nothing.

Description

Method; saves all open documents.

 NOTE If a file has never been saved, or has not been modified since the last time it was saved, the file isn't saved. To allow an unsaved or unmodified file to be saved, use `fl.saveDocumentAs()`.

Example

The following example saves all open documents.

```
fl.saveAll();
```

See also

`document.save()`, `document.saveAndCompact()`, `fl.saveDocument()`, `fl.saveDocumentAs()`

fl.saveDocument()

Availability

Flash MX 2004.

Usage

`fl.saveDocument( document [, fileURI] )`

Parameters

document   A Document object that specifies the document to be saved. If *document* is `null`, the active document is saved.

fileURI   A string, expressed as a file:/// URI, that specifies the name of the saved document. If the *fileURI* parameter is `null` or omitted, the document is saved with its current name. This parameter is optional.

Returns

A Boolean value: `true` if the save operation completes successfully; `false` otherwise.

 NOTE

> If the file has never been saved, or has not been modified since the last time it was saved, the file isn't saved and false is returned. To allow an unsaved or unmodified file to be saved, use `fl.saveDocumentAs()`.

Description

Method; saves the specified document as a FLA document.

Example

The following example saves the current document and two specified documents.

```
// Save the current document.
alert(fl.saveDocument(fl.getDocumentDOM()));
// Save the specified documents.
alert(fl.saveDocument(fl.documents[0], "file:///C|/example1.fla"));
alert(fl.saveDocument(fl.documents[1],"file:///C|/example2.fla"));
```

See also

`document.save()`, `document.saveAndCompact()`, `fl.saveAll()`, `fl.saveDocumentAs()`

fl.saveDocumentAs()

Availability

Flash MX 2004.

Usage

```
fl.saveDocumentAs( document )
```

Parameters

document   A Document object that specifies the document to save. If *document* is null, the active document is saved.

Returns

A Boolean value: true if the Save As operation completes successfully; false otherwise.

Description

Method; displays the Save As dialog box for the specified document.

Example

The following example prompts the user to save the specified document, and then displays an alert message that indicates whether the document was saved.

```
alert(fl.saveDocumentAs(fl.documents[1]));
```

See also

document.save(), document.saveAndCompact(), fl.saveAll(), fl.saveDocument()

fl.setActiveWindow()

Availability

Flash MX 2004.

Usage

```
fl.setActiveWindow( document [, bActivateFrame] )
```

Parameters

document   A Document object that specifies the document to select as the active window.

bActivateFrame   An optional parameter that is ignored by Flash and Fireworks and is present only for compatibility with Dreamweaver.

Returns

Nothing.

Description

Method; sets the active window to be the specified document. This method is also supported by Dreamweaver and Fireworks. If the document has multiple views (created by Edit In New Window), the first view is selected.

Example

The following example shows two ways to save a specified document.

```
fl.setActiveWindow(fl.documents[0]);
```

```
var theIndex = fl.findDocumentIndex("myFile.fla");
fl.setActiveWindow(fl.documents[theIndex]);
```

fl.showIdleMessage()

Availability

Flash 8.

Usage

```
fl.showIdleMessage( show )
```

Parameters

show   A Boolean value specifying whether to enable or disable the warning about a script running too long.

Returns

Nothing.

Description

Method; lets you disable the warning about a script running too long (pass `false` for *show*). You might want to do this when processing batch operations that take a long time to complete. To re-enable the alert, issue the command again, this time passing `true` for *show*.

Example

The following example illustrates how to disable and re-enable the warning about a script running too long.

```
fl.showIdleMessage(false);
var result = timeConsumingFunction();
fl.showIdleMessage(true);
```

fl.tools

Availability

Flash MX 2004.

Usage

```
fl.tools
```

Description

Read-only property; an array of Tools objects (see Tools object). This property is used only when creating extensible tools.

fl.trace()

Availability

Flash MX 2004.

Usage

```
fl.trace( message )
```

Parameters

message   A string that appears in the Output panel.

Returns

Nothing.

Description

Method; sends a text string to the Output panel, terminated by a new line, and displays the Output panel if it is not already visible. This method is identical to `outputPanel.trace()`, and works in the same way as the `trace()` statement in ActionScript.

To send a blank line, use `fl.trace("")` or `fl.trace("\n")`. You can use the latter command inline, making `\n` a part of the *message* string.

Example

The following example displays several lines of text in the Output panel:

```
fl.outputPanel.clear();
fl.trace("Hello World!!!");
var myPet = "cat";
fl.trace("\nI have a " + myPet);
fl.trace("");
fl.trace("I love my " + myPet);
fl.trace("Do you have a " + myPet +"?");
```

fl.version

Availability

Flash MX 2004.

Usage

```
fl.version
```

Description

Read-only property; the long string version of the Flash authoring tool, including platform.

Example

The following example displays the version of the Flash authoring tool in the Output panel.

```
alert( fl.version ); // For example, WIN 7,0,0,380
```

fl.xmlui

Availability

Flash MX 2004.

Usage

```
fl.xmlui
```

Description

Read-only property; an XMLUI object. This property lets you get and set XMLUI properties in a XMLUI dialog box and lets you accept or cancel the dialog box programmatically.

Example

See XMLUI object.

FLfile object

Availability

Flash MX 2004 7.2.

Description

The FLfile object lets you write Flash extensions that can access, modify, and remove files and folders on the local file system. The FLfile API is provided in the form of an extension to the JavaScript API. This extension is called a *shared library* and is located in the following folder:

- Windows 2000 or Windows XP:

  boot drive\Documents and Settings*user*\Local Settings\Application Data\Macromedia\Flash 8\ *language*\Configuration\External Libraries\FLfile.dll

- Mac OS X:

  Macintosh HD/Users/*userName*/Library/Application Support/Macromedia/Flash 8/ *language*/Configuration/External Libraries/FLfile.dll

> **NOTE** Don't confuse the shared libraries that contain symbols in your Flash documents with the JavaScript API shared libraries. They are two different things.

The FLfile methods work with files or folders (directories) on disk. Therefore, each method takes one or more parameters that specifies the location of a file or folder. The location of the file or folder is expressed as a string in a form very similar to a website URL. It is called a *file URI* (Uniform Resource Identifier) and is formatted as shown below (including the quote marks):

```
"file:///drive|/folder 1/folder 2/.../filename"
```

For example, if you want to create a folder on the C drive called config and place it in the Program Files/MyApp folder, use the following command:

```
FLfile.createFolder("file:///C|/Program Files/MyApp/config");
```

If you then want to place a file called config.ini in that folder, use the following command:

```
FLfile.write("file:///C|/Program Files/MyApp/config/config.ini", "");
```

To create a folder on the Macintosh, you could use the following command:

```
FLfile.createFolder("file:///Macintosh/MyApp/config");
```

Method summary for the FLfile object

The following methods can be used with the FLfile object.

Method	Description
FLfile.copy()	Copies a file.
FLfile.createFolder()	Creates one or more folders.
FLfile.exists()	Determines the existence of a file or folder.
FLfile.getAttributes()	Finds out if a file is writable, read-only, hidden, visible, or a system folder.
FLfile.getCreationDate()	Specifies how many seconds have passed between January 1, 1970, and the time the file or folder was created.
FLfile.getCreationDateObj()	Gets the date a file or folder was created.
FLfile.getModificationDate()	Specifies how many seconds have passed between January 1, 1970, and the time the file or folder was last modified.
FLfile.getModificationDateObj()	Gets the date a file or folder was last modified.
FLfile.getSize()	Gets the size of a file.
FLfile.listFolder()	Lists the contents of a folder.
FLfile.read()	Reads the contents of a file.
FLfile.remove()	Deletes a file or folder.
FLfile.setAttributes()	Makes a file or folder read-only, writable, hidden or visible.
FLfile.write()	Creates, writes to, or appends to a file.

FLfile.copy()

Availability

Flash MX 2004 7.2.

Usage

FLfile.copy(*fileURI*, *copyURI*)

Parameters

fileURI   A string, expressed as a file:/// URI, that specifies the file you want to copy.

copyURI   A string, expressed as a file:/// URI, that specifies the location and name of the copied file.

Returns

A Boolean value of true if successful; false otherwise.

Description

Method; copies a file from one location to another. This method returns false if *copyURI* already exists.

Example

The following example makes a backup copy of a configuration file named config.ini and places it inside the same folder in which it is located, with a new name.

```
var originalFileURI="file:///C|/Program Files/MyApp/config.ini";
var newFileURI="file:///C|/Program Files/MyApp/config_backup.ini";
Flfile.copy(originalFileURI, newFileURI);
```

If you prefer, you can perform the same task with a single command:

```
Flfile.copy("file:///C|:/Program Files/MyApp/config.ini",
  file:///C|/Program Files/MyApp/config_backup.ini");
```

FLfile.createFolder()

Availability

Flash MX 2004 7.2.

Usage

```
FLfile.createFolder( folderURI )
```

Parameters

folderURI   A folder URI that specifies the folder structure you want to create.

Returns

A Boolean value of true if successful; false if *folderURI* already exists.

Description

Method; creates one or more folders at the specified location.

You can create multiple folders at one time. For example, the following command creates both the MyData and the TempData folders if they don't already exist:

```
FLfile.createFolder("file:///c|/MyData/TempData")
```

Example

The following example creates two subfolders under the configuration folder (fl.configURI).

```
fl.trace(FLfile.createFolder(fl.configURI+"folder01/subfolder01"));
```

The following example attempts to create a folder called tempFolder at the root level on the C drive and displays an alert box indicating whether the operation was successful.

```
var folderURI = "file:///c|/tempFolder";
if (FLfile.createFolder(folderURI)) {
   alert("Created " + folderURI);
}
else {
   alert(folderURI + " already exists");
}
```

See also

FLfile.remove(), FLfile.write()

FLfile.exists()

Availability

Flash MX 2004 7.2.

Usage

```
FLfile.exists( fileURI )
```

Parameters

fileURI   A string, expressed as a file:/// URI, that specifies the file you want to verify.

Returns

A Boolean value of true if successful; false otherwise.

Description

Method; determines whether a specified file exists.

Examples

The following example checks for a file called mydata.txt and displays an alert box indicating whether the file exists.

```
var fileURI = "file:///c|/temp/mydata.txt";
if (FLfile.exists(fileURI)) {
   alert( fileURI + " exists!");
}
else {
   alert( fileURI + " does not exist.");
}
```

The following example checks to see if a required configuration file exists. If the file doesn't exist, it is created:

```
var configFile = "file:///C|/MyApplication/config.ini";
if (!FLfile.exists(configFile)) {
    FLfile.write(configFile,"")
}
```

See also

FLfile.write()

FLfile.getAttributes()

Availability

Flash MX 2004 7.2.

Usage

FLfile.getAttributes(*fileOrFolderURI*)

Parameters

fileOrFolderURI   A string, expressed as a file:/// URI, specifying the file or folder whose attributes you want to retrieve.

Returns

A string that represents the attributes of the specified file or folder.

> **NOTE**
> Results are unpredictable if the file or folder doesn't exist. You should use FLfile.exists() before using this method.

Description

Method; returns a string representing the attributes of the specified file or folder, or an empty string if the file has no specific attributes (that it, it is not read-only, not hidden, and so on). You should always use `FLfile.exists()` to test for the existence of a file or folder before using this method.

Characters in the string represent the attributes as follows:

R — *fileOrFolderURI* is read-only

D — *fileOrFolderURI* is a folder (directory)

H — *fileOrFolderURI* is hidden (Windows only)

S — *fileOrFolderURI* is a system file or folder (Windows only)

A — *fileOrFolderURI* is ready for archiving (Windows only)

For example, if *fileOrFolderURI* is a hidden folder, the string returned is `"DH"`.

Example

The following example gets the attributes of the file mydata.txt and displays an alert box if the file is read-only.

```
var URI = "file:///c|/temp/mydata.txt";
if (FLfile.exists(URI)){
  var attr = FLfile.getAttributes(URI);
    if (attr && (attr.indexOf("R") != -1)) { // Returned string contains R.
      alert(URI + " is read only!");
  }
}
```

See also

FLfile.setAttributes()

FLfile.getCreationDate()

Availability

Flash MX 2004 7.2.

Usage

FLfile.getCreationDate(*fileOrFolderURI*)

Parameters

fileOrFolderURI   A string, expressed as a file:/// URI, specifying the file or folder whose creation date and time you want to retrieve as a hexadecimal string.

Returns

A string containing a hexadecimal number that represents the number of seconds that have elapsed between January 1, 1970, and the time the file or folder was created, or "00000000" if the file or folder doesn't exist.

Description

Method; specifies how many seconds have passed between January 1, 1970, and the time the file or folder was created. This method is used primarily to compare the creation or modification dates of files or folders.

Example

The following example determines whether a file has been modified since it was created.

```
// Make sure the specified file exists.
var fileURI = "file:///C|/MyApplication/MyApp.fla";
var creationTime = FLfile.getCreationDate(fileURI)
var modificationTime = FLfile.getModificationDate(fileURI)
if ( modificationTime > creationTime ) {
    alert("The file has been modified since it was created")
}
else {
    alert("The file has not been modified since it was created")
}
```

See also

FLfile.getCreationDateObj(), FLfile.getModificationDate()

FLfile.getCreationDateObj()

Availability

Flash MX 2004 7.2.

Usage

FLfile.getCreationDateObj(*fileOrFolderURI*)

Parameters

fileOrFolderURI   A string, expressed as a file:/// URI, specifying the file or folder whose creation date and time you want to retrieve as a JavaScript Date object.

Returns

A JavaScript Date object that represents the date and time when the specified file or folder was created. If the file doesn't exist, the object contains information indicating that the file or folder was created at midnight GMT on December 31, 1969.

Description

Method; returns a JavaScript Date object that represents the date and time when the specified file or folder was created.

Example

The following example displays (in human-readable form) the date a file was created in the Output panel:

```
// Make sure the specified file exists.
var file1Date = FLfile.getCreationDateObj("file:///c|/temp/file1.txt");
fl.trace(file1Date);
```

See also

FLfile.getCreationDate(), FLfile.getModificationDateObj()

FLfile.getModificationDate()

Availability

Flash MX 2004 7.2.

Usage

FLfile.getModificationDate(fileOrFolderURI)

Parameters

fileOrFolderURI A string, expressed as a file:/// URI, specifying the file whose modification date and time you want to retrieve as a hexadecimal string.

Returns

A string containing a hexadecimal number that represents the number of seconds that have elapsed between January 1, 1970, and the time the file or folder was last modified, or "00000000" if the file doesn't exist.

Description

Method; specifies how many seconds have passed between January 1, 1970, and the time the file or folder was last modified. This method is used primarily to compare the creation or modification dates of files or folders.

Example

The following example compares the modification dates of two files and determines which of the two was modified most recently:

```
// Make sure the specified files exist.
file1 = "file:///C|/MyApplication/MyApp.fla"
file2 = "file:///C|/MyApplication/MyApp.as"
modificationTime1 = FLfile.getModificationDate(file1)
modificationTime2 = FLfile.getModificationDate(file2)

if(modificationTime1 > modificationTime2) {
    alert("File 2 is older than File 1")
}
else if(modificationTime1 < modificationTime2) {
    alert("File 1 is older than File 2")
}
else {
    alert("File 1 and File 2 were saved at the same time")
}
```

See also

FLfile.getCreationDate(), FLfile.getModificationDateObj()

FLfile.getModificationDateObj()

Availability

Flash MX 2004 7.2.

Usage

FLfile.getModificationDateObj(fileOrFolderURI)

Parameters

fileOrFolderURI   A string, expressed as a file:/// URI, specifying the file or folder whose modification date and time you want to retrieve as a JavaScript Date object.

Returns

A JavaScript Date object that represents the date and time when the specified file or folder was last modified. If the file or folder doesn't exist, the object contains information indicating that the file or folder was created at midnight GMT on December 31, 1969.

Description

Method; returns a JavaScript Date object that represents the date and time when the specified file or folder was last modified.

Example

The following example displays (in human-readable form) the date a file was last modified in the Output panel:

```
// Make sure the specified file exists.
var file1Date = FLfile.getModificationDateObj("file:///c|/temp/file1.txt");
trace(file1Date);
```

See also

`FLfile.getCreationDateObj()`, `FLfile.getModificationDate()`

FLfile.getSize()

Availability

Flash MX 2004 7.2.

Usage

`FLfile.getSize( fileURI )`

Parameters

fileURI   A string, expressed as a file:/// URI, specifying the file whose size you want to retrieve.

Returns

An integer that represents the size of the specified file, in bytes, or 0 if the file doesn't exist.

Description

Method; returns an integer that represents the size of the specified file, in bytes, or 0 if the file doesn't exist. If the return value is 0, you can use `FLfile.exists()` to determine whether the file is a zero-byte file or if the file doesn't exist.

Example

The following example stores the size of the mydata.txt file in the `fileSize` variable:

```
var URL = "file:///c|/temp/mydata.txt";
var fileSize = FLfile.getSize(URL);
```

FLfile.listFolder()

Availability

Flash MX 2004 7.2.

Usage

```
FLfile.listFolder( folderURI [, filesOrDirectories ] )
```

Parameters

folderURI   A string, expressed as a file:/// URI, specifying the folder whose contents you want to retrieve. You can include a wildcard mask as part of *folderURI*. Valid wildcards are * (matches one or more characters) and ? (matches a single character).

filesOrDirectories   An optional string that specifies whether to return only filenames or only folder (directory) names. If omitted, both filenames and folder names are returned. Acceptable values are "files" and "directories".

Returns

An array of strings representing the contents of the folder, or false if the folder doesn't exist.

Description

Method; returns an array of strings that represent the contents of the folder, or an empty array if the folder doesn't exist.

Examples

The following example returns an array representing the files, folders, or both files and folders in the Program Files directory.

```
var folderURI = "file:///C|/WINDOWS/Program Files" ;
var fileList = FLfile.listFolder(folderURI, "files") // files
var fileList = FLfile.listFolder("folderURI", "directories") //folders
var fileList = FLfile.listFolder(folderURI) //files and folders
```

The following example returns an array of all the text (.txt) files in the temp folder and displays the list in an alert box.

```
var folderURI = "file:///c|/temp";
var fileMask = "*.txt";
var list = FLfile.listFolder(folderURI + "/" + fileMask, "files");
if (list) {
  alert(folderURI + " contains: " + list.join(" "));
}
```

The following example uses a file mask in the specified *folderURI* to return the names of all the executable files in the Windows application folder:

```
var executables = FLfile.listFolder("file:///C|/WINDOWS/*.exe","files")
alert(executables.join("\n"))
```

FLfile.read()

Availability

Flash MX 2004 7.2.

Usage

```
FFLfile.read()
```

Parameters

fileOrFolderURI   A string, expressed as a file:/// URI, specifying the file or folder whose attributes you want to retrieve.

Returns

The contents of the specified file as a string, or null if the read fails.

Description

Method; returns the contents of the specified file as a string, or null if the read fails.

Examples

The following example reads the file mydata.txt and, if successful, displays an alert box with the contents of the file.

```
var fileURI = "file:///c|/temp/mydata.txt";
var str = FLfile.read( fileURI);
if (str) {
  alert( fileURL + " contains: " + str);
}
```

The following example reads the ActionScript code from a class file and stores it in the code variable:

```
var classFileURI = "file:///C|/MyApplication/TextCarousel.as";
var code = Flfile.read(classFileURI);
```

FLfile.remove()

Availability

Flash MX 2004 7.2.

Usage

```
FLfile.remove( fileOrFolderURI )
```

Parameters

fileOrFolderURI   A string, expressed as a file:/// URI, specifying the file or folder you want
to remove (delete).

Returns

A Boolean value of `true` if successful; `false` otherwise.

Description

Method; deletes the specified file or folder. If the folder contains files, those files will be
deleted as well. Files with the R (read-only) attribute cannot be removed.

Examples

The following example warns a user if a file exists and then deletes it if the user chooses to
do so.

```
var fileURI = prompt ("Enter file/folder to be deleted: ", "file:///c|/temp/
   delete.txt");
if (FLfile.exists(fileURI)) {
   var confirm = prompt("File exists. Delete it? (y/n)", "y");
   if (confirm == "y" || confirm == "Y") {
      if(FLfile.remove(fileURI)) {
         alert(fileURI + " is deleted.");
      }
      else {
         alert("fail to delete " + fileURI);
      }
   }
}
else {
   alert(fileURI + " does not exist");
}
```

The following example deletes a configuration file created by an application:

```
if(FLfile.remove("file:///C|/MyApplication/config.ini")) {
    alert("Configuration file deleted")
}
```

The following example deletes the Configuration folder and its contents:

```
FLfile.remove("file:///C|/MyApplication/Configuration/")
```

See also

```
FLfile.createFolder(), FLfile.getAttributes()
```

FLfile.setAttributes()

Availability

Flash MX 2004 7.2.

Usage

```
FLfile.setAttributes( fileURI, strAttrs )
```

Parameters

fileURI   A string, expressed as a file:/// URI, specifying the file whose attributes you want to set.

strAttrs   A string specifying values for the attribute(s) you want to set. For acceptable values for *strAttrs*, see the description below.

Returns

A Boolean value of `true` if successful.

 Results are unpredictable if the file or folder doesn't exist. You should use `FLfile.exists()` before using this method.

Description

Method; specifies system-level attributes for the specified file.

The following values are valid for *strAttrs*:

- N — No specific attributes (not read-only, not hidden, and so on)
- A — Ready for archiving (Windows only)
- R — Read-only (on the Macintosh, read-only means "locked")
- W — Writable (overrides R)
- H — Hidden (Windows only)
- V — Visible (overrides H, Windows only)

If you include both R and W in *strAttrs*, the R is ignored and the file is set as writable. Similarly, if you pass H and V, the H is ignored and the file is set as visible.

If you want to make sure the archive attribute is not set, use this command with the N parameter before setting attributes. That is, there is no direct counterpart to A that turns off the archive attribute.

Examples

The following example sets the file mydata.txt to be read-only and hidden. It has no effect on the archive attribute.

```
var URI = "file:///c|/temp/mydata.txt";
if (FLfile.exists(URI)) {
  FLfile.setAttributes(URI, "RH");
}
```

The following example sets the file mydata.txt to be read-only and hidden. It also ensures that the archive attribute is not set.

```
var URI = "file:///c|/temp/mydata.txt";

if (FLfile.exists(URI)) {
  FLfile.setAttributes(URI, "N");
  FLfile.setAttributes(URI, "RH");
}
```

See also

FLfile.getAttributes()

FLfile.write()

Availability

Flash MX 2004 7.2.

Usage

FLfile.write(*fileURI*, *textToWrite*, [, *strAppendMode*])

Parameters

fileURI   A string, expressed as a file:/// URI, specifying the file to which you want to write.

textToWrite   A string representing the text you want to place in the file.

strAppendMode   An optional string with the value "append", which specifies that you want to append *textToWrite* to the existing file. If omitted, *fileURI* is overwritten with *textToWrite*.

Returns

A Boolean value of `true` if successful; `false` otherwise.

Description

Method; writes the specified string to the specified file (as UTF-8). If the specified file does not exist, it is created. However, the folder in which you are placing the file must exist before you use this method. To create folders, use `FLfile.createFolder()`.

Example

The following example attempts to write the string "xxx" to the file mydata.txt and displays an alert message if the write succeeded. It then attempts to append the string "aaa" to the file and displays a second alert message if the write succeeded. After executing this script, the file mydata.txt will contain only the text "xxxaaa".

```
var URI = "file:///c|/temp/mydata.txt";
if (FLfile.write(URI, "xxx")) {
   alert("Wrote xxx to " + URI);
}
if (FLfile.write(URI, "aaa", "append")) {
   alert("Appended aaa to " + fileURI);
}
```

See also

`FLfile.createFolder()`, `FLfile.exists()`

folderItem object

Inheritance Item object > folderItem object

Availability

Flash MX 2004.

Description

The folderItem object is a subclass of the Item object. There are no unique methods or properties of folderItem. See Item object.

fontItem object

Inheritance   Item object > fontItem object

Availability

Flash MX 2004.

Description

The fontItem object is a subclass of the Item object. There are no unique methods or properties of fontItem. See Item object.

Frame object

Availability

Flash MX 2004.

Description

The Frame object represents frames in the layer.

Method summary for the Frame object

The following methods can be used with the Frame object.

Method	Description
frame.getCustomEase()	Returns an array of JavaScript objects, each of which has an x and y property.
frame.setCustomEase()	Specifies a cubic Bézier curve to be used as a custom ease curve.

Property summary for the Frame object

The following properties can be used with the Frame object:

Property	Description
frame.actionScript	A string representing ActionScript code.
frame.duration	Read-only; an integer that represents the number of frames in a frame sequence.
frame.elements	Read-only; an array of Element objects (see Element object).
frame.hasCustomEase	A Boolean value that specifies whether the frame gets its ease information from the custom ease curve.
frame.labelType	A string that specifies the type of Frame name.
frame.motionTweenOrientToPath	A Boolean value that specifies whether or not the tweened element rotates the element as it moves along a path to maintain its angle with respect to each point on the path.
frame.motionTweenRotate	A string that specifies how the tweened element rotates.

Property	Description
`frame.motionTweenRotateTimes`	An integer that specifies the number of times the tweened element rotates between the starting keyframe and the next keyframe.
`frame.motionTweenScale`	A Boolean value; specifies whether the tweened element scales to the size of the object in the following keyframe, increasing its size with each frame in the tween (`true`) or doesn't scale (`false`).
`frame.motionTweenSnap`	A Boolean value; specifies whether the tweened element automatically snaps to the nearest point on the motion guide layer associated with this frame's layer (`true`) or not (`false`).
`frame.motionTweenSync`	A Boolean value; if set to `true`, synchronizes the animation of the tweened object with the main timeline.
`frame.name`	A string that specifies the name of the frame.
`frame.shapeTweenBlend`	A string that specifies how a shape tween is blended between the shape in the keyframe at the start of the tween and the shape in the following keyframe.
`frame.soundEffect`	A string that specifies effects for a sound that is attached directly to a frame (`frame.soundLibraryItem`).
`frame.soundLibraryItem`	A library item (see SoundItem object) used to create a sound.
`frame.soundLoop`	An integer value that specifies the number of times a sound that is attached directly to a frame (`frame.soundLibraryItem`) plays.
`frame.soundLoopMode`	A string that specifies whether a sound that is attached directly to a frame (`frame.soundLibraryItem`) should play a specific number of times or loop indefinitely.
`frame.soundName`	A string that specifies the name of a sound that is attached directly to a frame (`frame.soundLibraryItem`), as stored in the library.
`frame.soundSync`	A string that specifies the sync behavior of a sound that is attached directly to a frame (`frame.soundLibraryItem`).
`frame.startFrame`	Read-only; the index of the first frame in a sequence.
`frame.tweenEasing`	An integer that specifies the amount of easing that should be applied to the tweened object.

Property	Description
frame.tweenType	A string that specifies the type of tween.
frame.useSingleEaseCurve	A Boolean value that specifies whether a single custom ease curve is used for easing information for all properties.

frame.actionScript

Availability

Flash MX 2004.

Usage

```
frame.actionScript
```

Description

Property; a string that represents ActionScript code. To insert a new line character, use "\\n".

Example

The following example assigns `stop()` to first frame top layer action:

```
fl.getDocumentDOM().getTimeline().layers[0].frames[0].actionScript =
  'stop();';
```

frame.duration

Availability

Flash MX 2004.

Usage

```
frame.duration
```

Description

Read-only property; an integer that represents the number of frames in a frame sequence.

Example

The following example stores the number of frames in a frame sequence that starts at first frame in the top layer in the `frameSpan` variable:

```
var frameSpan =
  fl.getDocumentDOM().getTimeline().layers[0].frames[0].duration;
```

frame.elements

Availability

Flash MX 2004.

Usage

```
frame.elements
```

Description

Read-only property; an array of Element objects (see Element object). The order of elements is the order in which they are stored in the FLA file. If there are multiple shapes on the Stage, and each is ungrouped, Flash treats them as one element. If each shape is grouped, so there are multiple groups on the Stage, Flash sees them as separate elements. In other words, Flash treats raw, ungrouped shapes as a single element, regardless of how many separate shapes are on the Stage. If a frame contains three raw, ungrouped shapes, for example, then `elements.length` in that frame returns a value of 1. Select each shape individually, and group it to work around this issue.

Example

The following example stores an array of current elements on the top layer, first frame in the `myElements` variable:

```
var myElements =
   fl.getDocumentDOM( ).getTimeline( ).layers[0].frames[0].elements;
```

frame.getCustomEase()

Availability

Flash 8.

Usage

```
Frame.getCustomEase( [ property ] )
```

Parameters

property An optional string that specifies the property for which you want to return the custom ease value. Acceptable values are `"all"`, `"position"`, `"rotation"`, `"scale"`, `"color"`, and `"filters"`. The default value is `"all"`.

Returns

Returns an array of JavaScript objects, each of which has an *x* and *y* property.

Description

Method; returns an array of objects that represent the control points for the cubic Bézier curve that defines the ease curve.

Example

The following example returns the custom ease value of the `position` property for the first frame in the top layer:

```
var theFrame = fl.getDocumentDOM().getTimeline().layers[0].frames[0]
var easeArray = theFrame.getCustomEase( "position" );
```

See also

`frame.hasCustomEase`, `frame.setCustomEase()`, `frame.useSingleEaseCurve`

frame.hasCustomEase

Availability

Flash 8.

Usage

`frame.hasCustomEase`

Description

Property; a Boolean value. If `true`, the frame gets its ease information from the custom ease curve. If `false`, the frame gets its ease information from the ease value.

Example

The following example specifies that the first frame in the top layer should get its ease information from the ease value rather than the custom ease curve:

```
var theFrame = fl.getDocumentDOM().getTimeline().layers[0].frames[0]
theFrame.hasCustomEase = false;
```

See also

`frame.getCustomEase()`, `frame.setCustomEase()`, `frame.useSingleEaseCurve`

frame.labelType

Availability

Flash MX 2004.

Usage

```
frame.labelType
```

Description

Property; a string that specifies the type of Frame name. Acceptable values are `"none"`, `"name"`, `"comment"`, and `"anchor"`. Setting a label to `"none"` clears the `frame.name` property.

Example

The following example sets the name of the first frame in the top layer to `"First Frame"` and then sets its label to `"comment"`:

```
fl.getDocumentDOM().getTimeline().layers[0].frames[0].name = 'First Frame';
fl.getDocumentDOM().getTimeline().layers[0].frames[0].labelType =
  'comment';
```

frame.motionTweenOrientToPath

Availability

Flash MX 2004.

Usage

```
frame.motionTweenOrientToPath
```

Description

Property; a Boolean value; specifies whether the tweened element rotates the element as it moves along a path to maintain its angle with respect to each point on the path (`true`) or whether it does not rotate (`false`).

If you want to specify a value for this property, you should set `frame.motionTweenRotate` to `"none"`.

frame.motionTweenRotate

Availability

Flash MX 2004.

Usage

```
frame.motionTweenRotate
```

Description

Property; a string that specifies how the tweened element rotates. Acceptable values are
`"none"`, `"auto"`, `"clockwise"`, and `"counter-clockwise"`. A value of `"auto"` means the
object will rotate in the direction requiring the least motion to match the rotation of the
object in the following keyframe.

If you want to specify a value for `frame.motionTweenOrientToPath`, set this property to
`"none"`.

Example

See `frame.motionTweenRotateTimes`.

frame.motionTweenRotateTimes

Availability

Flash MX 2004.

Usage

```
frame.motionTweenRotateTimes
```

Description

Property; an integer that specifies the number of times the tweened element rotates between
the starting keyframe and the next keyframe.

Example

The following example rotates the element in this frame counter-clockwise three times by the
time it reaches the next keyframe:

```
fl.getDocumentDOM().getTimeline().layers[0].frames[0].motionTweenRotate =
  "counter-clockwise";
fl.getDocumentDOM().getTimeline().layers[0].frames[0].motionTweenRotateTime
  s = 3;
```

frame.motionTweenScale

Availability

Flash MX 2004.

Usage

```
frame.motionTweenScale
```

Description

Property; a Boolean value; specifies whether the tweened element scales to the size of the object in the following keyframe, increasing its size with each frame in the tween (`true`) or doesn't scale (`false`).

Example

The following example specifies that the tweened element should scale to the size of the object in the following keyframe, increasing its size with each frame in the tween.

```
fl.getDocumentDOM().getTimeline().layers[0].frames[0].motionTweenScale =
    true;
```

frame.motionTweenSnap

Availability

Flash MX 2004.

Usage

```
frame.motionTweenSnap
```

Description

Property; a Boolean value; specifies whether the tweened element automatically snaps to the nearest point on the motion guide layer associated with this frame's layer (`true`) or not (`false`).

frame.motionTweenSync

Availability

Flash MX 2004.

Usage

```
frame.motionTweenSync
```

Description

Property; a Boolean value; if set to `true`, synchronizes the animation of the tweened object with the main timeline.

Example

The following example specifies that tweened object should be synchronized with the timeline:

```
fl.getDocumentDOM().getTimeline().layers[0].frames[0].motionTweenSync =
    true;
```

frame.name

Availability

Flash MX 2004.

Usage

```
frame.name
```

Description

Property; a string that specifies the name of the frame.

Example

The following example sets the name of the first frame, top layer to "First Frame" and then stores the `name` value in the `frameLabel` variable:

```
fl.getDocumentDOM().getTimeline().layers[0].frames[0].name = 'First Frame';
var frameLabel =
    fl.getDocumentDOM().getTimeline().layers[0].frames[0].name;
```

frame.setCustomEase()

Availability

Flash 8.

Usage

```
frame.setCustomEase( property, easeCurve )
```

Parameters

property A string that specifies the property the ease curve should be used for. Acceptable values are "all", "position", "rotation", "scale", "color", and "filters".

easeCurve An array of objects that defines the ease curve. Each array element must be a JavaScript object with *x* and *y* properties.

Returns

Nothing.

Description

Method; specifies an array of control point and tangent endpoint coordinates that describe a cubic Bézier curve to be used as a custom ease curve. This array is constructed by the horizontal (ordinal: left to right) position of the control points and tangent endpoints. For example, the following illustration shows an ease curve that would be created if the *easeCurve* array contained values for the seven points shown as *p1* through *p7*:

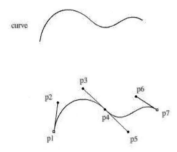

Example

The following example sets the ease curve for all properties of the first frame on the first layer to the Bézier curve specified by the control points and tangent end points stored in the myCurve array:

```
var theFrame = fl.getDocumentDOM().getTimeline().layers[0].frames[0]
var myCurve = [{x:100, y:200},{x:200, y:100}, {x:10, y:0}]
theFrame.setCustomEase("all", myCurve);
```

See also

frame.getCustomEase(), frame.hasCustomEase, frame.useSingleEaseCurve

frame.shapeTweenBlend

Availability

Flash MX 2004.

Usage

```
frame.shapeTweenBlend
```

Description

Property; a string that specifies how a shape tween is blended between the shape in the keyframe at the start of the tween and the shape in the following keyframe. Acceptable values are "distributive" and "angular".

frame.soundEffect

Availability

Flash MX 2004.

Usage

```
frame.soundEffect
```

Description

Property; a string that specifies effects for a sound that is attached directly to a frame (frame.soundLibraryItem). Acceptable values are "none", "left channel", "right channel", "fade left to right", "fade right to left", "fade in", "fade out", and "custom".

Example

The following example specifies that the sound attached to the first frame should fade in:

```
fl.getDocumentDOM().getTimeline().layers[0].frames[0].soundEffect = "fade
    in";
```

frame.soundLibraryItem

Availability

Flash MX 2004.

Usage

```
frame.soundLibraryItem
```

Description

Property; a library item (see SoundItem object) used to create a sound. The sound is attached directly to the frame.

Example

The following example assigns the first item in the library to the `soundLibraryItem` property of the first frame:

```
// The first item in the library must be a sound object
fl.getDocumentDOM().getTimeline().layers[0].frames[0].soundLibraryItem
  =fl.getDocumentDOM().library.items[0];
```

frame.soundLoop

Availability

Flash MX 2004.

Usage

```
frame.soundLoop
```

Description

Property; an integer value that specifies the number of times a sound that is attached directly to a frame (`frame.soundLibraryItem`) plays. If you want to specify a value for this property, set `frame.soundLoopMode` to `"repeat"`.

Example

See `frame.soundLoopMode`.

frame.soundLoopMode

Availability

Flash MX 2004.

Usage

```
frame.soundLoopMode
```

Description

Property; a string that specifies whether a sound that is attached directly to a frame (`frame.soundLibraryItem`) should play a specific number of times or loop indefinitely. Acceptable values are `"repeat"` and `"loop"`. To specify the number of times the sound should play, set a value for `frame.soundLoop`.

Example

The following example specifies that a sound should play two times:

```
fl.getDocumentDOM().getTimeline().layers[0].frames[0].soundLoopMode =
    "repeat";
fl.getDocumentDOM().getTimeline().layers[0].frames[0].soundLoop = 2;
```

frame.soundName

Availability

Flash MX 2004.

Usage

```
frame.soundName
```

Description

Property; a string that specifies the name of a sound that is attached directly to a frame (frame.soundLibraryItem), as stored in the library.

Example

The following example changes the soundName property of the first frame to "song1.mp3"; song1.mp3 must exist in the library:

```
fl.getDocumentDOM().getTimeline().layers[0].frames[0].soundName =
    "song1.mp3";
```

frame.soundSync

Availability

Flash MX 2004.

Usage

```
frame.soundSync
```

Description

Property; a string that specifies the sync behavior of a sound that is attached directly to a frame (frame.soundLibraryItem). Acceptable values are "event", "stop", "start", and "stream".

Example

The following example specifies that a sound should stream:

```
fl.getDocumentDOM().getTimeline().layers[0].frames[0].soundSync = 'stream';
```

frame.startFrame

Availability

Flash MX 2004.

Usage

```
frame.startFrame
```

Description

Read-only property; the index of the first frame in a sequence.

Example

In the following example, stFrame is the index of the first frame in the frame sequence. In this example, a frame sequence is spanning the six frames from Frame 5 to Frame 10. Therefore, the value of stFrame at any frame between Frame 5 and Frame 10 is 4 (remember that index values are different from frame number values).

```
var stFrame =
   fl.getDocumentDOM().getTimeline().layers[0].frames[4].startFrame;
fl.trace(stFrame); // 4
var stFrame =
   fl.getDocumentDOM().getTimeline().layers[0].frames[9].startFrame;
fl.trace(stFrame); // 4
```

frame.tweenEasing

Availability

Flash MX 2004.

Usage

```
frame.tweenEasing
```

Description

Property; an integer that specifies the amount of easing that should be applied to the tweened object. Acceptable values are -100 to 100. To begin the motion tween slowly and accelerate the tween toward the end of the animation, use a value between -1 and -100. To begin the motion tween rapidly and decelerate the tween toward the end of the animation, use a positive value between 1 and 100.

Example

The following example specifies that the motion of the tweened object should begin fairly rapidly and decelerate toward the end of the animation:

```
fl.getDocumentDOM().getTimeline().layers[0].frames[0].tweenEasing = 50;
```

frame.tweenType

Availability

Flash MX 2004.

Usage

```
frame.tweenType
```

Description

Property; a string that specifies the type of tween; acceptable values are `"motion"`, `"shape"`, or `"none"`. The value `"none"` removes the motion tween. Use the `timeline.createMotionTween()` method to create a tween.

If you specify `"motion"`, the object in the frame must be a symbol, text field, or grouped object. It will be tweened from its location in the current keyframe to the location in the following keyframe.

If you specify `"shape"`, the object in the frame must be a shape. It will blend from its shape in the current keyframe to the shape in the following keyframe.

Example

The following example specifies that the object is a motion tween, and therefore, it should be tweened from its location in the current keyframe to the location in the following keyframe:

```
fl.getDocumentDOM().getTimeline().layers[0].frames[0].tweenType = "motion";
```

frame.useSingleEaseCurve

Availability

Flash 8.

Usage

```
frame.useSingleEaseCurve
```

Description

Property; a Boolean value. If `true`, a single custom ease curve is used for easing information for all properties. If `false`, each property has its own ease curve.

This property is ignored if the frame doesn't have custom easing applied.

Example

The following example specifies that a single custom ease curve should be used for all properties of the first frame on the first layer:

```
var theFrame = fl.getDocumentDOM().getTimeline().layers[0].frames[0]
theFrame.useSingleEaseCurve = true;
```

See also

`frame.getCustomEase()`, `frame.hasCustomEase`, `frame.setCustomEase()`

HalfEdge object

Availability

Flash MX 2004.

Description

The HalfEdge object is the directed side of the edge of a Shape object. An edge has two half edges. You can transverse the contours of a shape by "walking around" these half edges. For example, starting from a half edge, you can trace all the half edges around a contour of a shape, and return to the original half edge.

Half edges are ordered. One half edge represents one side of the edge; the other half edge represents the other side.

Method summary for the HalfEdge object

The following methods are available for the HalfEdge object:

Method	Description
halfEdge.getEdge()	Gets the Edge object for the HalfEdge object.
halfEdge.getNext()	Gets the next half edge on the current contour.
halfEdge.getOppositeHalfEdge()	Gets the HalfEdge object on the other side of the edge.
halfEdge.getPrev()	Gets the preceding HalfEdge object on the current contour.
halfEdge.getVertex()	Gets the Vertex object at the head of the HalfEdge object.

Property summary for the HalfEdge object

The following properties are available for the HalfEdge object:

Property	Description
halfEdge.id	Read-only; a unique integer identifier for the HalfEdge object.
halfEdge.index	

halfEdge.getEdge()

Availability

Flash MX 2004.

Usage

```
halfEdge.getEdge()
```

Parameters

None.

Returns

An Edge object.

Description

Method; gets the Edge object for the HalfEdge object. See Edge object.

Example

The following example illustrates getting an edge and a half edge for the specified shape.

```
var shape = fl.getDocumentDOM().selection[0];
var hEdge = shape.edges[0].getHalfEdge(0);
var edge = hEdge.getEdge();
```

halfEdge.getNext()

Availability

Flash MX 2004.

Usage

```
halfEdge.getNext()
```

Parameters

None.

Returns

A HalfEdge object.

Description

Method; gets the next half edge on the current contour.

> **NOTE** Although half edges have a direction and a sequence order, edges do not.

Example

The following example stores the next half edge of the specified contour in the `nextHalfEdge` variable:

```
var shape = fl.getDocumentDOM().selection[0];
var hEdge = shape.edges[0].getHalfEdge( 0 );
var nextHalfEdge = hEdge.getNext();
```

halfEdge.getOppositeHalfEdge()

Availability

Flash MX 2004.

Usage

```
halfEdge.getOppositeHalfEdge()
```

Parameters

None.

Returns

A HalfEdge object.

Description

Method; gets the HalfEdge object on the other side of the edge.

Example

The following example stores the half edge opposite `hEdge` in the `otherHalfEdge` variable:

```
var shape = fl.getDocumentDOM().selection[0];
var hEdge = shape.edges[0].getHalfEdge(0);
var otherHalfEdge = hEdge.getOppositeHalfEdge();
```

halfEdge.getPrev()

Availability

Flash MX 2004.

Usage

```
halfEdge.getPrev()
```

Parameters

None.

Returns

A HalfEdge object.

Description

Method; gets the preceding HalfEdge object on the current contour.

> **NOTE** Although half edges have a direction and a sequence order, edges do not.

Example

The following example stores the previous half edge of the specified contour in the prevHalfEdge variable:

```
var shape = fl.getDocumentDOM().selection[0];
var hEdge = shape.edges[0].getHalfEdge( 0 );
var prevHalfEdge = hEdge.getPrev();
```

halfEdge.getVertex()

Availability

Flash MX 2004.

Usage

```
halfEdge.getVertex()
```

Parameters

None.

Returns

A Vertex object.

Description

Method; gets the Vertex object at the head of the HalfEdge object. See Vertex object.

Example

The following example stores the Vertex object at the head of hEdge in the vertex variable:

```
var shape = fl.getDocumentDOM().selection[0];
var edge = shape.edges[0];
var hEdge = edge.getHalfEdge(0);
var vertex = hEdge.getVertex();
```

halfEdge.id

Availability

Flash MX 2004.

Usage

```
halfEdge.id
```

Description

Read-only property; a unique integer identifier for the HalfEdge object.

Example

The following example displays a unique identifier for the specified half edge in the Output panel:

```
var shape = fl.getDocumentDOM().selection[0];
alert(shape.contours[0].getHalfEdge().id);
```

halfEdge.index

Availability

Flash MX 2004.

Usage

```
halfEdge.index
```

Description

Read-only property; an integer with a value of 0 or 1 that specifies the index for this HalfEdge object in the parent edge.

Example

The following example displays the index value for the specified half edge in the Output panel:

```
var shape = fl.getDocumentDOM().selection[0];
var hEdge = shape.edges[0].getHalfEdge(0);
var heIndex = hEdge.index;
```

Instance object

Inheritance   Element object > Instance object

Availability

Flash MX 2004.

Description

Instance is a subclass of the Element object.

Property summary for the Instance object

In addition to all of the Element object properties, Instance has the following properties:

Property	Description
instance.instanceType	Read-only; a string that represents the type of Instance.
instance.libraryItem	Library item used to instantiate this instance.

instance.instanceType

Availability

Flash MX 2004; acceptable value of "video" added in Flash 8.

Usage

instance.instanceType

Description

Read-only property; a string that represents the type of Instance. Acceptable values are "symbol", "bitmap", "embedded video", "linked video", "video", and "compiled clip".

> In Flash MX 2004, the value of instance.instanceType for an item added to the library using library.addNewItem("video") is "embedded_video". In Flash 8, the value is "video". See library.addNewItem().

Example

The following example shows that the instance type of a movie clip is "symbol":

```
// Select a movie clip, and then run this script.
var type = fl.getDocumentDOM().selection[0].instanceType;
fl.trace("This instance type is " + type);
```

instance.libraryItem

Availability

Flash MX 2004.

Usage

```
instance.libraryItem
```

Description

Property; a library item used to instantiate this instance. You can change this property only to another library item of the same type (that is, you cannot set a `symbol` instance to refer to a bitmap). See library object.

Example

The following example changes the selected symbol to refer to the first item in the library:

```
fl.getDocumentDOM().selection[0].libraryItem =
   fl.getDocumentDOM().library.items[0];
```

Item object

Availability

Flash MX 2004.

Description

The Item object is an abstract base class. Anything in the library derives from Item. See also library object.

Method summary for the Item object

The following methods are available for the Item object.

Method	Description
item.addData()	Adds specified data to a library item.
item.getData()	Retrieves the value of the specified data.
item.hasData()	Determines whether the library item has the named data.
item.removeData()	Removes persistent data from the library item.

Property summary for the Item object

The following properties are available for the Item object.

Property	Description
item.itemType	Read-only; a string that specifies the type of element.
item.linkageClassName	A string that specifies the ActionScript 2.0 class that will be associated with the symbol.
item.linkageExportForAS	A Boolean value. If true, the item is exported for ActionScript.
item.linkageExportForRS	A Boolean value. If true, the item is exported for runtime sharing.
item.linkageExportInFirstFrame	A Boolean value. If true, the item is exported in the first frame.
item.linkageIdentifier	A string that specifies the name Flash will use to identify the asset when linking to the destination SWF file.

Property	Description
item.linkageImportForRS	A Boolean value. If true, the item is imported for runtime sharing.
item.linkageURL	A string that specifies the URL where the SWF file containing the shared asset is located.
item.name	A string that specifies the name of the library item, which includes the folder structure.

item.addData()

Availability

Flash MX 2004.

Usage

```
item.addData( name, type, data )
```

Parameters

name   A string that specifies the name of the data.

type   A string that specifies the type of data. Valid types are "integer", "integerArray", "double", "doubleArray", "string", and "byteArray".

data   The data to add to the specified library item. The type of data depends on the value of the type parameter. For example, if type is "integer", the value of data must be an integer, and so on.

Returns

Nothing.

Description

Method; adds specified data to a library item.

Example

The following example adds data named myData with an integer value of 12 to the first item in the library:

```
fl.getDocumentDOM().library.items[0].addData("myData", "integer", 12);
```

item.getData()

Availability

Flash MX 2004.

Usage

```
item.getData( name )
```

Parameters

name   A string that specifies the name of the data to retrieve.

Returns

The data specified by the *name* parameter. The type of data returned depends on the type of stored data.

Description

Method; retrieves the value of the specified data.

Example

The following example gets the value of the data named myData from the first item in the library and stores it in the variable libData.

```
var libData = fl.getDocumentDOM().library.items[0].getData( "myData" );
```

item.hasData()

Availability

Flash MX 2004.

Usage

```
item.hasData( name )
```

Parameters

name   A string that specifies the name of the data to check for in the library item.

Returns

A Boolean value: true if the specified data exists; false otherwise.

Description

Method; determines whether the library item has the named data.

Example

The following example shows a message in the Output panel if the first item in the library contains data point named myData:

```
if ( fl.getDocumentDOM().library.items[0].hasData( "myData" ) ){
  fl.trace("Yep, it's there!");
}
```

item.itemType

Availability

Flash MX 2004.

Usage

```
item.itemType
```

Description

Read-only property; a string that specifies the type of element. The value is one of the following: "undefined", "component", "movie clip", "graphic", "button", "folder", "font", "sound", "bitmap", "compiled clip", "screen", and "video". If this property is "video", you can determine the type of video; see videoItem.videoType.

Example

The following example shows the type of the specified library item in the Output panel:

```
fl.trace(fl.getDocumentDOM().library.items[0].itemType);
```

item.linkageClassName

Availability

Flash MX 2004.

Usage

```
item.linkageClassName
```

Description

Property; a string that specifies the ActionScript 2.0 class that will be associated with the symbol. For this property to be defined, the item.linkageExportForAS and/or item.linkageExportForRS properties must be set to true, and the item.linkageImportForRS property must be set to false.

Example

The following example specifies that the ActionScript 2.0 class name associated with the first item in the library is myClass:

```
fl.getDocumentDOM().library.items[0].linkageClassName = "myClass";
```

item.linkageExportForAS

Availability

Flash MX 2004.

Usage

```
item.linkageExportForAS
```

Description

Property; a Boolean value. If this property is `true`, the item is exported for ActionScript. You can also set the `item.linkageExportForRS` and `item.linkageExportInFirstFrame` properties to `true`.

If you set this property to true, the `item.linkageImportForRS` property must be set to `false`. Also, you must specify an identifier (`item.linkageIdentifier`) and a URL (`item.linkageURL`).

Example

The following example sets this property for the specified library item:

```
fl.getDocumentDOM().library.items[0].linkageExportForAS = true;
```

item.linkageExportForRS

Availability

Flash MX 2004.

Usage

```
item.linkageExportForRS
```

Description

Property; a Boolean value. If this property is `true`, the item is exported for runtime sharing. You can also set the `item.linkageExportForAS` and `item.linkageExportInFirstFrame` properties to `true`.

If you set this property to true, the `item.linkageImportForRS` property must be set to `false`. Also, you must specify an identifier (`item.linkageIdentifier`) and a URL (`item.linkageURL`).

Example

The following example sets this property for the specified library item:

```
fl.getDocumentDOM().library.items[0].linkageExportForRS = true;
```

item.linkageExportInFirstFrame

Availability

Flash MX 2004.

Usage

```
item.linkageExportInFirstFrame
```

Description

Property; a Boolean value. If `true`, the item is exported in the first frame; if `false`, the item is exported on the frame of the first instance. If the item does not appear on the Stage, it isn't exported.

This property can be set to `true` only when `item.linkageExportForAS` and/or `item.linkageExportForRS` are set to `true`.

Example

The following example specifies that the specified library item is exported in the first frame:

```
fl.getDocumentDOM().library.items[0].linkageExportInFirstFrame = true;
```

item.linkageIdentifier

Availability

Flash MX 2004.

Usage

```
item.linkageIdentifier
```

Description

Property; a string that specifies the name Flash will use to identify the asset when linking to the destination SWF file. Flash ignores this property if `item.linkageImportForRS`, `item.linkageExportForAS`, and `item.linkageExportForRS` are set to `false`. Conversely, this property must be set when any of those properties are set to `true`.

Example

The following example specifies that the string `my_mc` will be used to identify the library item when it is linked to the destination SWF file to which it is being exported:

```
fl.getDocumentDOM().library.items[0].linkageIdentifier = "my_mc";
```

See also

```
item.linkageURL
```

item.linkageImportForRS

Availability

Flash MX 2004.

Usage

```
item.linkageImportForRS
```

Description

Property; a Boolean value: if `true`, the item is imported for runtime sharing. If this property is set to `true`, both `item.linkageExportForAS` and `item.linkageExportForRS` must be set to `false`. Also, you must specify an identifier (`item.linkageIdentifier`) and a URL (`item.linkageURL`).

Example

The following example sets this property to `true` for the specified library item:

```
fl.getDocumentDOM().library.items[0].linkageImportForRS = true;
```

item.linkageURL

Availability

Flash MX 2004.

Usage

```
item.linkageURL
```

Description

Property; a string that specifies the URL where the SWF file containing the shared asset is located. Flash ignores this property if `item.linkageImportForRS`, `item.linkageExportForAS`, and `item.linkageExportForRS` are set to `false`. Conversely, this property must be set when any of those properties are set to `true`. You can specify a web URL or a filename in platform-dependent format (that is, forward slashes [/] or backward slashes [\], depending on the platform).

Example

The following example specifies a linkage URL for the specified library item:

```
fl.getDocumentDOM().library.items[0].linkageURL = "theShareSWF.swf";
```

See also

```
item.linkageIdentifier
```

item.name

Availability

Flash MX 2004.

Usage

```
item.name
```

Description

Method; a string that specifies the name of the library item, which includes the folder structure. For example, if Symbol_1 is inside a folder called Folder_1, the `name` property of Symbol_1 is `"Folder_1/Symbol_1"`.

Example

The following example shows the name of the specified library item in the Output panel:

```
fl.trace(fl.getDocumentDOM().library.items[0].name);
```

item.removeData()

Availability

Flash MX 2004.

Usage

```
item.removeData( name )
```

Parameters

name   Specifies the name of the data to remove from the library item.

Returns

Nothing.

Description

Property; removes persistent data from the library item.

Example

The following example removes the data named myData from the first item in the library:

```
fl.getDocumentDOM().library.items[0].removeData( "myData" );
```

Layer object

Availability

Flash MX 2004.

Description

The Layer object represents a layer in the timeline. The `timeline.layers` property contains an array of Layer objects, which can be accessed by `fl.getDocumentDOM().getTimeline().layers`.

Property summary for the Layer object

The following properties are available for the Layer object:

Property	Description
layer.color	A string, hexadecimal value, or integer that specifies the color assigned to outline the layer.
layer.frameCount	Read-only; an integer that specifies the number of frames in the layer.
layer.frames	Read-only; an array of Frame objects.
layer.height	An integer that specifies the percentage layer height; equivalent to the Layer height value in the Layer Properties dialog box.
layer.layerType	A string that specifies the current use of the layer; equivalent to the Type setting in the Layer Properties dialog box.
layer.locked	A Boolean value that specifies the locked status of the layer.
layer.name	A string that specifies the name of the layer.
layer.outline	A Boolean value that specifies the status of outlines for all objects in the layer.
layer.parentLayer	A Layer object that represents the layer's containing folder, guiding, or masking layer.
layer.visible	A Boolean value that specifies whether the layer's objects on the Stage are shown or hidden.

layer.color

Availability

Flash MX 2004.

Usage

```
layer.color
```

Description

Property; the color assigned to outline the layer, in one of the following formats:

- A string in the format "#RRGGBB" or "#RRGGBBAA"
- A hexadecimal number in the format 0xRRGGBB
- An integer that represents the decimal equivalent of a hexadecimal number

This property is equivalent to the Outline color setting in the Layer Properties dialog box.

Example

The following example stores the value of the first layer in the colorValue variable:

```
var colorValue = fl.getDocumentDOM().getTimeline().layers[0].color;
```

The following example shows three ways to set the color of the first layer to red:

```
fl.getDocumentDOM().getTimeline().layers[0].color=16711680;
fl.getDocumentDOM().getTimeline().layers[0].color="#ff0000";
fl.getDocumentDOM().getTimeline().layers[0].color=0xFF0000;
```

layer.frameCount

Availability

Flash MX 2004.

Usage

```
layer.frameCount
```

Description

Read-only property; an integer that specifies the number of frames in the layer.

Example

The following example stores the number of frames in the first layer in the fcNum variable:

```
var fcNum = fl.getDocumentDOM().getTimeline().layers[0].frameCount;
```

layer.frames

Availability

Flash MX 2004.

Usage

```
layer.frames
```

Description

Read-only property; an array of Frame objects (see Frame object).

Example

The following example sets the variable `frameArray` to the array of Frame objects for the frames in the current document:

```
var frameArray = fl.getDocumentDOM().getTimeline().layers[0].frames;
```

To determine if a frame is a keyframe, check whether the `frame.startFrame` property matches the array index, as shown in the following example:

```
var frameArray = fl.getDocumentDOM().getTimeline().layers[0].frames;
var n = frameArray.length;
for (i=0; i<n; i++) {
  if (i==frameArray[i].startFrame) {
    alert("Keyframe at: " + i);
  }
}
```

layer.height

Availability

Flash MX 2004.

Usage

```
layer.height
```

Description

Property; an integer that specifies the percentage layer height; equivalent to the Layer height value in the Layer Properties dialog box. Acceptable values represent percentages of the default height: 100, 200, or 300.

Example

The following example stores the percentage value of the first layer's height setting:

```
var layerHeight = fl.getDocumentDOM().getTimeline().layers[0].height;
```

The following example sets the height of the first layer to 300 percent:

```
fl.getDocumentDOM().getTimeline().layers[0].height = 300;
```

layer.layerType

Availability

Flash MX 2004.

Usage

```
layer.layerType
```

Description

Property; a string that specifies the current use of the layer; equivalent to the Type setting in the Layer Properties dialog box. Acceptable values are `"normal"`, `"guide"`, `"guided"`, `"mask"`, `"masked"`, and `"folder"`.

Example

The following example sets the first layer in the timeline to type `"folder"`:

```
fl.getDocumentDOM().getTimeline().layers[0].layerType = "folder";
```

layer.locked

Availability

Flash MX 2004.

Usage

```
layer.locked
```

Description

Property; a Boolean value that specifies the locked status of the layer. If set to `true`, the layer is locked. The default value is `false`.

Example

The following example stores the Boolean value for the status of the first layer in the `lockStatus` variable:

```
var lockStatus = fl.getDocumentDOM().getTimeline().layers[0].locked;
```

The following example sets the status of the first layer to unlocked:

```
fl.getDocumentDOM().getTimeline().layers[0].locked = false;
```

layer.name

Availability

Flash MX 2004.

Usage

```
layer.name
```

Description

Property; a string that specifies the name of the layer.

Example

The following example sets the name of the first layer in the current document to "foreground":

```
fl.getDocumentDOM().getTimeline().layers[0].name = "foreground";
```

layer.outline

Availability

Flash MX 2004.

Usage

```
layer.outline
```

Description

Property; a Boolean value that specifies the status of outlines for all objects in the layer. If set to `true`, all objects in the layer appear only with outlines. If `false`, objects appear as they were created.

Example

The following example makes all objects on the first layer appear only with outlines:

```
fl.getDocumentDOM().getTimeline().layers[0].outline = true;
```

layer.parentLayer

Availability

Flash MX 2004.

Usage

```
layer.parentLayer
```

Description

Property; a Layer object that represents the layer's containing folder, guiding, or masking layer. Acceptable values for the parent layer are a folder, guide, or mask layer that precedes the layer, or the `parentLayer` of the preceding or following layer. Setting the layer's `parentLayer` does not move the layer's position in the list; trying to set a layer's `parentLayer` to a layer that would require moving it has no effect. Uses `null` for a top-level layer.

Example

The following example uses two layers at the same level on the same timeline. The first layer (layers[0]) is converted into a folder and then set as the parent folder of the second layer (layers[1]). This action moves the second layer inside the first layer.

```
var parLayer = fl.getDocumentDOM().getTimeline().layers[0];
parLayer.layerType = "folder";
fl.getDocumentDOM().getTimeline().layers[1].parentLayer = parLayer;
```

layer.visible

Availability

Flash MX 2004.

Usage

```
layer.visible
```

Description

Property; a Boolean value that specifies whether the layer's objects on the Stage are shown or hidden. If set to `true`, all objects in the layer are visible; if `false`, they are hidden. The default value is `true`.

Example

The following example makes all objects in the first layer invisible:

```
fl.getDocumentDOM().getTimeline().layers[0].visible = false;
```

library object

Availability

Flash MX 2004.

Description

The library object represents the Library panel. It is a property of the Document object (see `document.library`) and can be accessed by `fl.getDocumentDOM().library`.

The library object contains an array of items of different types, including symbols, bitmaps, sounds, and video.

Method summary for the library object

The following methods are available for the library object:

Method	Description
`library.addItemToDocument()`	Adds the current or specified item to the Stage at the specified position.
`library.addNewItem()`	Creates a new item of the specified type in the Library panel and sets the new item to the currently selected item.
`library.deleteItem()`	Deletes the current items or a specified item from the Library panel.
`library.duplicateItem()`	Makes a copy of the currently selected or specified item.
`library.editItem()`	Opens the currently selected or specified item in Edit mode.
`library.expandFolder()`	Expands or collapses the currently selected or specified folder in the library.
`library.findItemIndex()`	Returns the library item's index value (zero-based).
`library.getItemProperty()`	Gets the property for the selected item.
`library.getItemType()`	Gets the type of object currently selected or specified by a library path.
`library.getSelectedItems()`	Gets the array of all currently selected items in the library.
`library.importEmbeddedSWF()`	Imports a Shockwave (SWF) file into the library as a compiled clip.
`library.itemExists()`	Checks to see if a specified item exists in the library.
`library.moveToFolder()`	Moves the currently selected or specified library item to a specified folder.

Method	Description
`library.newFolder()`	Creates a new folder with the specified name, or a default name (`"untitled folder #"`) if no `folderName` parameter is provided, in the currently selected folder.
`library.renameItem()`	Renames the currently selected library item in the Library panel.
`library.selectAll()`	Selects or deselects all items in the library.
`library.selectItem()`	Selects a specified library item.
`library.selectNone()`	Selects all the library items.
`library.setItemProperty()`	Sets the property for all selected library items (ignoring folders).
`library.updateItem()`	Updates the specified item.

Property summary for the library object

The following property is available for the library object.

Property	Description
`library.items`	An array of item objects in the library

library.addItemToDocument()

Availability

Flash MX 2004.

Usage

`library.addItemToDocument( position [, namePath] )`

Parameters

position   A point that specifies the *x,y* position of the center of the item on the Stage.

namePath   A string that specifies the name of the item. If the item is in a folder, you can specify its name and path using slash notation. If *namePath* is not specified, the current library selection is used. This parameter is optional.

Returns

A Boolean value: `true` if the item is successfully added to the document; `false` otherwise.

Description

Method; adds the current or specified item to the Stage at the specified position.

Example

The following example adds the currently selected item to the Stage at the (3, 60) position:

```
fl.getDocumentDOM().library.addItemToDocument({x:3, y:60});
```

The following example adds the item Symbol1 located in folder1 of the library to the Stage at the (550, 485) position:

```
fl.getDocumentDOM().library.addItemToDocument({x:550.0, y:485.0}, "folder1/
    Symbol1");
```

library.addNewItem()

Availability

Flash MX 2004.

Usage

```
library.addNewItem( type [, namePath] )
```

Parameters

type   A string that specifies the type of item to create. The only acceptable values for *type* are "video", "movie clip", "button", "graphic", "bitmap", "screen", and "folder" (so, for example, you cannot add a sound to the library with this method). Specifying a folder path is the same as using library.newFolder() before calling this method.

namePath   A string that specifies the name of the item to be added. If the item is in a folder, specify its name and path using slash notation. This parameter is optional.

Returns

A Boolean value: true if the item is successfully created; false otherwise.

Description

Method; creates a new item of the specified type in the Library panel and sets the new item to the currently selected item. For more information on importing items into the library, including items such as sounds, see document.importFile().

Example

The following example creates a new button item named start in a new folder named folderTwo:

```
fl.getDocumentDOM().library.addNewItem("button", "folderTwo/start");
```

library.deleteItem()

Availability

Flash MX 2004.

Usage

```
library.deleteItem( [ namePath ] )
```

Parameters

namePath A string that specifies the name of the item to be deleted. If the item is in a folder, you can specify its name and path using slash notation. If you pass a folder name, the folder and all its items are deleted. If no name is specified, Flash deletes the currently selected item or items. To delete all the items in the Library panel, select all items before using this method. This parameter is optional.

Returns

A Boolean value: `true` if the items are successfully deleted; `false` otherwise.

Description

Method; deletes the current items or a specified item from the Library panel. This method can affect multiple items if several are selected.

Example

The following example deletes the currently selected item:

```
fl.getDocumentDOM().library.deleteItem();
```

The following example deletes the item Symbol_1 from the library folder Folder_1:

```
fl.getDocumentDOM().library.deleteItem("Folder_1/Symbol_1");
```

library.duplicateItem()

Availability

Flash MX 2004.

Usage

```
library.duplicateItem( [ namePath ] )
```

Parameters

namePath A string that specifies the name of the item to duplicate. If the item is in a folder, you can specify its name and path using slash notation. This parameter is optional.

Returns

A Boolean value: `true` if the item is duplicated successfully; `false` otherwise. If more than one item is selected, Flash returns `false`.

Description

Method; makes a copy of the currently selected or specified item. The new item has a default name (such as `item copy`) and is set as the currently selected item. If more than one item is selected, the command fails.

Example

The following example creates a copy of the item square in the library folder test:

```
fl.getDocumentDOM().library.duplicateItem("test/square");
```

library.editItem()

Availability

Flash MX 2004.

Usage

```
library.editItem( [ namePath ] )
```

Parameters

namePath   A string that specifies the name of the item. If the item is in a folder, you can specify its name and path using slash notation. If *namePath* is not specified, the single selected library item opens in Edit mode. If none or more than one item in the library is currently selected, the first scene in the main timeline appears for editing. This parameter is optional.

Returns

A Boolean value: `true` if the specified item exists and can be edited; `false` otherwise.

Description

Method; opens the currently selected or specified item in Edit mode.

Example

The following example opens the item circle in the test folder of the library for editing:

```
fl.getDocumentDOM().library.editItem("test/circle");
```

library.expandFolder()

Availability

Flash MX 2004.

Usage

```
library.expandFolder( bExpand [, bRecurseNestedParents [, namePath ] ] )
```

Parameters

bExpand   A Boolean value: if `true`, the folder is expanded; if `false` (the default), the folder is collapsed.

bRecurseNestedParents   A Boolean value: if `true`, all the folders within the specified folder are expanded or collapsed, based on the value of *bExpand*. The default value is `false`. This parameter is optional.

namePath   A string that specifies the name and, optionally, the path of the folder to expand or collapse. If this parameter is not specified, the method applies to the currently selected folder. This parameter is optional.

Returns

A Boolean value: `true` if the item is successfully expanded or collapsed; `false` if unsuccessful or the specified item is not a folder.

Description

Method; expands or collapses the currently selected or specified folder in the library.

Example

The following example collapses the test folder in the library as well as all the folders within the test folder (if any):

```
fl.getDocumentDOM().library.expandFolder(false, true, "test");
```

library.findItemIndex()

Availability

Flash MX 2004.

Usage

```
library.findItemIndex( namePath )
```

Parameters

namePath A string that specifies the name of the item. If the item is in a folder, you can specify its name and path using slash notation.

Returns

An integer value representing the item's zero-based index value.

Description

Method; returns the library item's index value (zero-based). The library index is flat, so folders are considered part of the main index. Folder paths can be used to specify a nested item.

Example

The following example stores the zero-based index value of the library item square, which is in the test folder, in the variable `sqIndex`, and then displays the index value in a dialog box:

```
var sqIndex = fl.getDocumentDOM().library.findItemIndex("test/square");
alert(sqIndex);
```

library.getItemProperty()

Availability

Flash MX 2004.

Usage

```
library.getItemProperty( property )
```

Parameters

property A string. For a list of values that you can use as a *property* parameter, see the Property summary for the Item object, along with property summaries for its subclasses.

Returns

A string value for the property.

Description

Method; gets the property for the selected item.

Example

The following example shows a dialog box that contains the Linkage Identifier value for the symbol when referencing it using ActionScript or for runtime sharing:

```
alert(fl.getDocumentDOM().library.getItemProperty("linkageIdentifier"));
```

library.getItemType()

Availability

Flash MX 2004.

Usage

```
library.getItemType( [ namePath ] )
```

Parameters

namePath A string that specifies the name of the item. If the item is in a folder, specify its name and path using slash notation. If *namePath* is not specified, Flash provides the type of the current selection. If more than one item is currently selected and no *namePath* is provided, Flash ignores the command. This parameter is optional.

Returns

A string value specifying the type of object. For possible return values, see item.itemType.

Description

Method; gets the type of object currently selected or specified by a library path.

Example

The following example shows a dialog box that contains the item type of Symbol_1 located in the Folder_1/Folder_2 folder:

```
alert(fl.getDocumentDOM().library.getItemType("Folder_1/Folder_2/
  Symbol_1"));
```

library.getSelectedItems()

Availability

Flash MX 2004.

Parameters

None.

Returns

An array of values for all currently selected items in the library.

Description

Method; gets the array of all currently selected items in the library.

Example

The following example stores the array of currently selected library items (in this case, several audio files) in the selItems variable and then changes the sampleRate property of the first audio file in the array to "11 kHz":

```
var selItems = fl.getDocumentDOM().library.getSelectedItems();
selItems[0].sampleRate = "11 kHz";
```

library.importEmbeddedSWF()

Availability

Flash MX 2004.

Usage

```
library.importEmbeddedSWF( linkageName, swfData [, libName] )
```

Parameters

linkageName A string that provides the name of the SWF linkage of the root movie clip.

swfData An array of binary SWF data, which comes from an external library or DLL.

libName A string that specifies the library name for the created item. If the name is already used, the method creates an alternate name. This parameter is optional.

Returns

Nothing.

Description

Method; imports a Shockwave (SWF) file into the library as a compiled clip. Unlike File > Import > SWF, this method lets you embed a compiled SWF file inside the library. There is no corresponding user interface functionality, and this method must be used with an external library or DLL (see Chapter 3, "C-Level Extensibility," on page 533).

The SWF file that you are importing must have one top-level movie clip that contains all the content. That movie clip should have its linkage identifier set to the same value as the *linkageName* parameter passed to this method.

Example

The following example adds the SWF file with the *linkageName* value of MyMovie to the library as a compiled clip named Intro:

```
fl.getDocumentDOM().library.importEmbeddedSWF("MyMovie", swfData, "Intro");
```

library.itemExists()

Availability

Flash MX 2004.

Usage

```
library.itemExists( namePath )
```

Parameters

namePath A string that specifies the name of the item. If the item is in a folder, specify its name and path using slash notation.

Returns

A Boolean value: `true` if the specified item exists in the library; `false` otherwise.

Description

Method; checks to see if a specified item exists in the library.

Example

The following example displays `true` or `false` in a dialog box, depending on whether the item Symbol_1 exists in the Folder_1 library folder:

```
alert(fl.getDocumentDOM().library.itemExists('Folder_1/Symbol_1'));
```

library.items

Availability

Flash MX 2004.

Usage

```
library.items
```

Description

Property; an array of item objects in the library.

Example

The following example stores the array of all library items in the `itemArray` variable:

```
var itemArray = fl.getDocumentDOM().library.items;
```

library.moveToFolder()

Availability

Flash MX 2004.

Usage

```
library.moveToFolder( folderPath [, itemToMove [, bReplace ] ] )
```

Parameters

folderPath   A string that specifies the path to the folder in the form `"FolderName"` or
`"FolderName/FolderName"`. To move an item to the top level, specify an empty string (`""`)
for *folderPath*.

itemToMove   A string that specifies the name of the item to move. If *itemToMove* is not
specified, the currently selected items move. This parameter is optional.

bReplace   A Boolean value. If an item with the same name already exists, specifying `true`
for the *bReplace* parameter replaces the existing item with the item being moved. If `false`,
the name of the dropped item changes to a unique name. The default value is `false`. This
parameter is optional.

Returns

A Boolean value: `true` if the item moves successfully; `false` otherwise.

Description

Method; moves the currently selected or specified library item to a specified folder. If the
folderPath parameter is empty, the items move to the top level.

Example

The following example moves the item Symbol_1 to the library folder new and replaces the
item in that folder with the same name:

```
fl.getDocumentDOM().library.moveToFolder("new", "Symbol_1", true);
```

library.newFolder()

Availability

Flash MX 2004.

Usage

```
library.newFolder( [folderPath] )
```

Parameters

folderPath   A string that specifies the name of the folder to be created. If it is specified as a path, and the path doesn't exist, the path is created. This parameter is optional.

Returns

A Boolean value: `true` if folder is created successfully; `false` otherwise.

Description

Method; creates a new folder with the specified name, or a default name (`"untitled folder #"`) if no *folderName* parameter is provided, in the currently selected folder.

Example

The following example creates two new library folders; the second folder is a subfolder of the first folder:

```
fl.getDocumentDOM().library.newFolder("first/second");
```

library.renameItem()

Availability

Flash MX 2004.

Usage

```
library.renameItem(name)
```

Parameters

name   A string that specifies a new name for the library item.

Returns

A Boolean value of `true` if the name of the item changes successfully, `false` otherwise. If multiple items are selected, no names are changed, and the return value is `false` (to match user interface behavior).

Description

Method; renames the currently selected library item in the Library panel.

Example

The following example renames the currently selected library item to `new name`:

```
fl.getDocumentDOM().library.renameItem("new name");
```

library.selectAll()

Availability

Flash MX 2004.

Usage

```
library.selectAll( [ bSelectAll ] )
```

Parameters

bSelectAll A Boolean value that specifies whether to select or deselect all items in the library. Omit this parameter or use the default value of `true` to select all the items in the library; `false` deselects all library items. This parameter is optional.

Returns

Nothing.

Description

Method; selects or deselects all items in the library.

Example

The following examples select all the items in the library:

```
fl.getDocumentDOM().library.selectAll();
fl.getDocumentDOM().library.selectAll(true);
```

The following examples deselect all the items in the library:

```
fl.getDocumentDOM().library.selectAll(false);
fl.getDocumentDOM().library.selectNone();
```

library.selectItem()

Availability

Flash MX 2004.

Usage

```
library.selectItem( namePath [, bReplaceCurrentSelection [, bSelect ] ] )
```

Parameters

namePath   A string that specifies the name of the item. If the item is in a folder, you can specify its name and path using slash notation.

bReplaceCurrentSelection   A Boolean value that specifies whether to replace the current selection or add the item to the current selection. The default value is `true` (replace current selection). This parameter is optional.

bSelect   A Boolean value that specifies whether to select or deselect an item. The default value is `true` (select). This parameter is optional.

Returns

A Boolean value: `true` if the specified item exists; `false` otherwise.

Description

Method; selects a specified library item.

Example

The following example changes the current selection in the library to symbol 1 inside untitled folder 1:

```
fl.getDocumentDOM().library.selectItem("untitled Folder_1/Symbol_1");
```

The following example extends what is currently selected in the library to include symbol 1 inside untitled folder 1:

```
fl.getDocumentDOM().library.selectItem("untitled Folder_1/Symbol_1",
    false);
```

The following example deselects symbol 1 inside untitled folder 1 and does not change other selected items:

```
fl.getDocumentDOM().library.selectItem("untitled Folder_1/Symbol_1", true,
    false);
```

library.selectNone()

Availability

Flash MX 2004.

Parameters

None.

Returns

Nothing.

Description

Method; deselects all the library items.

Example

The following examples deselect all the items in the library:

```
fl.getDocumentDOM().library.selectNone();
fl.getDocumentDOM().library.selectAll(false);
```

library.setItemProperty()

Availability

Flash MX 2004.

Usage

```
library.setItemProperty( property, value )
```

Parameters

property   A string that is the name of the property to set. For a list of properties, see the Property summary for the Item object and property summaries for its subclasses. To see which objects are subclasses of the Item object, see Summary of the DOM structure.

value   The value to assign to the specified property.

Returns

Nothing.

Description

Method; sets the property for all selected library items (ignoring folders).

Example

The following example assigns the value button to the `symbolType` property for the selected library item or items. In this case, the item must be a SymbolItem object; `symbolType` is a valid property for SymbolItem objects.

```
fl.getDocumentDOM().library.setItemProperty("symbolType", "button");
```

library.updateItem()

Availability

Flash MX 2004.

Usage

```
library.updateItem( [ namePath ] )
```

Parameters

namePath   A string that specifies the name of the item. If the item is in a folder, specify its name and path using slash notation. This is the same as right-clicking on an item and selecting Update from the menu in the user interface. If no name is provided, the current selection is updated. This parameter is optional.

Returns

A Boolean value: `true` if Flash updated the item successfully; `false` otherwise.

Description

Method; updates the specified item.

Example

The following example displays a dialog box that shows whether the currently selected item is updated (`true`) or not (`false`):

```
alert(fl.getDocumentDOM().library.updateItem());
```

Math object

Availability
Flash MX 2004.

Description
The Math object is available as a read-only property of the flash object; see `fl.Math`. This object provides methods that perform common mathematical operations.

Method summary for the Math object
The following methods are available for the Math object:

Method	Description
`Math.concatMatrix()`	Performs a matrix concatenation and returns the result.
`Math.invertMatrix()`	Returns the inverse of the specified matrix.
`Math.pointDistance()`	Computes the distance between two points.

Math.concatMatrix()

Availability
Flash MX 2004.

Usage
`Math.concatMatrix(mat1, mat2)`

Parameters
mat1 and *mat2*   Specify the Matrix objects to be concatenated (see Matrix object). Each parameter must be an object with fields a, b, c, d, tx, and ty.

Returns
A concatenated object matrix.

Description

Method; performs a matrix concatenation and returns the result.

Example

The following example stores the currently selected object in the `elt` variable, multiplies the object matrix by the view matrix, and stores that value in the `mat` variable:

```
var elt = fl.getDocumentDOM().selection[0];
var mat = fl.Math.concatMatrix( elt.matrix , fl.getDocumentDOM().viewMatrix
    );
```

Math.invertMatrix()

Availability

Flash MX 2004.

Usage

```
Math.invertMatrix(mat)
```

Parameters

mat   Indicates the Matrix object to invert (see Matrix object). It must have the following fields: a, b, c, d, tx, and ty.

Returns

A Matrix object that is the inverse of the original matrix.

Description

Method; returns the inverse of the specified matrix.

Example

The following example stores the currently selected object in the `elt` variable, assigns that matrix to the `mat` variable, and stores the inverse of the matrix in the `inv` variable:

```
var elt = fl.getDocumentDOM().selection[0];
var mat = elt.matrix;
var inv = fl.Math.invertMatrix( mat );
```

Math.pointDistance()

Availability

Flash MX 2004.

Usage

```
Math.pointDistance(pt1, pt2)
```

Parameters

pt1 and *pt2*   Specify the points between which distance is measured.

Returns

A floating-point value that represents the distance between the points.

Description

Method; computes the distance between two points.

Example

The following example stores the value for the distance between *pt1* and *pt2* in the `dist` variable:

```
var pt1 = {x:10, y:20}
var pt2 = {x:100, y:200}
var dist = fl.Math.pointDistance(pt1, pt2);
```

Matrix object

Availability

Flash MX 2004.

Description

The Matrix object represents a transformation matrix.

Property summary for the Matrix object

The following properties are available for the Matrix object:

Property	Description
matrix.a	A floating-point value that specifies the (0,0) element in the transformation matrix.
matrix.b	A floating-point value that specifies the (0,1) element in the matrix.
matrix.c	A floating-point value that specifies the (1,0) element in the matrix.
matrix.d	A floating-point value that specifies the (1,1) element in the matrix.
matrix.tx	A floating-point value that specifies the x-axis location of a symbol's registration point or the center of a shape.
matrix.ty	A floating-point value that specifies the y-axis location of a symbol's registration point or the center of a shape.

matrix.a

Availability

Flash MX 2004.

Usage

matrix.a

Description

Property; a floating-point value that specifies the (0,0) element in the transformation matrix. This value represents the scale factor of the object's x-axis.

Example

The a and d properties in a matrix represent scaling. In the following example, the values are set to 2 and 3, respectively, to scale the selected object to two times its width and three times its height:

```
var mat = fl.getDocumentDOM().selection[0].matrix;
mat.a = 2;
mat.d = 3;
fl.getDocumentDOM().selection[0].matrix = mat;
```

You can rotate an object by setting the a, b, c, and d matrix properties relative to one another, where a = d and b = -c. For example, values of 0.5, 0.8, -0.8, and 0.5 rotate the object 60°:

```
var mat = fl.getDocumentDOM().selection[0].matrix;
mat.a = 0.5;
mat.b = 0.8;
mat.c = 0.8*(-1);
mat.d = 0.5;
fl.getDocumentDOM().selection[0].matrix = mat;
```

You can set a = d = 1 and c = b = 0 to reset the object back to its original shape.

matrix.b

Availability

Flash MX 2004.

Usage

```
matrix.b
```

Description

Property; a floating-point value that specifies the (0,1) element in the matrix. This value represents the vertical skew of a shape; it causes Flash to move the shape's right edge along the vertical axis.

The matrix.b and matrix.c properties in a matrix represent skewing (see matrix.c).

Example

In the following example, you can set b and c to -1 and 0, respectively; these settings skew the object at a 45° vertical angle:

```
var mat = fl.getDocumentDOM().selection[0].matrix;
mat.b = -1;
mat.c = 0;
fl.getDocumentDOM().selection[0].matrix = mat;
```

To skew the object back to its original shape, you can set b and c to 0.

See also the matrix.a example.

matrix.c

Availability

Flash MX 2004.

Usage

matrix.c

Description

Property; a floating-point value that specifies the (1,0) element in the matrix. This value causes Flash to skew the object by moving its bottom edge along a horizontal axis.

The matrix.b and matrix.c properties in a matrix represent skewing.

Example

See the matrix.b example.

matrix.d

Availability

Flash MX 2004.

Usage

matrix.d

Description

Property; a floating-point value that specifies the (1,1) element in the matrix. This value represents the scale factor of the object's *y*-axis.

Example

See the matrix.a example.

matrix.tx

Availability

Flash MX 2004.

Usage

```
matrix.tx
```

Description

Property; a floating-point value that specifies the *x*-axis location of a symbol's registration point or the center of a shape. It defines the *x* translation of the transformation.

You can move an object by setting the `matrix.tx` and `matrix.ty` properties (see `matrix.ty`).

Example

In the following example, setting `tx` and `ty` to 0 moves the registration point of the object to point 0,0 in the document:

```
var mat = fl.getDocumentDOM().selection[0].matrix;
mat.tx = 0;
mat.ty = 0;
fl.getDocumentDOM().selection[0].matrix = mat;
```

matrix.ty

Availability

Flash MX 2004.

Usage

```
matrix.ty
```

Description

Property; a floating-point value that specifies the *y*-axis location of a symbol's registration point or the center of a shape. It defines the *y* translation of the transformation.

You can move an object by setting the `matrix.tx` and `matrix.ty` properties.

Example

See the `matrix.tx` example.

outputPanel object

Availability

Flash MX 2004.

Description

This object represents the Output panel, which displays troubleshooting information such as syntax errors. To access this object, use `fl.outputPanel` (or `flash.outputPanel`). See `fl.outputPanel`.

Method summary for the outputPanel object

The outputPanel object uses the following methods.

Method	Description
outputPanel.clear()	Clears the contents of the Output panel.
outputPanel.save()	Saves the contents of the Output panel to a local text file.
outputPanel.trace()	Adds a line to the contents of the Output panel, terminated by a new line.

outputPanel.clear()

Availability

Flash MX 2004.

Usage

`outputPanel.clear()`

Parameters

None.

Returns

Nothing.

Description

Method; clears the contents of the Output panel. You can use this method in a batch processing application to clear a list of errors, or to save them incrementally by using this method with `outputPanel.save()`.

Example

The following example clears the current contents of the Output panel:

```
fl.outputPanel.clear();
```

outputPanel.save()

Availability

Flash MX 2004; *bUseSystemEncoding* parameter added in Flash 8.

Usage

```
outputPanel.save(fileURI [, bAppendToFile [ , bUseSystemEncoding ] ])
```

Parameters

fileURI   A string, expressed as a file:/// URI, that specifies the local file to contain the contents of the Output panel.

bAppendToFile   An optional Boolean value. If true, it appends the Output panel's contents to the output file, and if false, the method overwrites the output file if it already exists. The default value is false.

bUseSystemEncoding   An optional Boolean value. If true, it saves the Output panel text using the system encoding; if false, it saves the Output panel text using UTF-8 encoding, with Byte Order Mark characters at the beginning of the text. The default value is false.

Returns

Nothing.

Description

Method; saves the contents of the Output panel to a local text file. You can also specify that the contents be appended to the contents of a local file, rather than being overwritten. If *fileURI* is invalid or unspecified, an error is reported.

This method is useful for batch processing. For example, you can create a JSFL file that compiles several components. Any compile errors appear in the Output panel, and you can use this method to save the resulting errors to a text file, which can be automatically parsed by the build system in use.

Example

The following example saves the Output panel's contents to the batch.log file in the /tests folder, overwriting the batch.log file if it already exists:

```
fl.outputPanel.save("file:///c|/tests/batch.log");
```

outputPanel.trace()

Availability

Flash MX 2004.

Usage

```
outputPanel.trace(message)
```

Parameters

The *message* parameter is a string that contains the text to add to the Output panel.

Returns

Nothing.

Description

Method; sends a text string to the Output panel, terminated by a new line, and displays the Output panel if it is not already visible. This method is identical to `fl.trace()`, and works in the same way as the `trace()` statement in ActionScript.

To send a blank line, use `outputPanel.trace("")` or `outputPanel.trace("\n")`. You can use the latter command inline, making `\n` a part of the *message* string.

Example

The following example displays several lines of text in the Output panel:

```
fl.outputPanel.clear();
fl.outputPanel.trace("Hello World!!!");
var myPet = "cat";
fl.outputPanel.trace("\nI have a " + myPet);
fl.outputPanel.trace("");
fl.outputPanel.trace("I love my " + myPet);
fl.outputPanel.trace("Do you have a " + myPet +"?");
```

Parameter object

Availability

Flash MX 2004.

Description

The Parameter object type is accessed from the `screen.parameters` array (which corresponds to the screen Property inspector in the Flash authoring tool) or by the `componentInstance.parameters` array (which corresponds to the component Property inspector in the authoring tool). See `screen.parameters` and `componentInstance.parameters`.

Method summary for the Parameter object

The following methods are available for the Parameter object:

Method	Description
`parameter.insertItem()`	Inserts an item into a list, object, or array.
`parameter.removeItem()`	Removes an element of the list, object, or array type of a screen or component parameter.

Property summary for the Parameter object

The following properties are available for the Parameter object:

Property	Description
`parameter.category`	Property; string that specifies the `category` property for the `screen` parameter or `componentInstance` parameter.
`parameter.listIndex`	An integer that specifies the value of the selected list item.
`parameter.name`	Read-only; a string that specifies the name of the parameter.
`parameter.value`	Property; corresponds to the Value field in the Parameters tab of the Component inspector, the Parameters tab of the Property inspector, or the screen Property inspector.
`parameter.valueType`	Read-only; a string that indicates the type of the screen or component parameter.
`parameter.verbose`	Specifies where the parameter is displayed.

parameter.category

Availability

Flash MX 2004.

Usage

```
parameter.category
```

Description

Property; a string that specifies the `category` property for the `screen` parameter or `componentInstance` parameter. This property provides an alternative way of presenting a list of parameters. This functionality is not available through the Flash user interface.

parameter.insertItem()

Availability

Flash MX 2004.

Usage

```
parameter.insertItem(index, name, value, type)
```

Parameters

index   A zero-based integer index that indicates where the item will be inserted in the list, object, or array. If the index is 0, the item is inserted at the beginning of the list. If the index is greater than the list size, the new item is inserted at the end of the array.

name   A string that specifies the name of the item to insert. This is a required parameter for object parameters.

value   A string that specifies the value of the item to insert.

type   A string that specifies the type of item to insert.

Returns

Nothing.

Description

Method; inserts an item in a list, object, or array. If a parameter is a list, object, or array, the *value* property is an array.

Example

The following example inserts the value of `"New Value"` into the `labelPlacement` parameter:

```
// Select an instance of a Button component on the Stage.
var parms = fl.getDocument.DOM().selection[0].parameters;
parms[2].insertItem(0, "name", "New Value", "String");
var values = parms[2].value;
for(var prop in values){
    fl.trace("labelPlacement parameter value = " + values[prop].value);
}
```

parameter.listIndex

Availability

Flash MX 2004.

Usage

```
parameter.listIndex
```

Description

Property; the value of the selected list item. This property is valid only if the `valueType` parameter is `"List"`.

Example

The following example sets the first parameter for a Slide, which is the `autoKeyNav` parameter. To set the parameter to one of its acceptable values (`true`, `false`, or `inherit`) `parameter.listIndex` is set to the index of the item in the list (0 for `true`, 1 for `false`, 2 for `inherit`).

```
var parms = fl.getDocumentDOM().screenOutline.screens[1].parameters;
parms[0].listIndex = 1;
```

parameter.name

Availability

Flash MX 2004.

Usage

```
parameter.name
```

Description

Read-only property; a string that specifies the name of the parameter.

Example

The following example shows the name of the fifth parameter for the selected component:

```
var parms = fl.getDocumentDOM().selection[0].parameters;
fl.trace("name: " + parms[4].name);
```

The following example shows the name of the fifth parameter for the specified screen:

```
var parms = fl.getDocumentDOM().screenOutline.screens[1].parameters;
  fl.trace("name: " + parms[4].name);
```

parameter.removeItem()

Availability

Flash MX 2004.

Usage

```
parameter.removeItem(index)
```

Parameters

index   The zero-based integer index of the item to remove from the screen or component property.

Returns

Nothing.

Description

Method; removes an element of the list, object, or array type of a screen or component parameter.

Example

The following example removes the element at index 1 from the `labelPlacement` parameter of a component:

```
// Select an instance of a Button component on the Stage.
var parms = fl.getDocumentDOM().selection[0].parameters;
var values = parms[2].value;
fl.trace("--Original--");
for(var prop in values){
  fl.trace("labelPlacement value = " + values[prop].value);
}
parms[2].removeItem(1);

var newValues = parms[2].value;
fl.trace("--After Removing Item--");
for(var prop in newValues){
  fl.trace("labelPlacement value = " + newValues[prop].value);
}
```

The following example removes the element at index 1 from the `autoKeyNav` parameter of a screen:

```
// Open a presentation document.
var parms = fl.getDocumentDOM().screenOutline.screens[1].parameters;
var values = parms[0].value;
fl.trace("--Original--");
for(var prop in values){
  fl.trace("autoKeyNav value = " + values[prop].value);
}
parms[0].removeItem(1);

var newValues = parms[0].value;
fl.trace("--After Removing Item--");
for(var prop in newValues){
  fl.trace("autoKeyNav value = " + newValues[prop].value);
}
```

parameter.value

Availability

Flash MX 2004.

Usage

```
parameter.value
```

Description

Property; corresponds to the Value field in the Parameters tab of the Component inspector, the Parameters tab of the Property inspector, or the screen Property inspector. The type of the `value` property is determined by the `valueType` property for the parameter (see `parameter.valueType`).

parameter.valueType

Availability

Flash MX 2004.

Usage

`parameter.valueType`

Description

Read-only property; a string that indicates the type of the screen or component parameter. The type can be one of the following values: `"Default"`, `"Array"`, `"Object"`, `"List"`, `"String"`, `"Number"`, `"Boolean"`, `"Font Name"`, `"Color"`, `"Collection"`, `"Web Service URL"`, or `"Web Service Operation"`.

See also

`parameter.value`

parameter.verbose

Availability

Flash MX 2004.

Usage

`parameter.verbose`

Description

Property; specifies where the parameter is displayed. If the value of this property is 0 (nonverbose), the parameter is displayed only in the Component inspector. If it is 1 (verbose), the parameter is displayed in the Component inspector and in the Parameters tab of the Property inspector.

Path object

Availability

Flash MX 2004.

Description

The Path object defines a sequence of line segments (straight, curved, or both), which you typically use when creating extensible tools. The following example shows an instance of a Path object being returned from the flash object:

```
path = fl.drawingLayer.newPath();
```

See also the drawingLayer object.

Method summary for the Path object

The following methods are available for the Path object:

Method	Description
path.addCubicCurve()	Appends a cubic Bézier curve segment to the path.
path.addCurve()	Appends a quadratic Bézier segment to the path.
path.addPoint()	Adds a point to the path.
path.clear()	Removes all points from the path.
path.close()	Appends a point at the location of the first point of the path and extends the path to that point, which closes the path.
path.makeShape()	Creates a shape on the Stage by using the current stroke and fill settings.
path.newContour()	Starts a new contour in the path.

Property summary for the Path object

The following properties are available for the Path object:

Property	Description
path.nPts	Read-only; an integer representing the number of points in the path.

path.addCubicCurve()

Availability

Flash MX 2004.

Usage

```
path.addCubicCurve(xAnchor, yAnchor, x2, y2, x3, y3, x4, y4)
```

Parameters

xAnchor   A floating-point number that specifies the *x* position of the first control point.

yAnchor   A floating-point number that specifies the *y* position of the first control point.

x2   A floating-point number that specifies the *x* position of the second control point.

y2   A floating-point number that specifies the *y* position of the second control point.

x3   A floating-point number that specifies the *x* position of the third control point.

y3   A floating-point number that specifies the *y* position of the third control point.

x4   A floating-point number that specifies the *x* position of the fourth control point.

y4   A floating-point number that specifies the *y* position of the fourth control point.

Returns

Nothing.

Description

Method; appends a cubic Bézier curve segment to the path.

Example

The following example creates a new path, stores it in the `myPath` variable, and assigns the curve to the path:

```
var myPath = fl.drawingLayer.newPath();
myPath.addCubicCurve(0, 0, 10, 20, 20, 20, 30, 0);
```

path.addCurve()

Availability

Flash MX 2004.

Usage

```
path.addCurve(xAnchor, yAnchor, x2, y2, x3, y3)
```

Parameters

xAnchor   A floating-point value that specifies the *x* position of the first control point.

yAnchor   A floating-point value that specifies the *y* position of the first control point.

x2   A floating-point value that specifies the *x* position of the second control point.

y2   A floating-point value that specifies the *y* position of the second control point.

x3   A floating-point value that specifies the *x* position of the third control point.

y3   A floating-point value that specifies the *y* position of the third control point.

Returns

Nothing.

Description

Method; appends a quadratic Bézier segment to the path.

Example

The following example creates a new path, stores it in the `myPath` variable, and assigns the curve to the path:

```
var myPath = fl.drawingLayer.newPath();
myPath.addCurve(0, 0, 10, 20, 20, 0);
```

path.addPoint()

Availability

Flash MX 2004.

Usage

```
path.addPoint(x, y)
```

Parameters

x   A floating-point value that specifies the *x* position of the point.

y   A floating-point value that specifies the *y* position of the point.

Returns

Nothing.

Description

Method; adds a point to the path.

Example

The following example creates a new path, stores it in the `myPath` variable, and assigns the new point to the path:

```
var myPath = fl.drawingLayer.newPath();
myPath.addPoint(10, 100);
```

path.clear()

Availability

Flash MX 2004.

Usage

```
path.clear()
```

Parameters

None.

Returns

Nothing.

Description

Method; removes all points from the path.

Example

The following example removes all points from a path stored in the `myPath` variable:

```
var myPath = fl.drawingLayer.newPath();
myPath.clear();
```

path.close()

Availability

Flash MX 2004.

Usage

```
path.close()
```

Parameters

None.

Returns

Nothing.

Description

Method; appends a point at the location of the first point of the path and extends the path to that point, which closes the path. If the path has no points, no points are added.

Example

The following example creates a closed path:

```
var myPath = fl.drawingLayer.newPath();
myPath.close();
```

path.makeShape()

Availability

Flash MX 2004.

Usage

```
path.makeShape([bSupressFill [, bSupressStroke]])
```

Parameters

bSupressFill   A Boolean value that, if set to `true`, suppresses the fill that would be applied to the shape. The default value is `false`. This parameter is optional.

bSupressStroke   A Boolean value that, if set to `true`, suppresses the stroke that would be applied to the shape. The default value is `false`. This parameter is optional.

Returns

Nothing.

Description

Method; creates a shape on the Stage by using the current stroke and fill settings. The path is cleared after the shape is created. This method has two optional parameters for suppressing the fill and stroke of the resulting shape object. If you omit these parameters or set them to `false`, the current values for fill and stroke are used.

Example

The following example creates a shape with the current fill and no stroke:

```
var myPath = fl.drawingLayer.newPath();
myPath.makeShape(false, true);
```

path.newContour()

Availability

Flash MX 2004.

Usage

```
path.newContour()
```

Parameters

None.

Returns

Nothing.

Description

Method; starts a new contour in the path.

Example

The following example creates a hollow square:

```
var myPath = fl.drawingLayer.newPath();
myPath.addPoint( 0,  0);
myPath.addPoint( 0, 30);
myPath.addPoint(30, 30);
myPath.addPoint(30,  0);
myPath.addPoint( 0,  0);

myPath.newContour();
myPath.addPoint(10, 10);
myPath.addPoint(10, 20);
myPath.addPoint(20, 20);
myPath.addPoint(20, 10);
myPath.addPoint(10, 10);

myPath.makeShape();
```

path.nPts

Availability

Flash MX 2004.

Usage

```
path.nPts
```

Description

Read-only property; an integer representing the number of points in the path. A new path has 0 points.

Example

The following example uses the Output panel to show the number of points in the path referenced by the `myPath` variable:

```
var myPath = fl.drawingLayer.newPath();
var numOfPoints = myPath.nPts;
fl.trace("Number of points in the path: " + numOfPoints);
// Displays: Number of points in the path: 0
```

Project object

Availability

Flash 8.

Description

The Project object represents a Flash Project (FLP) file. You can use the following commands to return a Project object:

- To create a new project file, use `fl.createProject()`.
- To open an existing project file, use `fl.openProject()`.
- To return a Project object for the currently open project, use `fl.getProject()`.

Method summary for the Project object

The following methods can be used with the Project object.

Method	Description
`project.addFile()`	Adds the specified file to the project.
`project.canPublishProject()`	Determines whether the project can be published.
`project.canTestProject()`	Determines whether the project can be tested.
`project.findProjectItem()`	Searches for a specified file in the project.
`project.publishProject()`	Publishes the FLA files in a project.
`project.testProject()`	Tests the project.

Property summary for the Project object

The following properties can be used with the Project object.

Property	Description
`project.defaultItem`	Specifies the ProjectItem object that represents the default document in the project.
`project.items`	An array of ProjectItem objects (see ProjectItem object) contained in the project (read-only property).
`project.name`	The name of the project that appears in the Project panel.
`project.projectURI`	A string representing the path and name of the project file, expressed as a file:/// URI (read-only property).

project.addFile()

Availability

Flash 8.

Usage

```
project.addFile( fileURI [ , autoCreateFolder ] )
```

Parameters

fileURI   A string specifying the file to be added to the project, expressed as a file:/// URI.

autoCreateFolder   An optional Boolean value specifying if folders should be automatically created in the Project panel to mirror the path in *fileURI*; the default value is false.

Returns

If successful, returns a ProjectItem object; otherwise, returns undefined. See ProjectItem object.

Description

Method; adds the specified file to the project. You can use *autoCreateFolder* to determine where the new file should be positioned in the Project panel:

- If you omit *autoCreateFolder* or pass a value of false, the file is added at the root level of the project.

- If you pass a value of true for *autoCreateFolder*, and *fileURI* is below the FLP file in the folder structure on disk, the folder structure of the files is mirrored in the Project panel. That is, new folders are added to the Project panel if necessary to reflect the location of the file on disk.

- If you pass a value of true for *autoCreateFolder*, and *fileURI* is above the FLP file in the folder structure on disk, the file is added at the root level. That is, *autoCreateFolder* is ignored.

Example

The following example illustrates several ways to use this command. In this case, the open project file is in the c:\Projects directory, and the only files currently in the project have been added at the root level.

```
// Get the project object
var myProject = fl.getProject();

// The following command creates a folder named "files" below the root level
   in the project, and places myFile.fla in that folder.
var newFile = myProject.addFile("file:///C|Projects/files/myFile.fla",
   true)
fl.trace(newFile.isMissing); // false

// The following two commands have the same effect: placing myFile_02.fla in
   the root level of the project.
var newFile = myProject.addFile("file:///C|Projects/files/myFile_02.fla" ,
   false)
var newFile = myProject.addFile("file:///C|Projects/files/myFile_02.fla")
fl.trace(newFile.isMissing); // false

// The following command places myFile_03 in the root level of the project
   as a missing file.
var newFile = myProject.addFile("file:///C|myFile_03.fla")
fl.trace(newFile.isMissing); // true
```

The following example attempts to add a new file to the project, and displays a message in the Output panel indicating whether the file was added.

```
var myProject = fl.getProject();
var newItem = myProject.addFile("file:///C|Projects/files/Integra.fla",
   true);
fl.trace( "Item " + ( newItem ? "was" : "was not" ) + " added!" );
```

See also

`fl.getProject()`, `project.items`, ProjectItem object

project.canPublishProject()

Availability

Flash 8.

Usage

```
project.canPublishProject()
```

Parameters

None.

Returns

A Boolean value specifying whether the project can be published.

Description

Method; determines whether the project can be published. A project can be published if it contains at least one FLA file.

Example

The following example displays a message in the Output panel if the project cannot be published:

```
if (!fl.getProject().canPublishProject()) {
    fl.trace("Project cannot be published!");
}
```

See also

`fl.getProject()`, `project.publishProject()`, `projectItem.canPublish()`

project.canTestProject()

Availability

Flash 8.

Usage

`project.canTestProject()`

Parameters

None.

Returns

A Boolean value specifying whether the project can be tested.

Description

Method; determines whether the project can be tested. A project can be tested if a default document has been specified.

Example

The following example displays a message in the Output panel if the project cannot be tested:

```
if (!fl.getProject().canTestProject()) {
  fl.trace("Project cannot be tested!");
}
```

See also

`fl.getProject()`, `project.testProject()`, `projectItem.canTest()`

project.defaultItem

Availability

Flash 8.

Usage

`project.defaultItem`

Description

Property; specifies the ProjectItem object that represents the default document in the project. You must specify a default item if you want to test the project. See ProjectItem object.

Example

The following example sets the default document in the project to the Flower.fla file:

```
var myProject = fl.getProject();
var item = myProject.findProjectItem("file:///C|/Projects/files/
  Flower.fla");
fl.myProject.defaultItem = item;
```

The following example displays the name of the default document in the Output panel:

```
fl.trace(fl.getProject().defaultItem.displayName);
```

See also

`fl.getProject()`, `project.findProjectItem()`, ProjectItem object

project.findProjectItem()

Availability

Flash 8.

Usage

```
project.findProjectItem( fileURI )
```

Parameters

fileURI   A string specifying the file to search for in the project, expressed as a file:/// URI.

Returns

A ProjectItem object for the item if successful; otherwise, returns `false`. See ProjectItem object.

Description

Method; searches for a specified file in the project.

Example

The following example displays an error message in the Output panel if a specified file is not found in the project:

```
var myProject = fl.getProject();
var item = myProject.findProjectItem("file:///C|Projects/files/
  Integra.fla");
if (item == undefined) {
  fl.trace("Integra.fla is missing!");
}
```

See also

`fl.getProject()`, ProjectItem object, `projectItem.isMissing`

project.items

Availability

Flash 8.

Usage

```
project.items
```

Description

Read-only property; an array of ProjectItem objects (see ProjectItem object) contained in the project.

Example

The following example displays the names of all the items in the project in the Output panel:

```
for (i = 0; i < fl.getProject().items.length; i++) {
    fl.trace(fl.getProject().items[i].displayName);
}
```

See also

fl.getProject(), ProjectItem object

project.name

Availability

Flash 8.

Usage

```
project.name
```

Description

Property; the name of the project that appears in the Project panel.

Example

The following example specifies a new name to be displayed in the Project panel:

```
fl.getProject().name = "New project name";
```

See also

fl.getProject(), project.projectURI

project.projectURI

Availability

Flash 8.

Usage

```
project.projectURI
```

Description

Read-only property; a string representing the path and name of the project file, expressed as a file:/// URI.

Example

The following example displays the path and name of the currently open project file in the Output panel:

```
fl.trace("Project is located at: " + fl.getProject().projectURI);
```

See also

`fl.getProject()`, `project.name`

project.publishProject()

Availability

Flash 8.

Usage

```
project.publishProject()
```

Parameters

None.

Returns

A Boolean value indicating if the project was successfully published.

Description

Method; publishes the FLA files in a project.

Example

The following example publishes the project after confirming that it can be published, and then indicates whether the project was published in the Output panel:

```
if (fl.getProject().canPublishProject()) {
    var bSucceeded = fl.getProject().publishProject();
}
fl.trace(bSucceeded);
```

See also

`fl.getProject()`, `project.canPublishProject()`, `projectItem.publish()`

project.testProject()

Availability

Flash 8.

Usage

```
project.testProject()
```

Parameters

None.

Returns

A Boolean value indicating if the project was successfully tested.

Description

Method; tests the project. A project must have a default document to be tested.

Example

The following example tests the project after confirming that it can be tested, and then indicates whether the project was tested in the Output panel:

```
if (fl.getProject().canTestProject()) {
  var bSucceeded = fl.getProject().testProject();
}
fl.trace(bSucceeded);
```

See also

fl.getProject(), project.canTestProject(), project.defaultItem,
projectItem.test()

ProjectItem object

Availability

Flash 8.

Description

The ProjectItem object represents an item (file on disk) that has been added to a project. This object is a property of the Project object (see `project.items`). You can use the following commands to return a ProjectItem object.

- To add a new file to a project, use `project.addFile()`.
- To locate an item that has already been added to a project, use `project.findProjectItem()`.

Method summary for the ProjectItem object

The following methods can be used with the ProjectItem object.

Method	Description
`projectItem.canPublish()`	Determines whether a project item can be published.
`projectItem.canTest()`	Determines whether a project item can be tested.
`projectItem.publish()`	Publishes a project item.
`projectItem.test()`	Tests a project item.

Property summary for the ProjectItem object

The following properties can be used with the ProjectItem object.

Property	Description
`projectItem.displayName`	Read-only; a string that specifies the name of a project item.
`projectItem.isMissing`	Read-only; a Boolean value that specifies whether a file is missing from the disk.
`projectItem.itemURI`	Read-only; a string that specifies the path and name of the project item.
`projectItem.publishProfile`	A string that specifies the publish profile to use when publishing a project item (FLA file).

projectItem.canPublish()

Availability

Flash 8.

Usage

```
projectItem.canPublish()
```

Parameters

None.

Returns

A Boolean value specifying whether a project item can be published.

Description

Method; determines whether an item can be published. An item can be published only if it is a FLA file.

Example

The following example displays a message in the Output panel if the first item in the project cannot be published.

```
var item = fl.getProject().items[0];
if (!item.canPublish()) {
   fl.trace(item.displayName + " cannot be published!");
}
```

See also

`fl.getProject()`, `project.canPublishProject()`, `project.items`, `projectItem.publish()`

projectItem.canTest()

Availability

Flash 8.

Usage

```
projectItem.canTest()
```

Parameters

None.

Returns

A Boolean value specifying whether a project item can be tested.

Description

Method; determines whether an item can be tested. An item can be tested if it is a FLA or HTML file.

Example

The following example displays a message in the Output panel if the first item in the project cannot be tested.

```
var item = fl.getProject().items[0];
if (!item.canTest()) {
  fl.trace(item.name + " cannot be tested!");
}
```

See also

fl.getProject(), project.canTestProject(), project.items, projectItem.test()

projectItem.displayName

Availability

Flash 8.

Usage

```
projectItem.displayName
```

Description

Read-only property; a string that specifies the name of a project item, such as "file.fla".

Example

The following example displays the names of all the files in the project in the Output panel.

```
fl.trace( "These are all the files in the project: ");
var files = fl.getProject().items;
for (i = 0; i < files.length; i++) {
  fl.trace(files[i].displayName + " ");
}
```

See also

fl.getProject(), project.items, projectItem.itemURI

projectItem.isMissing

Availability

Flash 8.

Usage

```
projectItem.isMissing
```

Description

Read-only property; a Boolean value that specifies whether a file is missing from the disk (for example, if the item has been moved, deleted or renamed).

Example

The following example displays a message in the Output panel that indicates whether a specific file is on the disk in the expected folder.

```
var item = fl.getProject().findProjectItem("file:///C|/Projects/files/
    DynamicHighAscii.fla");
fl.trace("DynamicHighAscii.fla is missing: " + item.isMissing);
```

See also

```
fl.getProject(), project.findProjectItem(), project.items
```

projectItem.itemURI

Availability

Flash 8.

Usage

```
projectItem.itemURI
```

Description

Read-only property; a string, specified as a file:/// URI, that specifies the path and name of the project item. Folder items contain an empty string ("").

Example

The following example displays the path and name of each item in the project in the
Output panel.

```
files = fl.getProject().items;
for (i = 0; i < files.length; i++) {
  fl.trace(files[i].itemURI);
}
```

See also

`fl.getProject(), projectItem.displayName, project.items`

projectItem.publish()

Availability

Flash 8.

Usage

`projectItem.publish()`

Parameters

None.

Returns

A Boolean value of `true` if successful; `false` otherwise.

Description

Method; publishes a project item. Only FLA files can be published.

Example

The following example publishes all of the publishable items in the project.

```
for (var i in fl.getProject().items) {
  var item = fl.getProject().items[i];
  if (item.canPublish()) {
    item.publish();
  }
}
```

See also

`fl.getProject(), project.canPublishProject(), project.items,`
`projectItem.canPublish(), projectItem.publishProfile`

projectItem.publishProfile

Availability

Flash 8.

Usage

```
projectItem.publishProfile
```

Description

Property; a string that specifies the publish profile to use when publishing a project item (FLA file). The publish profile must be an existing profile in the item, or a subsequent call to `projectItem.publish()` will fail. See `projectItem.publish()`.

If the item is not a FLA file, this property is an empty string (""), and any attempts to set this property fail.

Example

The following example sets the publish profile of all the items in the project to a specified profile that already exists in the item, and then publishes each item. If the profile doesn't exist in a file, the file isn't published.

```
var items = fl.getProject().items;
for ( i = 0 ; i < items.length ; i++ ) {
  items[i].publishProfile = "mySpecialProfile";
  items[i].publish();
}
```

See also

`fl.getProject()`, `project.canPublishProject()`, `project.items`, `projectItem.canPublish()`, `projectItem.publish()`

projectItem.test()

Availability

Flash 8.

Usage

```
projectItem.test()
```

Parameters

None.

Returns

A Boolean value that indicates whether the item was successfully tested or not.

Descriptionn

Method; tests a project item. If the test operation fails because the item is not a FLA or HTML file, this method returns `false`.

Example

The following example tests all the FLA and HTML files in the project:

```
for (var i in fl.getProject().items) {
  var item = fl.getProject().items[i];
  if (item.canTest()) {
    item.test();
  }
}
```

See also

`fl.getProject()`, `project.canTestProject()`, `project.items`, `projectItem.canTest()`

Screen object

Availability

Flash MX 2004.

Description

The Screen object represents a single screen in a slide or form document. This object contains properties related to the slide or form. For access to the array of all Screen objects in the document, use the following code:

```
fl.getDocumentDOM().screenOutline.screens
```

Property summary for the Screen object

The Screen object has the following properties:

Properties	Description
screen.accName	A string that is equivalent to the Name field in the Accessibility panel.
screen.childScreens	Read-only; the array of child screens for this screen. The array is empty if there are no child screens.
screen.description	A string that is equivalent to the Description field in the Accessibility panel.
screen.forceSimple	A Boolean value that enables and disables accessibility for the object's children.
screen.hidden	A Boolean value that specifies whether a screen is visible.
screen.instanceName	Read-only; a string that represents the instance name used to access the object from ActionScript.
screen.name	Read-only; a string that represents the name of the screen.
screen.nextScreen	Read-only; an object that represents the next peer screen in the parent's childScreens array.
screen.parameters	Read-only; an array of ActionScript 2.0 properties that are accessible from the screen Property inspector.
screen.parentScreen	Read-only; an object that represents the parent screen.
screen.prevScreen	Read-only; an object that represents the previous peer screen in the parent's childScreens array.
screen.silent	A Boolean value that specifies whether the object is accessible.

Properties	Description
screen.tabIndex	Property; equivalent to the Tab Index field in the Accessibility panel.
screen.timeline	Read-only; the Timeline object for the screen. See Timeline object.

screen.accName

Availability

Flash MX 2004.

Usage

```
screen.accName
```

Description

Property; a string that is equivalent to the Name field in the Accessibility panel. Screen readers identify objects by reading the name aloud.

Example

The following example stores the value of the name of the object in the theName variable:

```
var theName = fl.getDocumentDOM().screenOutline.screens[1].accName;
```

The following example sets the name of the object to "Home Button":

```
fl.getDocumentDOM().screenOutline.screens[1].accName = 'Home Button';
```

screen.childScreens

Availability

Flash MX 2004.

Usage

```
screen.childScreens
```

Description

Read-only property; the array of child screens for this screen. The array is empty if there are no child screens.

Example

The following example checks to see if the current document is a slide or form, and if it is, stores the array of child screens in the myChildren variable and displays their names in the Output panel:

```
var myChildren = new Array();
if(fl.getDocumentDOM().allowScreens) {
  var myParent = fl.getDocumentDOM().screenOutline.rootScreen.name
  for (i in fl.getDocumentDOM().screenOutline.rootScreen.childScreens) {
    myChildren.push("
    "+fl.getDocumentDOM().screenOutline.rootScreen.childScreens[i].name);
    }
  fl.trace(" The child screens of "+myParent+" are "+myChildren+". ");
}
```

screen.description

Availability

Flash MX 2004.

Usage

```
screen.description
```

Description

Property; a string that is equivalent to the Description field in the Accessibility panel. The description is read by the screen reader.

Example

The following example gets the description of the object and stores it in the theDescription variable:

```
var theDescription =
  fl.getDocumentDOM().screenOutline.screens[1].description;
```

The following example sets the description of the object to "This is Screen 1":

```
fl.getDocumentDOM().screenOutline.screens[1].description = "This is Screen
  1"
```

screen.forceSimple

Availability

Flash MX 2004.

Usage

```
screen.forceSimple
```

Description

Property; a Boolean value that enables or disables accessibility for the object's children. This is equivalent to the inverse logic of the Make Child Objects Accessible setting in the Accessibility panel. That is, if `forceSimple` is `true`, it is the same as the Make Child Object Accessible option being deselected. If `forceSimple` is `false`, it is the same as the Make Child Object Accessible option being selected.

Example

The following example stores the value of `forceSimple` in the `areChildrenAccessible` variable (a value of `false` means the children of the object are accessible):

```
var areChildrenAccessible =
  fl.getDocumentDOM().screenOutline.screens[1].forceSimple
```

The following example makes the children of the object accessible:

```
fl.getDocumentDOM().screenOutline.screens[1].forceSimple = false;
```

screen.hidden

Availability

Flash MX 2004.

Usage

```
screen.hidden
```

Description

Property; a Boolean value that specifies whether the screen is visible. A screen with the `hidden` property set to `true` is not visible in any other screen.

Example

The following example checks to see if the first screen in the outline is hidden and changes the visibility of the screen accordingly. Then, a message in the Output panel shows what the visibility of the screen was before the change:

```
if (fl.getDocumentDOM().screenOutline.screens[0].hidden) {
  fl.getDocumentDOM().screenOutline.setScreenProperty("hidden", false);
  fl.trace(fl.getDocumentDOM().screenOutline.screens[0].name+" had its
  'hidden' property set to 'false'");
}
else {
  fl.getDocumentDOM().screenOutline.setScreenProperty("hidden", true);
  fl.trace(fl.getDocumentDOM().screenOutline.screens[0].name+" had its
  'hidden' property set to 'true'");
}
```

screen.instanceName

Availability

Flash MX 2004.

Usage

```
screen.instanceName
```

Description

Read-only property; a string that represents the instance name used to access the object from ActionScript.

Example

The following example checks to see if the current document allows screens (because it is a slide or form). Then, it assigns the instanceName value of the first child screen in the array to the myInstanceName variable and opens the Output panel to show the instance name of the screen:

```
var myChildren = new Array();
if(fl.getDocumentDOM().allowScreens) {
  var myInstanceName =
  fl.getDocumentDOM().screenOutline.rootScreen.childScreens[0].instanceNam
  e;
  fl.trace(" The instanceName is "+myInstanceName+". ");
}
```

screen.name

Availability

Flash MX 2004.

Usage

```
screen.name
```

Description

Read-only property; a string that represents the name of the screen.

Example

The following example checks to see if the current document allows screens (because it is a slide or form document). Then, it assigns the `name` value of the first child screen in the array to the `myName` variable and opens the Output panel to show the name of the screen:

```
var myChildren = new Array();
if(fl.getDocumentDOM().allowScreens) {
  var myName =
  fl.getDocumentDOM().screenOutline.rootScreen.childScreens[0].name;
  fl.trace("The name of the screen is "+myName+". ");
}
```

screen.nextScreen

Availability

Flash MX 2004.

Usage

```
screen.nextScreen
```

Description

Read-only property; an object that represents the next peer screen in the parent's `childScreens` array. That is, `screen.NextScreen` is found by moving down an array of child screens to the next screen in the array. See `screen.prevScreen`.

If there isn't a peer screen, the value is `null`.

Example

The following example first checks to see if the current document is a slide or form, and if it is, retrieves and shows the sequence of screens in the Output panel:

```
if(fl.getDocumentDOM().allowScreens) {
  var myCurrent =
  fl.getDocumentDOM().screenOutline.rootScreen.childScreens[0].name;
  var myNext =
  fl.getDocumentDOM().screenOutline.rootScreen.childScreens[0].nextScreen.
  name;
  fl.trace(" The next screen to "+myCurrent+" is "+myNext+". ");
}
```

screen.parameters

Availability

Flash MX 2004.

Usage

```
screen.parameters
```

Description

Read-only property; an array of ActionScript 2.0 properties that are accessible from the screen Property inspector.

Example

The following example stores the parameters for the second screen in the outline to the `parms` variable and then assigns the `"some value"` value to the first property:

```
var parms = fl.getDocumentDOM().screenOutline.screens[1].parameters;
parms[0].value = "some value";
```

See also

Parameter object

screen.parentScreen

Availability

Flash MX 2004.

Usage

```
screen.parentScreen
```

Description

Read-only property; an object that represents the parent screen. If `parentScreen` is `null`, the screen is a top-level screen.

Example

The following example stores the values for the `childScreens` and `parentScreen` properties in variables and then shows those values and their parent/child relationship in the Output panel:

```
if(fl.getDocumentDOM().allowScreens) {
  var myCurrent =
  fl.getDocumentDOM().screenOutline.rootScreen.childScreens[1].name;
  var myParent =
  fl.getDocumentDOM().screenOutline.rootScreen.childScreens[1].parentScree
  n.name;
  fl.trace(" The parent screen to "+myCurrent+" is "+myParent+". ");
}
```

screen.prevScreen

Availability

Flash MX 2004.

Usage

```
screen.prevScreen
```

Description

Read-only property; an object that represents the previous peer screen in the parent's `childScreens` array. If there isn't a peer screen, the value is `null`. See also `screen.nextScreen`.

Example

The following example checks to see if the current document is a slide or form, and if it is, retrieves and shows the sequence of screens in the Output panel:

```
if(fl.getDocumentDOM().allowScreens) {
    var myCurrent =
    fl.getDocumentDOM().screenOutline.rootScreen.childScreens[1].name;
    var myNext =
    fl.getDocumentDOM().screenOutline.rootScreen.childScreens[1].prevScreen.
    name;
    fl.trace(" The previous screen to "+myCurrent+" is "+myNext+". ");
}
```

screen.silent

Availability

Flash MX 2004.

Usage

```
screen.silent
```

Description

Property; a Boolean value that specifies whether the object is accessible. This is equivalent to the inverse logic of the Make Object Accessible setting in the Accessibility panel. That is, if silent is true, it is the same as having the Make Object Accessible option deselected in the Accessibility panel. If silent is false, it is the same as having the Make Object Accessible option selected in the Accessibility panel.

Example

The following example retrieves the silent value of the object (a value of false means the object is accessible):

```
var isSilent = fl.getDocumentDOM().screenOutline.screens[1].silent;
```

The following example sets the object to be accessible:

```
fl.getDocumentDOM().screenOutline.screens[1].silent = false;
```

screen.tabIndex

Availability

Flash MX 2004.

Usage

```
screen.tabIndex
```

Description

Property; equivalent to the Tab Index field in the Accessibility panel. This value lets you determine the order in which objects are accessed when the user presses the Tab key.

Example

The following example gets the tab index of the object:

```
var theTabIndex = fl.getDocumentDOM().screenOutline.screens[1].tabIndex;
```

The following example sets the tab index of the object to 1:

```
fl.getDocumentDOM().screenOutline.screens[1].tabIndex = 1;
```

screen.timeline

Availability

Flash MX 2004.

Usage

```
screen.timeline
```

Description

Read-only property; the Timeline object for the screen.

Example

The following example gets the `screenOutline` property of the current slide document, assigns the array of `timeline` properties for the first screen to `myArray`, and displays those properties in the Output panel:

```
myArray = new Array();
if(fl.getDocumentDOM().screenOutline) {
   for(i in fl.getDocumentDOM().screenOutline.screens[0].timeline) {
   myArray.push(" "+i+" :
   "+fl.getDocumentDOM().screenOutline.screens[0].timeline[i]+" ") ;
   }
   fl.trace("Here are the properties of the screen named "+
   fl.getDocumentDOM().screenOutline.screens[0].name+": "+myArray);
}
```

ScreenOutline object

Availability

Flash MX 2004.

Description

The ScreenOutline object represents the group of screens in a slide or form document. The object is accessed by using `fl.getDocumentDOM().screenOutline`.

The ScreenOutline object exists only if the document is a slide or form document, so before accessing the property, use `document.allowScreens()` to verify that a Screens document exists, as shown in the following example:

```
if(fl.getDocumentDOM().allowScreens) {
    var myName =
        fl.getDocumentDOM().screenOutline.rootScreen.childScreens[0].name;
    fl.trace("The name of the screen is " + myName + ". ");
}
```

Method summary for the ScreenOutline object

You can use the following methods with the ScreenOutline object:

Method	Description
screenOutline.copyScreenFromFile()	Inserts all the screens, or a named screen and its children, from a specified document under the currently selected screen.
screenOutline.deleteScreen()	Deletes the currently selected screen(s), or a specified screen, and the children of the screen(s).
screenOutline.duplicateScreen()	Duplicates the currently selected screen(s) or a specified screen.
screenOutline.getSelectedScreens()	Returns an array of Screen objects that are currently selected in the screen outline.
screenOutline.insertNestedScreen()	Inserts a nested screen of a specific type into a particular location in the screen outline.
screenOutline.insertScreen()	Inserts a new blank screen of a specified type into the document at a specified location.
screenOutline.moveScreen()	Moves the specified screen in relation to the value of the referenceScreen parameter; either before, after, as the first child, or as the last child.

Method	Description
screenOutline.renameScreen()	Changes the screen with a specified name to a new name.
screenOutline.setCurrentScreen()	Sets the current selection in the screen outline to the specified screen.
screenOutline.setScreenProperty()	Lets the specified property with the specified value for the selected screens.
screenOutline.setSelectedScreens()	Selects the specified screens in the Screen Outline pane.

Property summary for the ScreenOutline object

You can use the following properties with the ScreenOutline object:

Property	Description
screenOutline.currentScreen	A Screen object; the currently selected screen.
screenOutline.rootScreen	Read-only; the first screen in the screen outline.
screenOutline.screens	Read-only ; the array of top level Screen objects contained in the document (see Screen object).

screenOutline.copyScreenFromFile()

Availability

Flash MX 2004.

Usage

screenOutline.copyScreenFromFile(fileURI [, screenName])

Parameters

fileURI   A string, expressed as a file:/// URI, that specifies a filename for the authoring file that contains the screens to copy into the document.

screenName   The name of the screen to copy. If the *screenName* parameter is present, Flash copies that screen and its children. If the *screenName* is not specified, Flash copies the whole document. This parameter is optional.

Returns

Nothing. If the file is not found or is not a valid FLA file, or if the specified screen is not found, an error is reported and the script is cancelled.

Description

Method; inserts all the screens, or a named screen and its children, from a specified document under the currently selected screen. If more than one screen is selected, the screen(s) are inserted under the last selected screen, as its sibling.

Example

The following example copies the "slide1" screen from the myTarget.fla file on the Desktop into the current document (substitute your user name for *userName*):

```
fl.getDocumentDOM().screenOutline.copyScreenFromFile("file:///C|/Documents
   and Settings/userName/Desktop/myTarget.fla", "slide1");
```

screenOutline.currentScreen

Availability

Flash MX 2004.

Usage

```
screenOutline.currentScreen
```

Description

Property; a Screen object, the currently selected screen (see Screen object).

Example

The following example stores the currentScreen object in the myScreen variable and then displays the name of that screen in the Output panel:

```
var myScreen = fl.getDocumentDOM().screenOutline.currentScreen;
fl.trace(myScreen.name);
```

screenOutline.deleteScreen()

Availability

Flash MX 2004.

Usage

```
screenOutline.deleteScreen( [screenName] )
```

Parameters

screenName   A string that specifies the name of the screen to be deleted. If you don't pass a value for *screenName*, the currently selected screen(s) and their children are deleted. This parameter is optional.

Returns

Nothing.

Description

Method; deletes the currently selected screen(s), or a specified screen, and the children of the screen(s).

Example

The following example removes the screen named apple and all its children:

```
fl.getDocumentDOM().screenOutline.deleteScreen("apple");
```

screenOutline.duplicateScreen()

Availability

Flash MX 2004.

Usage

```
screenOutline.duplicateScreen( [screenName] )
```

Parameters

screenName   A string value that specifies the screen name to duplicate. If you don't pass a value for *screenName*, the currently selected screen(s) are duplicated. This parameter is optional.

Returns

A Boolean value: true if the screen is successfully duplicated; false otherwise.

Description

Method; duplicates the currently selected screen(s) or a specified screen. The duplicate screens are given a default name by appending _copy to the original name, such as Screen_copy, Screen_copy2, and so on. If you duplicate multiple screens, the duplicates are placed directly below the selected screen that is lowest in the screen outline hierarchy.

Example

The following example duplicates a screen named apple:

```
fl.getDocumentDOM().screenOutline.duplicateScreen("apple");
```

screenOutline.getSelectedScreens()

Availability

Flash MX 2004.

Usage

```
screenOutline.getSelectedScreens()
```

Parameters

None.

Returns

An array of selected Screen objects (see Screen object).

Description

Method; returns an array of Screen objects that are currently selected in the screen outline.

Example

The following example stores the selected Screen objects in the `myArray` variable and displays the screen names in the Output panel:

```
var myArray = fl.getDocumentDOM().screenOutline.getSelectedScreens();
for (var i in myArray) {
  fl.trace(myArray[i].name)
}
```

screenOutline.insertNestedScreen()

Availability

Flash MX 2004.

Usage

```
screenOutline.insertNestedScreen( [ name [, referenceScreen [,
  screenTypeName ] ] ])
```

Parameters

name   A string indicating the name of the new screen to insert. An empty name will insert a screen with a default screen name, such as Slide *n* or Form *n* (where *n* is the first available unique number). This parameter is optional.

referenceScreen   A string indicating the name of the screen into which the new screen is inserted as a child. If this parameter is omitted, the new screen is inserted as a child of the currently selected screen. This parameter is optional.

screenTypeName   A string that specifies the screen type to attach to the new nested screen. The screen type and class name are set for this screen. Acceptable values are "Form" and "Slide". This parameter is optional. If this parameter is omitted, the type is inherited from the parent screen.

Returns

A Screen object.

Description

Method; inserts a nested screen of a specific type into a particular location in the screen outline.

Example

The following example inserts slide2 as a child of slide1:

```
fl.getDocumentDOM().screenOutline.insertNestedScreen("slide2", "slide1",
  "Slide");
```

screenOutline.insertScreen()

Availability

Flash MX 2004.

Usage

```
screenOutline.insertScreen( [name [, referenceScreen [, screenTypeName ] ]
  ])
```

Parameters

name A string indicating the name of the new screen to insert. If this parameter is omitted, the method inserts a screen with a default screen name, such as Slide *n* or Form *n* (where *n* is the first available unique number). This parameter is optional.

referenceScreen A string indicating the name of the screen before the new screen. If this parameter is omitted, the new screen is inserted after the currently selected screen. If the *referenceScreen* parameter identifies a child screen, the new screen will be a peer of the child screen, and a child screen of the same parent. This parameter is optional.

screenTypeName A string that specifies the screen type to attach to the new screen. The screen type and classname are set for this screen. Acceptable values are "Form" and "Slide". This parameter is optional.

Returns

A Screen object.

Description

Method; inserts a new blank screen of a specified type into the document at a specified location.

Example

The following example inserts a form named slide2 after the screen named slide1:

```
fl.getDocumentDOM().screenOutline.insertScreen("slide2","slide1","Form");
```

The following example inserts a slide named slide4 after the screen slide3:

```
fl.getDocumentDOM().screenOutline.insertScreen("slide4","slide3","Slide");
```

screenOutline.moveScreen()

Availability

Flash MX 2004.

Usage

```
screenOutline.moveScreen( screenToMove, referenceScreen, position )
```

Parameters

screenToMove   A string that is the screen name to move.

referenceScreen   A string that specifies the screen near which *screenToMove* will be placed.

position   A string that specifies where to move the screen in relation to *referenceScreen*. Acceptable values are "before", "after", "firstChild", and "lastChild".

Returns

A Boolean value: true if the move is successful; false otherwise.

Description

Method; moves the specified screen in relation to the value of the *referenceScreen* parameter; either before, after, as the first child, or as the last child.

Example

The following example moves screen slide1 to be the first child of slide2:

```
fl.getDocumentDOM().screenOutline.moveScreen("slide1", "slide2",
  "firstChild");
```

screenOutline.renameScreen()

Availability

Flash MX 2004.

Usage

```
screenOutline.renameScreen( newScreenName [, oldScreenName [,
  bDisplayError] ] )
```

Parameters

newScreenName   A string that specifies the new name of the screen

oldScreenName   A string that specifies the name of the existing screen to change. If not specified, the name of the currently selected screen changes. This parameter is optional.

bDisplayError   A Boolean value that, if set to true, shows an error message if an error occurs, for example, if a screen with the same name as the value passed to *newScreenName* already exists. The default value is false.

Returns

A Boolean value: true if the renaming is successful; false otherwise.

Description

Method; changes the screen with a specified name to a new name.

Example

The following example changes the name of slide1 to Intro:

```
fl.getDocumentDOM().screenOutline.renameScreen("Intro", "slide1");
```

screenOutline.rootScreen

Availability

Flash MX 2004.

Usage

```
screenOutline.rootScreen
```

Description

Read-only property; the first screen in the screen outline. You can use
`screenOutline.rootScreen` as a shortcut for `screenOutline.screens[0]`.

Example

The following example displays the name of the first child of the first screen in the
screen outline:

```
fl.trace(fl.getDocumentDOM().screenOutline.rootScreen.childScreens[0].name)
  ;
```

screenOutline.screens

Availability

Flash MX 2004.

Usage

```
screenOutline.screens
```

Description

Read-only property; the array of top level Screen objects contained in the document (see
Screen object).

Example

The following example stores the array of Screen objects in the `myArray` variable and then displays their names in the Output panel:

```
var myArray = new Array();
if(fl.getDocumentDOM().allowScreens) {
  for(var i in fl.getDocumentDOM().screenOutline.screens) {

    myArray.push(" "+fl.getDocumentDOM().screenOutline.screens[i].name);

  }
  fl.trace("The screens array contains objects whose names are:
  "+myArray+". ");
}
```

screenOutline.setCurrentScreen()

Availability

Flash MX 2004.

Usage

```
screenOutline.setCurrentScreen( name )
```

Parameters

name   A string that specifies the name screen which should become the currently selected screen. If the screen is a child of another screen, you do not need to indicate a path or hierarchy.

Returns

Nothing.

Description

Method; sets the current selection in the screen outline to the specified screen.

Example

The following example sets the current screen to the screen named ChildOfSlide_1:

```
fl.getDocumentDOM().screenOutline.setCurrentScreen("ChildOfSlide_1");
```

screenOutline.setScreenProperty()

Availability

Flash MX 2004.

Usage

```
screenOutline.setScreenProperty( property, value )
```

Parameters

property   A string that specifies the property to set.

value   The new value for the property. The type of value depends on the property being set.

For a list of available properties and values, see Property summary for the Screen object.

Returns

Nothing.

Description

Method; sets the specified property with the specified value for the selected screens.

Example

The following example changes the visibility of the currently selected screens from hidden to visible:

```
fl.getDocumentDOM().screenOutline.setScreenProperty("hidden", false);
```

screenOutline.setSelectedScreens()

Availability

Flash MX 2004.

Usage

```
screenOutline.setSelectedScreens ( selection [, bReplaceCurrentSelection ]
  )
```

Parameters

selection   An array of screen names to be selected in the screen outline.

bReplaceCurrentSelection   A Boolean value that, if true, lets you deselect the current selection. The default value is true. If false, Flash extends the current selection to include the specified screens. This parameter is optional.

Returns

Nothing.

Description

Method; selects the specified screens in the screen outline. If multiple screens are specified, the screen with the last index value of the selection array is focused on the Stage.

Example

The following example deselects any currently selected screens, and then selects screens slide1, slide2, slide3, and slide4 in the screen outline:

```
myArray = new Array("slide1", "slide2", "slide3", "slide4");
fl.getDocumentDOM().screenOutline.setSelectedScreens(myArray, true);
```

Shape object

Inheritance   Element object > Shape object

Availability

Flash MX 2004.

Description

The Shape object is a subclass of the Element object. The Shape object provides more precise control than the Drawing APIs when manipulating or creating geometry on the Stage. This control is necessary so that scripts can create useful effects and other drawing commands. (See Element object.)

All Shape methods and properties that change a shape or any of its subordinate parts must be placed between `shape.beginEdit()` and `shape.endEdit()` calls to function correctly.

Method summary for the Shape object

In addition to the Element object methods, you can use the following methods with the Shape object:

Method	Description
`shape.beginEdit()`	Defines the start of an edit session.
`shape.deleteEdge()`	Deletes the specified edge.
`shape.endEdit()`	Defines the end of an edit session for the shape.

Property summary for the Shape object

In addition to the Element object properties, the following properties are available for the Shape object:

Property	Description
`shape.contours`	Read-only; an array of Contour objects for the shape (see Contour object).
`shape.edges`	Read-only; an array of Edge objects (see Edge object).
`shape.isDrawingObject`	Read-only; if `true`, the shape is a drawing object.
`shape.isGroup`	Read-only; if `true`, the shape is a group.
`shape.vertices`	Read-only; an array of Vertex objects (see Vertex object).

shape.beginEdit()

Availability

Flash MX 2004.

Usage

```
shape.beginEdit()
```

Parameters

None.

Returns

Nothing.

Description

Method; defines the start of an edit session. You must use this method before issuing any commands that change the Shape object or any of its subordinate parts.

Example

The following example takes the currently selected shape and removes the first edge in the edge array from it:

```
var shape = fl.getDocumentDOM().selection[0];
shape.beginEdit();
shape.deleteEdge(0);
shape.endEdit();
```

shape.contours

Availability

Flash MX 2004.

Usage

```
shape.contours
```

Description

Read-only property; an array of Contour objects for the shape (see Contour object).

Example

The following example stores the first contour in the contours array in the *c* variable and then stores the HalfEdge object of that contour in the he variable:

```
var c = fl.getDocumentDOM().selection[0].contours[0];
var he = c.getHalfEdge();
```

shape.deleteEdge()

Availability

Flash MX 2004.

Usage

```
shape.deleteEdge( index )
```

Parameters

index   A zero-based index that specifies the edge to delete from the shape.edges array. This method changes the length of the shape.edges array.

Returns

Nothing.

Description

Method; deletes the specified edge. You must call shape.beginEdit() before using this method.

Example

The following example takes the currently selected shape and removes the first edge in the edge array:

```
var shape = fl.getDocumentDOM().selection[0];
shape.beginEdit();
shape.deleteEdge(0);
shape.endEdit();
```

shape.edges

Availability

Flash MX 2004.

Usage

```
shape.edges
```

Description

Read-only property; an array of Edge objects (see Edge object).

shape.endEdit()

Availability

Flash MX 2004.

Usage

```
shape.endEdit()
```

Parameters

None.

Returns

Nothing.

Description

Method; defines the end of an edit session for the shape. All changes made to the Shape object or any of its subordinate parts will be applied to the shape. You must use this method after issuing any commands that change the Shape object or any of its subordinate parts.

Example

The following example takes the currently selected shape and removes the first edge in the edge array from it:

```
var shape = fl.getDocumentDOM().selection[0];
shape.beginEdit();
shape.deleteEdge(0);
shape.endEdit();
```

shape.isDrawingObject

Availability

Flash 8.

Usage

```
shape.isDrawingObject
```

Description

Read-only property; if true, the shape is a drawing object.

Example

The following example stores the first selected item object in the sel variable and then uses the element.elementType and shape.isDrawingObject properties to determine if the selected item is a drawing object.

```
var sel = fl.getDocumentDOM().selection[0];
var shapeDrawingObject = (sel.elementType == "shape") &&
    sel.isDrawingObject;
fl.trace(shapeDrawingObject);
```

See also

document.crop(), document.deleteEnvelope(), document.intersect(), document.punch(), document.union(), shape.isGroup

shape.isGroup

Availability

Flash MX 2004.

Usage

shape.isGroup

Description

Read-only property; if true, the shape is a group.

Example

The following example stores the first selected item object in the sel variable and then uses the element.elementType and shape.isGroup properties to determine if the selected item is a group:

```
var sel = fl.getDocumentDOM().selection[0];
var shapeGroup = (sel.elementType == "shape") && sel.isGroup;
fl.trace(shapeGroup);
```

See also

shape.isDrawingObject

shape.vertices

Availability

Flash MX 2004.

Usage

```
shape.vertices
```

Description

Read-only property; an array of Vertex objects (see Vertex object).

Example

The following example stores the first selected item object in the someShape variable and then shows the number of vertices for that object in the Output panel:

```
var someShape = fl.getDocumentDOM().selection[0];
fl.trace("The shape has " + someShape.vertices.length + " vertices.");
```

SoundItem object

Inheritance   Item object > SoundItem object

Availability

Flash MX 2004.

Description

The SoundItem object is a subclass of the Item object. It represents a library item used to create a sound. See also `frame.soundLibraryItem` and Item object.

Property summary for the SoundItem object

In addition to the Item object properties, the following properties are available for the SoundItem object:

Property	Description
soundItem.bitRate	A string that specifies the bit rate of a sound in the library. Available only for the MP3 compression type.
soundItem.bits	A string that specifies the bits value for a sound in the library that has ADPCM compression.
soundItem.compressionType	A string that specifies the compression type for a sound in the library.
soundItem.convertStereoToMono	A Boolean value available only for MP3 and Raw compression types.
soundItem.quality	A string that specifies the playback quality of a sound in the library. Available only for MP3 compression type.
soundItem.sampleRate	A string that specifies the sample rate for the audio clip.
soundItem.useImportedMP3Quality	A Boolean value; if `true`, all other properties are ignored and the imported MP3 quality is used.

soundItem.bitRate

Availability

Flash MX 2004.

Usage

`soundItem.bitRate`

Description

Property; a string that specifies the bit rate of a sound in the library. This property is available only for the MP3 compression type. Acceptable values are `"8 kbps"`, `"16 kbps"`, `"20 kbps"`, `"24 kbps"`, `"32 kbps"`, `"48 kbps"`, `"56 kbps"`, `"64 kbps"`, `"80 kbps"`, `"112 kbps"`, `"128 kbps"`, and `"160 kbps"`. Stereo sounds exported at 8 or 16 kbps are converted to mono. The property is undefined for other compression types.

> **NOTE** If you want to specify a value for this property, set `soundItem.useImportedMP3Quality` to `false`.

Example

The following example displays the `bitRate` value in the Output panel if the specified item in the library has MP3 compression type:

```
alert(fl.getDocumentDOM().library.items[0].bitRate);
```

See also

`soundItem.compressionType`, `soundItem.convertStereoToMono`

soundItem.bits

Availability

Flash MX 2004.

Usage

```
soundItem.bits
```

Description

Property; a string that specifies the bits value for a sound in the library that has ADPCM compression. Acceptable values are `"2 bit"`, `"3 bit"`, `"4 bit"`, and `"5 bit"`.

> **NOTE** If you want to specify a value for this property, set `soundItem.useImportedMP3Quality` to `false`.

Example

The following example displays the bits value in the Output panel if the currently selected item in the library has ADPCM compression type:

```
alert(fl.getDocumentDOM().library.items[0].bits);
```

See also

`soundItem.compressionType`

soundItem.compressionType

Availability

Flash MX 2004.

Usage

```
soundItem.compressionType
```

Description

Property; a string that specifies that compression type for a sound in the library. Acceptable values are "Default", "ADPCM", "MP3", "Raw", and "Speech".

 If you want to specify a value for this property, set soundItem.useImportedMP3Quality to false.

Example

The following example changes an item in the library to compression type Raw:

```
fl.getDocumentDOM().library.items[0].compressionType = "Raw";
```

The following example changes a selected item's compression type to Speech:

```
fl.getDocumentDOM().library.getSelectedItems()[0].compressionType =
    "Speech";
```

soundItem.convertStereoToMono

Availability

Flash MX 2004.

Usage

```
soundItem.convertStereoToMono
```

Description

Property; a Boolean value available only for MP3 and Raw compression types. Setting this to true converts a stereo sound to mono; false leaves it as stereo. For MP3 compression type, if soundItem.bitRate is less than 20 Kbps, this property is ignored and forced to true (see soundItem.bitRate).

 If you want to specify a value for this property, set soundItem.useImportedMP3Quality to false.

Example

The following example converts an item in the library to mono, only if the item has MP3 or Raw compression type:

```
fl.getDocumentDOM().library.items[0].convertStereoToMono = true;
```

See also

soundItem.compressionType

soundItem.quality

Availability

Flash MX 2004.

Usage

soundItem.quality

Description

Property; a string that specifies the playback quality of a sound in the library. This property is available only for MP3 compression type. Acceptable values are "Fast", "Medium", and "Best".

> **NOTE** If you want to specify a value for this property, set soundItem.useImportedMP3Quality to false.

Example

The following example sets the playback quality of an item in the library to Best, if the item has MP3 compression type:

```
fl.getDocumentDOM().library.items[0].quality = "Best";
```

See also

soundItem.compressionType

soundItem.sampleRate

Availability

Flash MX 2004.

Usage

soundItem.sampleRate

Description

Property; a string that specifies the sample rate for the audio clip. This property is available only for ADPCM, Raw, and Speech compression types. Acceptable values are `"5 kHz"`, `"11 kHz"`, `"22 kHz"`, and `"44 kHz"`.

 NOTE If you want to specify a value for this property, set `soundItem.useImportedMP3Quality` to `false`.

Example

The following example sets the sample rate of an item in the library to 5 kHz, if the item has ADPCM, Raw, or Speech compression type:

```
fl.getDocumentDOM().library.items[0].sampleRate = "5 kHz";
```

See also

`soundItem.compressionType`

soundItem.useImportedMP3Quality

Availability

Flash MX 2004.

Usage

```
soundItem.useImportedMP3Quality
```

Description

Property; a Boolean value. If `true`, all other properties are ignored and the imported MP3 quality is used.

Example

The following example sets an item in the library to use the imported MP3 quality:

```
fl.getDocumentDOM().library.items[0].useImportedMP3Quality = true;
```

See also

`soundItem.compressionType`

Stroke object

Availability

Flash MX 2004.

Description

The Stroke object contains all the settings for a stroke, including the custom settings. This object represents the information contained in the Property inspector. Using the Stroke object together with the `document.setCustomStroke()` method, you can change the stroke settings for the Tools panel, the Property inspector, and the current selection. You can also get the stroke settings of the Tools panel and Property inspector, or of the current selection, by using the `document.getCustomStroke()` method.

This object always has the following four properties: `style`, `thickness`, `color`, and `breakAtCorners`. Other properties can be set, depending on the value of the `stroke.style` property.

Property summary for the Stroke object

The following properties are available for the Stroke object:

Property	Description
stroke.breakAtCorners	Same as the Sharp Corners setting in the custom Stroke Style dialog box.
stroke.capType	A string that specifies the type of cap for the stroke.
stroke.color	A string, hexadecimal value, or integer that represents the stroke color.
stroke.curve	A string that specifies type of hatching for the stroke.
stroke.dash1	An integer that specifies the lengths of the solid part of a dashed line.
stroke.dash2	An integer that specifies the lengths of the blank part of a dashed line.
stroke.density	A string that specifies the density of a stippled line.
stroke.dotSize	A string that specifies the dot size of a stippled line.
stroke.dotSpace	An integer that specifies the spacing between dots in a dotted line.
stroke.hatchThickness	A string that specifies the thickness of a hatch line.

Property	Description
stroke.jiggle	A string that specifies the jiggle property of a hatched line.
stroke.joinType	A string that specifies the type of join for the stroke.
stroke.length	A string that specifies the length of a hatch line.
stroke.miterLimit	A float value that specifies the angle above which the tip of the miter will be truncated by a segment.
stroke.pattern	A string that specifies the pattern of a ragged line.
stroke.rotate	A string that specifies the rotation of a hatch line.
stroke.scaleType	A string that specifies the type of scale to be applied to the stroke.
stroke.shapeFill	A Fill object that represents the fill settings of the stroke.
stroke.space	A string that specifies the spacing of a hatched line.
stroke.strokeHinting	A Boolean value that specifies whether stroke hinting is set on the stroke.
stroke.style	A string that describes the stroke style.
stroke.thickness	An integer that specifies the stroke size.
stroke.variation	A string that specifies the variation of a stippled line.
stroke.waveHeight	A string that specifies the wave height of a ragged line.
stroke.waveLength	A string that specifies the wave length of a ragged line.

stroke.breakAtCorners

Availability

Flash MX 2004.

Usage

stroke.breakAtCorners

Description

Property; a Boolean value. This property is the same as the Sharp Corners setting in the custom Stroke Style dialog box.

Example

The following example sets the `breakAtCorners` property to `true`:

```
var myStroke = fl.getDocumentDOM().getCustomStroke();
myStroke.breakAtCorners = true;
fl.getDocumentDOM().setCustomStroke( myStroke );
```

stroke.capType

Availability

Flash 8.

Usage

```
stroke.capType
```

Description

Property; a string that specifies the type of cap for the stroke. Acceptable values are `"none"`, `"round"`, and `"square"`.

Example

The following example sets the stroke cap type to `"round"`:

```
var myStroke = fl.getDocumentDOM().getCustomStroke();
myStroke.capType = "round";
fl.getDocumentDOM().setCustomStroke(myStroke);
```

stroke.color

Availability

Flash MX 2004.

Usage

```
stroke.color
```

Description

Property; the color of the stroke, in one of the following formats:

- A string in the format `"#RRGGBB"` or `"#RRGGBBAA"`
- A hexadecimal number in the format `0xRRGGBB`
- An integer that represents the decimal equivalent of a hexadecimal number

Example

The following example sets the stroke color:

```
var myStroke = fl.getDocumentDOM().getCustomStroke();
myStroke.color = "#000000";
fl.getDocumentDOM().setCustomStroke( myStroke );
```

stroke.curve

Availability

Flash MX 2004.

Usage

```
stroke.curve
```

Description

Property; a string that specifies type of hatching for the stroke. This property can be set only if the `stroke.style` property is `"hatched"` (see `stroke.style`). Acceptable values are `"straight"`, `"slight curve"`, `"medium curve"`, and `"very curved"`.

Example

The following example sets the curve property, as well as others, for a stroke having the `"hatched"` style:

```
var myStroke = fl.getDocumentDOM().getCustomStroke();
myStroke.style = "hatched";
myStroke.curve = "straight";
myStroke.space = "close";
myStroke.jiggle = "wild";
myStroke.rotate = "free";
myStroke.length = "slight";
myStroke.hatchThickness = "thin";
fl.getDocumentDOM().setCustomStroke( myStroke );
```

stroke.dash1

Availability

Flash MX 2004.

Usage

```
stroke.dash1
```

Description

Property; an integer that specifies the lengths of the solid parts of a dashed line. This property is available only if the `stroke.style` property is set to "dashed" (see `stroke.style`).

Example

The following example sets the `dash1` and `dash2` properties for a stroke style of `dashed`:

```
var myStroke = fl.getDocumentDOM().getCustomStroke();
myStroke.style = "dashed";
myStroke.dash1 = 1;
myStroke.dash2 = 2;
fl.getDocumentDOM().setCustomStroke( myStroke );
```

stroke.dash2

Availability

Flash MX 2004.

Usage

`stroke.dash2`

Description

Property; an integer that specifies the lengths of the blank parts of a dashed line. This property is available only if the `stroke.style` property is set to "dashed" (see `stroke.style`).

Example

See `stroke.dash1`.

stroke.density

Availability

Flash MX 2004.

Usage

`stroke.density`

Description

Property; a string that specifies the density of a stippled line. This property is available only if the `stroke.style` property is set to "stipple" (see `stroke.style`). Acceptable values are "very dense", "dense", "sparse", and "very sparse".

Example

The following example sets the density property to "`sparse`" for the stroke style of `stipple`:

```
var myStroke = fl.getDocumentDOM().getCustomStroke();
myStroke.style = "stipple";
myStroke.dotSpace= 3;
myStroke.variation = "random sizes";
myStroke.density = "sparse";
fl.getDocumentDOM().setCustomStroke( myStroke );
```

stroke.dotSize

Availability

Flash MX 2004.

Usage

```
stroke.dotSize
```

Description

Property; a string that specifies the dot size of a stippled line. This property is available only if the `stroke.style` property is set to "`stipple`" (see `stroke.style`). Acceptable values are "`tiny`", "`small`", "`medium`", and "`large`".

The following example sets the `dotsize` property to "`tiny`" for the stroke style of `stipple`:

```
var myStroke = fl.getDocumentDOM().getCustomStroke();
myStroke.style = "stipple";
myStroke.dotSpace= 3;
myStroke.dotsize = "tiny";
myStroke.variation = "random sizes";
myStroke.density = "sparse";
fl.getDocumentDOM().setCustomStroke( myStroke );
```

stroke.dotSpace

Availability

Flash MX 2004.

Usage

```
stroke.dotSpace
```

Description

Property; an integer that specifies the spacing between dots in a dotted line. This property is available only if the `stroke.style` property is set to "`dotted`". See `stroke.style`.

Example

The following example sets the `dotSpace` property to 3 for a stroke style of `dotted`:

```
var myStroke = fl.getDocumentDOM().getCustomStroke();
myStroke.style = "dotted";
myStroke.dotSpace= 3;
fl.getDocumentDOM().setCustomStroke( myStroke );
```

stroke.hatchThickness

Availability

Flash MX 2004.

Usage

```
stroke.hatchThickness
```

Description

Property; a string that specifies the thickness of a hatch line. This property is available only if the `stroke.style` property is set to `"hatched"` (see `stroke.style`). Acceptable values are `"hairline"`, `"thin"`, `"medium"`, and `"thick"`.

Example

The following example sets the `hatchThickness` property to `"thin"` for a stroke style of `hatched`:

```
var myStroke = fl.getDocumentDOM().getCustomStroke();
myStroke.style = "hatched";
myStroke.curve = "straight";
myStroke.space = "close";
myStroke.jiggle = "wild";
myStroke.rotate = "free";
myStroke.length = "slight";
myStroke.hatchThickness = "thin";
fl.getDocumentDOM().setCustomStroke( myStroke );
```

stroke.jiggle

Availability

Flash MX 2004.

Usage

```
stroke.jiggle
```

Description

Property; a string that specifies the jiggle property of a hatched line. This property is available only if the `stroke.style` property is set to `"hatched"` (see `stroke.style`). Acceptable values are `"none"`, `"bounce"`, `"loose"`, and `"wild"`.

Example

The following example sets the `jiggle` property to `"wild"` for a stroke style of `hatched`:

```
var myStroke = fl.getDocumentDOM().getCustomStroke();
myStroke.style = "hatched";
myStroke.curve = "straight";
myStroke.space = "close";
myStroke.jiggle = "wild";
myStroke.rotate = "free";
myStroke.length = "slight";
myStroke.hatchThickness = "thin";
fl.getDocumentDOM().setCustomStroke( myStroke );
```

stroke.joinType

Availability

Flash 8.

Usage

`stroke.joinType`

Description

Property; a string that specifies the type of join for the stroke. Acceptable values are `"miter"`, `"round"`, and `"bevel"`.

See also

`stroke.capType`

stroke.length

Availability

Flash MX 2004.

Usage

`stroke.length`

Description

Property; a string that specifies the length of a hatch line. This property is available only if the stroke.style property is set to "hatched" (see stroke.style). Acceptable values are "equal", "slight", "variation", "medium variation", and "random".

Example

The following example sets the length property to "slight" for a stroke style of hatched:

```
var myStroke = fl.getDocumentDOM().getCustomStroke();
myStroke.style = "hatched";
myStroke.curve = "straight";
myStroke.space = "close";
myStroke.jiggle = "wild";
myStroke.rotate = "free";
myStroke.length = "slight";
myStroke.hatchThickness = "thin";
fl.getDocumentDOM().setCustomStroke( myStroke );
```

stroke.miterLimit

Availability

Flash 8.

Usage

```
stroke.miterLimit
```

Description

Property; a float value that specifies the angle above which the tip of the miter will be truncated by a segment. That means the miter is truncated only if the miter angle is greater than the value of miterLimit.

Example

The following example changes the miter limit of the stroke setting to 3. If the miter angle is greater than 3, the miter is truncated.

```
var myStroke = fl.getDocumentDOM().getCustomStroke();
myStroke.miterLimit = 3;
var myStroke = fl.getDocumentDOM().setCustomStroke();
```

stroke.pattern

Availability

Flash MX 2004.

Usage

```
stroke.pattern
```

Description

Property; a string that specifies the pattern of a ragged line. This property is available only if the `stroke.style` property is set to `"ragged"` (see `stroke.style`). Acceptable values are `"solid"`, `"simple"`, `"random"`, `"dotted"`, `"random dotted"`, `"triple dotted"`, and `"random triple dotted"`.

Example

The following example sets the `pattern` property to `"random"` for a stroke style of `ragged`:

```
var myStroke = fl.getDocumentDOM().getCustomStroke();
myStroke.style = "ragged";
myStroke.pattern = "random";
fl.getDocumentDOM().setCustomStroke( myStroke );
```

stroke.rotate

Availability

Flash MX 2004.

Usage

```
stroke.rotate
```

Description

Property; a string that specifies the rotation of a hatch line. This property is available only if the `stroke.style` property is set to `"hatched"` (see `stroke.style`). Acceptable values are `"none"`, `"slight"`, `"medium"`, and `"free"`.

Example

The following example sets the `rotate` property to `"free"` for a style stroke of `hatched`:

```
var myStroke = fl.getDocumentDOM().getCustomStroke();
myStroke.style = "hatched";
myStroke.curve = "straight";
myStroke.space = "close";
myStroke.jiggle = "wild";
myStroke.rotate = "free";
myStroke.length = "slight";
myStroke.hatchThickness = "thin";
```

stroke.scaleType

Availability

Flash 8.

Usage

`stroke.scaleType`

Description

Property; a string that specifies the type of scale to be applied to the stroke. Acceptable values are `"normal"`, `"horizontal"`, `"vertical"`, and `"none"`.

Example

The following example sets the scale type of the stroke to `"horizontal"`:

```
var myStroke = fl.getDocumentDOM().getCustomStroke();
myStroke.scaleType = "horizontal";
fl.getDocumentDOM().setCustomStroke(myStroke);
```

stroke.shapeFill

Availability

Flash 8.

Usage

`stroke.shapeFill`

Description

Property; a Fill object that represents the fill settings of the stroke.

Example

The following example specifies fill settings and then applies them to the stroke:

```
var fill = fl.getDocumentDOM().getCustomFill();
fill.linearGradient = true;
fill.colorArray = [ 00ff00, ff0000, fffff ];
var stroke = fl.getDocumentDOM().getCustomStroke();
stroke.shapeFill = fill;
fl.getDocumentDOM().setCustomStroke(stroke);
```

stroke.space

Availability

Flash MX 2004.

Usage

```
stroke.space
```

Description

Property; a string that specifies the spacing of a hatched line. This property is available only if the stroke.style property is set to "hatched" (see stroke.style). Acceptable values are "very close", "close", "distant", and "very distant".

Example

The following example sets the space property to "close" for a stroke style of hatched:

```
var myStroke = fl.getDocumentDOM().getCustomStroke();
myStroke.style = "hatched";
myStroke.curve = "straight";
myStroke.space = "close";
myStroke.jiggle = "wild";
myStroke.rotate = "free";
myStroke.length = "slight";
myStroke.hatchThickness = "thin";
fl.getDocumentDOM().setCustomStroke( myStroke );
```

stroke.strokeHinting

Availability

Flash 8.

Usage

```
stroke.strokeHinting
```

Description

Property; a Boolean value that specifies whether stroke hinting is set on the stroke.

Example

The following example enables stroke hinting for the stroke:

```
var myStroke = fl.getDocumentDOM().getCustomStroke();
myStroke.strokeHinting = true;
fl.getDocumentDOM().setCustomStroke(myStroke);
```

stroke.style

Availability

Flash MX 2004.

Usage

```
stroke.style
```

Description

Property; a string that describes the stroke style. Acceptable values are `"noStroke"`, `"solid"`, `"dashed"`, `"dotted"`, `"ragged"`, `"stipple"`, and `"hatched"`. Some of these values require additional properties of the stroke object to be set, as described in the following list:

- If value is `"solid"` or `"noStroke"`, there are no other properties.
- If value is `"dashed"`, there are two additional properties: `"dash1"` and `"dash2"`.
- If value is `"dotted"`, there is one additional property: `"dotSpace"`.
- If value is `"ragged"`, there are three additional properties: `"pattern"`, `"waveHeight"`, and `"waveLength"`.
- If value is `"stipple"`, there are three additional properties: `"dotSize"`, `"variation"`, and `"density"`.
- If value is `"hatched"`, there are six additional properties: `"hatchThickness"`, `"space"`, `"jiggle"`, `"rotate"`, `"curve"`, and `"length"`.

Example

The following example sets the stroke style to "`ragged`":

```
var myStroke = fl.getDocumentDOM().getCustomStroke();
myStroke.style = "ragged";
fl.getDocumentDOM().setCustomStroke( myStroke );
```

stroke.thickness

Availability

Flash MX 2004.

Usage

```
stroke.thickness
```

Description

Property; an integer that specifies the stroke size.

Example

The following example sets the `thickness` property of the stroke to a value of 2:

```
var myStroke = fl.getDocumentDOM().getCustomStroke();
myStroke.thickness = 2;
fl.getDocumentDOM().setCustomStroke( myStroke );
```

stroke.variation

Availability

Flash MX 2004.

Usage

```
stroke.variation
```

Description

Property; a string that specifies the variation of a stippled line. This property is available only if the `stroke.style` property is set to "`stipple`" (see `stroke.style`). Acceptable values are "`one size`", "`small variation`", "`varied sizes`", and "`random sizes`".

Example

The following example sets the variation property to "`random sizes`" for a stroke style of `stipple`:

```
var myStroke = fl.getDocumentDOM().getCustomStroke();
myStroke.style = "stipple";
```

```
myStroke.dotSpace= 3;
myStroke.variation = "random sizes";
myStroke.density = "sparse";
fl.getDocumentDOM().setCustomStroke( myStroke );
```

stroke.waveHeight

Availability

Flash MX 2004.

Usage

```
stroke.waveHeight
```

Description

Property; a string that specifies the wave height of a ragged line. This property is available only
if the `stroke.style` property is set to `"ragged"` (see `stroke.style`). Acceptable values are
`"flat"`, `"wavy"`, `"very wavy"`, and `"wild"`.

Example

The following example sets the `waveHeight` property to `"flat"` for a stroke style of `ragged`:

```
var myStroke = fl.getDocumentDOM().getCustomStroke();
myStroke.style = "ragged";
myStroke.pattern = "random";
myStroke.waveHeight = "flat";
myStroke.waveLength = "short";
fl.getDocumentDOM().setCustomStroke( myStroke );
```

stroke.waveLength

Availability

Flash MX 2004.

Usage

```
stroke.waveLength
```

Description

Property; a string that specifies the wave length of a ragged line. This property is available only
if the `stroke.style` property is set to `"ragged"` (see `stroke.style`). Acceptable values are
`"very short"`, `"short"`, `"medium"`, and `"long"`.

Example

The following example sets the waveLength property to "short" for a stroke style of ragged:

```
var myStroke = fl.getDocumentDOM().getCustomStroke();
myStroke.style = "ragged";
myStroke.pattern = "random";
myStroke.waveHeight = 'flat';
myStroke.waveLength = "short";
fl.getDocumentDOM().setCustomStroke( myStroke );
```

SymbolInstance object

Inheritance   Element object > Instance object > SymbolInstance object

Availability
Flash MX 2004.

Description
SymbolInstance is a subclass of the Instance object and represents a symbol in a frame (see Instance object).

Property summary for the SymbolInstance object

In addition to the Instance object properties, the SymbolInstance object has the following properties:

Property	Description
symbolInstance.accName	A string that is equivalent to the Name field in the Accessibility panel.
symbolInstance.actionScript	A string that specifies the actions assigned to the symbol.
symbolInstance.blendMode	A string that specifies the blend mode to be applied to a movie clip symbol.
symbolInstance.buttonTracking	A string that, for button symbols only, sets the same property as the pop-up menu for Track as Button or Track as Menu Item in the Property inspector.
symbolInstance.cacheAsBitmap	A Boolean value that specifies whether runtime bitmap caching is enabled.
symbolInstance.colorAlphaAmount	An integer that is part of the color transformation for the instance, specifying the Advanced Effect Alpha settings; equivalent to using the Color > Advanced setting in the Property inspector and adjusting the controls on the right of the dialog box.
symbolInstance.colorAlphaPercent	An integer that specifies part of the color transformation for the instance; equivalent to using the Color > Advanced setting in the instance Property inspector (the percentage controls on the left of the dialog box).
symbolInstance.colorBlueAmount	An integer that is part of the color transformation for the instance; equivalent to using the Color > Advanced setting in the instance Property inspector.

Property	Description
symbolInstance.colorBluePercent	An integer that is part of the color transformation for the instance; equivalent to using the Color › Advanced setting in the instance Property inspector (the percentage controls on the left of the dialog box).
symbolInstance.colorGreenAmount	An integer that is part of the color transformation for the instance; equivalent to using the Color › Advanced setting in the instance Property inspector. Allowable values are from -255 to 255.
symbolInstance.colorGreenPercent	Part of the color transformation for the instance; equivalent to using the Color › Advanced setting in the instance Property inspector (the percentage controls on the left of the dialog box).
symbolInstance.colorMode	A string that specifies the color mode as identified in the symbol Property inspector Color pop-up menu.
symbolInstance.colorRedAmount	An integer that is part of the color transformation for the instance, equivalent to using the Color › Advanced setting in the instance Property inspector.
symbolInstance.colorRedPercent	Part of the color transformation for the instance; equivalent to using the Color › Advanced setting in the instance Property inspector (the percentage controls on the left of the dialog box).
symbolInstance.description	A string that is equivalent to the Description field in the Accessibility panel.
symbolInstance.filters	An array of Filter objects (see Filter object).
symbolInstance.firstFrame	A zero-based integer that specifies the first frame to appear in the timeline of the graphic.
symbolInstance.forceSimple	A Boolean value that enables and disables the accessibility of the object's children; equivalent to the inverse logic of the Make Child Objects Accessible setting in the Accessibility panel.
symbolInstance.loop	A string that, for graphic symbols, sets the same property as the Loop pop-up menu in the Property inspector.
symbolInstance.shortcut	A string that is equivalent to the shortcut key associated with the symbol; equivalent to the Shortcut field in the Accessibility panel.

Property	Description
symbolInstance.silent	A Boolean value that enables or disables the accessibility of the object; equivalent to the inverse logic of the Make Object Accessible setting in the Accessibility panel.
symbolInstance.symbolType	A string that specifies the type of symbol; equivalent to the value for Behavior in the Create New Symbol and Convert To Symbol dialog boxes.
symbolInstance.tabIndex	An integer that is equivalent to the Tab index field in the Accessibility panel.

symbolInstance.accName

Availability

Flash MX 2004.

Usage

```
symbolInstance.accName
```

Description

Property; a string that is equivalent to the Name field in the Accessibility panel. Screen readers identify objects by reading the name aloud. This property is not available for graphic symbols.

Example

The following example stores the value for the Accessibility panel name of the object in the theName variable:

```
var theName = fl.getDocumentDOM().selection[0].accName;
```

The following example sets the value for the Accessibility panel name of the object to "Home Button":

```
fl.getDocumentDOM().selection[0].accName = "Home Button";
```

symbolInstance.actionScript

Availability

Flash MX 2004.

Usage

```
symbolInstance.actionScript
```

Description

Property; a string that specifies the actions assigned to the symbol. This applies only to movie clip and button instances. For a graphic symbol instance, the value returns undefined.

Example

The following example assigns an `onClipEvent` action to the first item in the first frame of the first layer in the timeline:

```
fl.getDocumentDOM().getTimeline().layers[0].frames[0].elements[0].actionScr
  ipt
  = "onClipEvent(enterFrame) {trace('movie clip enterFrame');}";
```

symbolInstance.blendMode

Availability

Flash 8.

Usage

```
symbolInstance.blendMode
```

Description

Property; a string that specifies the blend mode to be applied to a movie clip symbol. Acceptable values are `"normal"`, `"layer"`, `"multiply"`, `"screen"`, `"overlay"`, `"hardlight"`, `"lighten"`, `"darken"`, `"difference"`, `"add"`, `"subtract"`, `"invert"`, `"alpha"`, and `"erase"`.

Example

The following example sets the blend mode for the first movie clip symbol in the first frame on the first level to `"add"`:

```
fl.getDocumentDOM().getTimeline().layers[0].frames[0].elements[0].blendMode
  = 'add';
```

See also

```
document.setBlendMode()
```

symbolInstance.buttonTracking

Availability

Flash MX 2004.

Usage

```
symbolInstance.buttonTracking
```

Description

Property; a string that, for button symbols only, sets the same property as the pop-up menu for Track as Button or Track as Menu Item in the Property inspector. For other types of symbols, this property is ignored. Acceptable values are `"button"` or `"menu"`.

Example

The following example sets the first symbol in the first frame of the first layer in the timeline to Track as Menu Item, as long as that symbol is a button:

```
fl.getDocumentDOM().getTimeline().layers[0].frames[0].elements[0].buttonTra
  cking = "menu";
```

symbolInstance.cacheAsBitmap

Availability

Flash 8.

Usage

```
symbolInstance.cacheAsBitmap
```

Description

Property; a Boolean value that specifies whether runtime bitmap caching is enabled.

Example

The following example enables runtime bitmap caching for the first element in the first frame on the first layer:

```
fl.getDocumentDOM().getTimeline().layers[0].frames[0].elements[0].cacheAsBi
  tmap = true;
```

symbolInstance.colorAlphaAmount

Availability

Flash MX 2004.

Usage

```
symbolInstance.colorAlphaAmount
```

Description

Property; an integer that is part of the color transformation for the instance, specifying the Advanced Effect Alpha settings. This property is equivalent to using the Color > Advanced setting in the Property inspector and adjusting the controls on the right of the dialog box. This value either reduces or increases the tint and alpha values by a constant amount. This value is added to the current value. This property is most useful if used with `symbolInstance.colorAlphaPercent`. Allowable values are from -255 to 255.

Example

The following example subtracts 100 from the alpha setting of the selected symbol instance:

```
fl.getDocumentDOM().selection[0].colorAlphaAmount = -100;
```

symbolInstance.colorAlphaPercent

Availability

Flash MX 2004.

Usage

```
symbolInstance.colorAlphaPercent
```

Description

Property; an integer that specifies part of the color transformation for the instance. This property is equivalent to using the Color > Advanced setting in the instance Property inspector (the percentage controls on the left of the dialog box). This value changes the tint and alpha values to a specified percentage. Allowable values are from -100 to 100. See also `symbolInstance.colorAlphaAmount`.

Example

The following example sets the `colorAlphaPercent` of the selected symbol instance to 80:

```
fl.getDocumentDOM().selection[0].colorAlphaPercent = 80;
```

symbolInstance.colorBlueAmount

Availability

Flash MX 2004.

Usage

```
symbolInstance.colorBlueAmount
```

Description

Property; an integer that is part of the color transformation for the instance. This property is equivalent to using the Color > Advanced setting in the instance Property inspector. Allowable values are from -255 to 255.

symbolInstance.colorBluePercent

Availability

Flash MX 2004.

Usage

```
symbolInstance.colorBluePercent
```

Description

Property; an integer that is part of the color transformation for the instance. This property is equivalent to using the Color > Advanced setting in the instance Property inspector (the percentage controls on the left of the dialog box). This value sets the blue values to a specified percentage. Allowable values are from -100 to 100.

Example

The following example sets the `colorBluePercent` of the selected symbol instance to 80:

```
fl.getDocumentDOM().selection[0].colorBluePercent = 80;
```

symbolInstance.colorGreenAmount

Availability

Flash MX 2004.

Usage

```
symbolInstance.colorGreenAmount
```

Description

Property; an integer that is part of the color transformation for the instance. This property is equivalent to using the Color > Advanced setting in the instance Property inspector. Allowable values are from -255 to 255.

symbolInstance.colorGreenPercent

Availability

Flash MX 2004.

Usage

```
symbolInstance.colorGreenPercent
```

Description

Property; part of the color transformation for the instance. This property is equivalent to using the Color > Advanced setting in the instance Property inspector (the percentage controls on the left of the dialog box). This value sets the green values by a specified percentage. Allowable values are from -100 to 100.

Example

The following example sets the `colorGreenPercent` of the selected symbol instance to 70:

```
fl.getDocumentDOM().selection[0].colorGreenPercent = 70;
```

symbolInstance.colorMode

Availability

Flash MX 2004.

Usage

```
symbolInstance.colorMode
```

Description

Property; a string that specifies the color mode as identified in the symbol Property inspector Color pop-up menu. Acceptable values are `"none"`, `"brightness"`, `"tint"`, `"alpha"`, and `"advanced"`.

Example

The following example changes the `colorMode` property of the first element in the first frame of the first layer in the timeline to `"alpha"`:

```
fl.getDocumentDOM().getTimeline().layers[0].frames[0].elements[0].colorMode
  = "alpha";
```

symbolInstance.colorRedAmount

Availability

Flash MX 2004.

Usage

`symbolInstance.colorRedAmount`

Description

Property; an integer that is part of the color transformation for the instance. This property is equivalent to using the Color > Advanced setting in the instance Property inspector. Allowable values are from -255 to 255.

Example

The following example sets the `colorRedAmount` of the selected symbol instance to 255:

```
fl.getDocumentDOM().selection[0].colorRedAmount = 255;
```

symbolInstance.colorRedPercent

Availability

Flash MX 2004.

Usage

`symbolInstance.colorRedPercent`

Description

Property; part of the color transformation for the instance. This property is equivalent to using the Color > Advanced setting in the instance Property inspector (the percentage controls on the left of the dialog box). This value sets the red values to a specified percentage. Allowable values are from -100 to 100.

Example

The following example sets the `colorRedPercent` of the selected symbol instance to 10:

```
fl.getDocumentDOM().selection[0].colorRedPercent = 10;
```

symbolInstance.description

Availability

Flash MX 2004.

Usage

```
symbolInstance.description
```

Description

Property; a string that is equivalent to the Description field in the Accessibility panel. The description is read by the screen reader. This property is not available for graphic symbols.

Example

The following example stores the value for the Accessibility panel description of the object in the theDescription variable:

```
var theDescription = fl.getDocumentDOM().selection[0].description;
```

The following example sets the value for the Accessibility panel description to "Click the home button to go to home":

```
fl.getDocumentDOM().selection[0].description= "Click the home button to go
    to home";
```

symbolInstance.filters

Availability

Flash 8.

Usage

```
symbolInstance.filters
```

Description

Property; an array of Filter objects (see Filter object). To modify filter properties, you don't write to this array directly. Instead, retrieve the array, set the individual properties, and then set the array to reflect the new properties.

Example

The following example traces the name of the filter at index 0. If it is a Glow filter, its `blurX` property is set to 100 and the new value is written to the filters array.

```
var filterName =
    fl.getDocumentDOM().getTimeline().layers[0].frames[0].elements[0].filter
    s[0].name;
fl.trace(filterName);
var filterArray =
    fl.getDocumentDOM().getTimeline().layers[0].frames[0].elements[0].filter
    s;
if (filterName == 'glowFilter'){
    filterArray[0].blurX = 100;
}
fl.getDocumentDOM().getTimeline().layers[0].frames[0].elements[0].filters =
    filterArray;
```

symbolInstance.firstFrame

Availability

Flash MX 2004.

Usage

```
symbolInstance.firstFrame
```

Description

Property; a zero-based integer that specifies the first frame to appear in the timeline of the graphic. This property applies only to graphic symbols and sets the same property as the First field in the Property inspector. For other types of symbols, this property is `undefined`.

Example

The following example specifies that Frame 11 should be the first frame to appear in the timeline of the specified element:

```
fl.getDocumentDOM().getTimeline().layers[0].frames[0].elements[0].firstFram
    e = 10;
```

symbolInstance.forceSimple

Availability

Flash MX 2004.

Usage

```
symbolInstance.forceSimple
```

Description

Property; a Boolean value that enables and disables the accessibility of the object's children. This property is equivalent to the inverse logic of the Make Child Objects Accessible setting in the Accessibility panel. For example, if forceSimple is true, it is the same as the Make Child Object Accessible option being unchecked. If forceSimple is false, it is the same as the Make Child Object Accessible option being checked.

This property is available only for movie clip objects.

Example

The following example checks to see if the children of the object are accessible; a return value of false means the children are accessible:

```
var areChildrenAccessible = fl.getDocumentDOM().selection[0].forceSimple;
```

The following example allows the children of the object to be accessible:

```
fl.getDocumentDOM().selection[0].forceSimple = false;
```

symbolInstance.loop

Availability

Flash MX 2004.

Usage

```
symbolInstance.loop
```

Description

Property; a string that, for graphic symbols, sets the same property as the Loop pop-up menu in the Property inspector. For other types of symbols, this property is undefined. Acceptable values are "loop", "play once", and "single frame" to set the graphic's animation accordingly.

Example

The following example sets the first symbol in the first frame of the first layer in the timeline to Single Frame (display one specified frame of the graphic timeline), as long as that symbol is a graphic:

```
fl.getDocumentDOM().getTimeline().layers[0].frames[0].elements[0].loop =
  'single frame';
```

symbolInstance.shortcut

Availability

Flash MX 2004.

Usage

```
symbolInstance.shortcut
```

Description

Property; a string that is equivalent to the shortcut key associated with the symbol. This property is equivalent to the Shortcut field in the Accessibility panel. This key is read by the screen readers. This property is not available for graphic symbols.

Example

The following example stores the value for the shortcut key of the object in the theShortcut variable:

```
var theShortcut = fl.getDocumentDOM().selection[0].shortcut;
```

The following example sets the shortcut key of the object to "Ctrl+i":

```
fl.getDocumentDOM().selection[0].shortcut = "Ctrl+i";
```

symbolInstance.silent

Availability

Flash MX 2004.

Usage

```
symbolInstance.silent
```

Description

Property; a Boolean value that enables or disables the accessibility of the object. This property is equivalent to the inverse logic of the Make Object Accessible setting in the Accessibility panel. For example, if `silent` is `true`, it is the same as the Make Object Accessible option being unchecked. If `silent` is `false`, it is the same as the Make Object Accessible option being checked.

This property is not available for graphic objects.

Example

The following example checks to see if the object is accessible; a return value of `false` means the object is accessible:

```
var isSilent = fl.getDocumentDOM().selection[0].silent;
```

The following example sets the object to be accessible:

```
fl.getDocumentDOM().selection[0].silent = false;
```

symbolInstance.symbolType

Availability

Flash MX 2004.

Usage

```
symbolInstance.symbolType
```

Description

Property; a string that specifies the type of symbol. This property is equivalent to the value for Behavior in the Create New Symbol and Convert To Symbol dialog boxes. Acceptable values are `"button"`, `"movie clip"`, and `"graphic"`.

Example

The following example sets the first symbol in the first frame of the first layer in the timeline of the current document to behave as a graphic symbol:

```
fl.getDocumentDOM().getTimeline().layers[0].frames[0].elements[0].symbolTyp
  e = "graphic";
```

symbolInstance.tabIndex

Availability

Flash MX 2004.

Usage

```
symbolInstance.tabIndex
```

Description

Property; an integer that is equivalent to the Tab index field in the Accessibility panel. Creates a tab order in which objects are accessed when the user presses the Tab key. This property is not available for graphic symbols.

Example

The following example sets the tabIndex property of the mySymbol object to 3 and displays that value in the Output panel:

```
var mySymbol = fl.getDocumentDOM().selection[0];
mySymbol.tabIndex = 3;
fl.trace(mySymbol.tabIndex);
```

SymbolItem object

Inheritance   Item object > SymbolItem object

Availability

Flash MX 2004.

Description

The SymbolItem object is a subclass of the Item object.

Method summary for the SymbolItem object

In addition to the Item object methods, you can use the following methods with the SymbolItem object:

Method	Description
symbolItem.convertToCompiledClip()	Converts a symbol item in the library to a compiled movie clip.
symbolItem.exportSWC()	Exports the symbol item to a SWC file.
symbolItem.exportSWF()	Exports the symbol item to a SWF file.

Property summary for the SymbolItem object

In addition to the Item object properties, the following properties are available for the SymbolItem object:

Property	Description
symbolItem.scalingGrid	A Boolean value that specifies whether 9-slice scaling is enabled for the item.
symbolItem.scalingGridRect	A Boolean value that specifies whether 9-slice scaling is enabled for the item.
symbolItem.sourceAutoUpdate	A Boolean value that specifies whether the item is updated when the FLA file is published.
symbolItem.sourceFilePath	A string that specifies the path for the source FLA file as a file:/// URI.
symbolItem.sourceLibraryName	A string that specifies the name of the item in the source file library.

Property	Description
symbolItem.symbolType	A string that specifies the type of symbol.
symbolItem.timeline	Read-only; a Timeline object.

symbolItem.convertToCompiledClip()

Availability

Flash MX 2004.

Usage

```
symbolItem.convertToCompiledClip()
```

Parameters

None.

Returns

Nothing.

Description

Method; converts a symbol item in the library to a compiled movie clip.

Example

The following example converts an item in the library to a compiled movie clip:

```
fl.getDocumentDOM().library.items[3].convertToCompiledClip();
```

symbolItem.exportSWC()

Availability

Flash MX 2004.

Usage

```
symbolItem.exportSWC( outputURI )
```

Parameters

outputURI   A string, expressed as a file:/// URI, that specifies the SWC file to which the method will export the symbol. The *outputURI* must reference a local file. Flash does not create a folder if *outputURI* does not exist.

Returns

Nothing.

Description

Method; exports the symbol item to a SWC file.

Example

The following example exports an item in the library to the SWC file named my.swc in the tests folder:

```
fl.getDocumentDOM().library.items[0].exportSWC("file:///c|/tests/my.swc");
```

symbolItem.exportSWF()

Availability

Flash MX 2004.

Usage

```
symbolItem.exportSWF( outputURI )
```

Parameters

outputURI   A string, expressed as a file:/// URI, that specifies the SWF file to which the method will export the symbol. The *outputURI* must reference a local file. Flash does not create a folder if *outputURI* doesn't exist.

Returns

Nothing.

Description

Method; exports the symbol item to a SWF file.

Example

The following example exports an item in the library to the my.swf file in the tests folder:

```
fl.getDocumentDOM().library.items[0].exportSWF("file:///c|/tests/my.swf");
```

symbolItem.scalingGrid

Availability

Flash 8.

Usage

```
symbolItem.scalingGrid
```

Description

Property; a Boolean value that specifies whether 9-slice scaling is enabled for the item.

Example

The following example enables 9-slice scaling for an item in the library:

```
fl.getDocumentDOM().library.items[0].scalingGrid = true;
```

See also

```
symbolItem.scalingGridRect
```

symbolItem.scalingGridRect

Availability

Flash 8.

Usage

```
symbolItem.scalingGridRect
```

Description

Property; a rectangle object that specifies the locations of the four 9-slice guides. For information on the format of the rectangle, see `document.addNewRectangle()`.

Example

The following example specifies the locations of the 9-slice guides:

```
fl.getDocumentDOM().library.items[0].scalingGridRect = {left:338, top:237,
   right:3859, bottom:713};
```

See also

```
symbolItem.scalingGrid
```

symbolItem.sourceAutoUpdate

Availability

Flash MX 2004.

Usage

```
symbolItem.sourceAutoUpdate
```

Description

Property; a Boolean value that specifies whether the item is updated when the FLA file is published. The default value is `false`. Used for shared library symbols.

Example

The following example sets the `sourceAutoUpdate` property for a library item:

```
fl.getDocumentDOM().library.items[0].sourceAutoUpdate = true;
```

symbolItem.sourceFilePath

Availability

Flash MX 2004.

Usage

```
symbolItem.sourceFilePath
```

Description

Property; a string that specifies the path for the source FLA file as a file:/// URI. The path must be an absolute path, not a relative path. This property is used for shared library symbols.

Example

The following example shows the value of the `sourceFilePath` property in the Output panel:

```
fl.trace(fl.getDocumentDOM().library.items[0].sourceFilePath);
```

symbolItem.sourceLibraryName

Availability

Flash MX 2004.

Usage

```
symbolItem.sourceLibraryName
```

Description

Property; a string that specifies the name of the item in the source file library. It is used for shared library symbols.

Example

The following example shows the value of the sourceLibraryName property in the Output panel:

```
fl.trace(fl.getDocumentDOM().library.items[0].sourceLibraryName);
```

symbolItem.symbolType

Availability

Flash MX 2004.

Usage

```
symbolItem.symbolType
```

Description

Property; a string that specifies the type of symbol. Acceptable values are "movie clip", "button", and "graphic".

Example

The following example shows the current value of the symbolType property, changes it to "button", and shows it again:

```
alert(fl.getDocumentDOM().library.items[0].symbolType);
fl.getDocumentDOM().library.items[0].symbolType = "button";
alert(fl.getDocumentDOM().library.items[0].symbolType);
```

symbolltem.timeline

Availability

Flash MX 2004.

Usage

```
symbolItem.timeline
```

Description

Read-only property; a Timeline object.

Example

The following example obtains and shows the number of layers that the selected movie clip in the library contains:

```
var tl = fl.getDocumentDOM().library.getSelectedItems()[0].timeline;
alert(tl.layerCount);
```

Text object

Inheritance   Element object > Text object

Availability

Flash MX 2004.

Description

The Text object represents a single text item in a document. All properties of the text pertain to the entire text block.

To set properties of a text run within the text field, see "Property summary for the TextRun object" on page 467. To change properties of a selection within a text field, you can use `document.setElementTextAttr()` and specify a range of text, or use the current selection.

To set text properties of the selected text field, use `document.setElementProperty()`. The following example assigns the currently selected text field to the variable `textVar`:

`fl.getDocumentDOM().setElementProperty("variableName", "textVar");`

Method summary for the Text object

In addition to the Element object methods, you can use the following methods with the Text object:

Method	Description
`text.getTextAttr()`	Retrieves the specified attribute for the text identified by the optional `startIndex` and `endIndex` parameters.
`text.getTextString()`	Retrieves the specified range of text.
`text.setTextAttr()`	Sets the specified attribute associated with the text identified by `startIndex` and `endIndex`.
`text.setTextString()`	Changes the text string within this text object.

Property summary for the Text object

In addition to the Element object properties, the following properties are available for the Text object:

Property	Description
text.accName	A string that is equivalent to the Name field in the Accessibility panel.
text.antiAliasSharpness	A float value that specifies the anti-aliasing sharpness of the text.
text.antiAliasThickness	A float value that specifies the anti-aliasing thickness of the text.
text.autoExpand	A Boolean value that controls the expansion of the bounding width for static text fields or the bounding width and height for dynamic or input text.
text.border	A Boolean value that controls whether Flash shows (true) or hides (false) a border around dynamic or input text.
text.description	A string that is equivalent to the Description field in the Accessibility panel.
text.embeddedCharacters	A string that specifies characters to embed. This is equivalent to entering text in the Character Options dialog box.
text.embedRanges	A string that consists of delimited integers that correspond to the items that can be selected in the Character Options dialog box.
text.fontRenderingMode	A string that specifies the rendering mode for the text.
text.length	Read-only; an integer that represents the number of characters in the text object.
text.lineType	A string that sets the line type to "single line", "multiline", "multiline no wrap", or "password".
text.maxCharacters	An integer that specifies the maximum characters the user can enter into this text object.
text.orientation	A string that specifies the orientation of the text field.
text.renderAsHTML	A Boolean value that controls whether Flash draws the text as HTML and interprets embedded HTML tags.
text.scrollable	A Boolean value that controls whether the text can (true) or cannot (false) be scrolled.
text.selectable	A Boolean value that controls whether the text can (true) or cannot (false) be selected. Input text is always selectable.

Property	Description
text.selectionEnd	A zero-based integer that specifies the offset of the end of a text subselection.
text.selectionStart	A zero-based integer that specifies the offset of the beginning of a text subselection.
text.shortcut	A string that is equivalent to the Shortcut field in the Accessibility panel.
text.silent	A Boolean value that specifies whether the object is accessible.
text.tabIndex	An integer that is equivalent to the Tab Index field in the Accessibility panel.
text.textRuns	Read-only; an array of TextRun objects.
text.textType	A string that specifies the type of text field. Acceptable values are "static", "dynamic", and "input".
text.useDeviceFonts	A Boolean value. A value of true causes Flash to draw text using device fonts.
text.variableName	A string that contains the contents of the text object.

text.antiAliasSharpness

Availability
Flash 8.

Usage
text.antiAliasSharpness

Description
Property; a float value that specifies the anti-aliasing sharpness of the text. This property controls how crisply the text is drawn; higher values specify sharper (or crisper) text. A value of 0 specifies normal sharpness. This property is available only if text.fontRenderingMode is set to "customThicknessSharpness".

Example
See text.fontRenderingMode.

See also
text.antiAliasThickness, text.fontRenderingMode

text.antiAliasThickness

Availability

Flash 8.

Usage

```
text.antiAliasThickness
```

Description

Property; a float value that specifies the anti-aliasing thickness of the text. This property controls how thickly the text is drawn, with higher values specifying thicker text. A value of 0 specifies normal thickness. This property is available only if `text.fontRenderingMode` is set to `"customThicknessSharpness"`.

Example

See `text.fontRenderingMode`.

See also

`text.antiAliasSharpness`, `text.fontRenderingMode`

text.accName

Availability

Flash MX 2004.

Usage

```
text.accName
```

Description

Property; a string that is equivalent to the Name field in the Accessibility panel. Screen readers identify objects by reading the name aloud. This property cannot be used with dynamic text.

Example

The following example retrieves the name of the object:

```
var theName =
  fl.getDocumentDOM().getTimeline().layers[0].frames[0].elements[0].accNam
  e;
```

The following example sets the name of the currently selected object:

```
fl.getDocumentDOM().selection[0].accName = "Home Button";
```

text.autoExpand

Availability

Flash MX 2004.

Usage

```
text.autoExpand
```

Description

Property; a Boolean value. For static text fields, a value of true causes the bounding width to expand to show all text. For dynamic or input text fields, a value of true causes the bounding width and height to expand to show all text.

Example

The following example sets the autoExpand property to a value of true:

```
fl.getDocumentDOM().selection[0].autoExpand = true;
```

text.border

Availability

Flash MX 2004.

Usage

```
text.border
```

Description

Property; a Boolean value. A value of true causes Flash to show a border around text.

Example

The following example sets the border property to a value of true:

```
fl.getDocumentDOM().getTimeline().layers[0].frames[0].elements[0].border =
    true;
```

text.description

Availability

Flash MX 2004.

Usage

```
text.description
```

Description

Property; a string that is equivalent to the Description field in the Accessibility panel. The description is read by the screen reader.

Example

The following example retrieves the description of the object:

```
var theDescription =
  fl.getDocumentDOM().getTimeline().layers[0].frames[0].elements[0].descri
  ption;
```

The following example sets the description of the object:

```
fl.getDocumentDOM().getTimeline().layers[0].frames[0].elements[0].descripti
  on= "Enter your name here";
```

text.embeddedCharacters

Availability

Flash MX 2004.

Usage

```
text.embeddedCharacters
```

Description

Property; a string that specifies characters to embed. This is equivalent to entering text in the Character Options dialog box.

This property works only with dynamic or input text; it generates a warning if used with other text types.

Example

The following example sets the embeddedCharacters property to "abc":

```
fl.getDocumentDOM().selection[0].embeddedCharacters = "abc";
```

text.embedRanges

Availability

Flash MX 2004.

Usage

```
text.embedRanges
```

Description

Property; a string that consists of delimited integers that correspond to the items that can be selected in the Character Options dialog box. This property works only with dynamic or input text; it is ignored if used with static text.

 NOTE This property corresponds to the XML file in the Configuration/Font Embedding folder.

Example

The following example sets the `embedRanges` property to `"1|3|7"`:

```
fl.getDocumentDOM().getTimeline().layers[0].frames[0].elements[0].embedRang
    es = "1|3|7";
```

The following example resets the property:

```
fl.getDocumentDOM().getTimeline().layers[0].frames[0].elements[0].embedRang
    es = "";
```

text.fontRenderingMode

Availability

Flash 8.

Usage

```
text.fontRenderingMode
```

Description

Property; a string that specifies the rendering mode for the text. This property affects how the text is displayed both on the Stage and in Flash Player. Acceptable values are described in the following table.

Property value	How text is rendered
device	Renders the text with device fonts.
bitmap	Renders aliased text as a bitmap, or as a pixel font would.
standard	Renders text using the standard anti-aliasing method used by Flash MX 2004. This is the best setting to use for animated, very large, or skewed text.

Property value	How text is rendered
advanced	Renders text using the FlashType font rendering technology implemented in Flash 8, which produces better anti-aliasing and improves readability, especially for small text.
customThicknessSharpness	Lets you specify custom settings for the sharpness and thickness of the text when using the FlashType font rendering technology implemented in Flash 8.

Example

The following example shows how you can use the customThicknessSharpness value to specify the sharpness and thickness of the text:

```
fl.getDocumentDOM().setElementProperty("fontRenderingMode",
  "customThicknessSharpness");
fl.getDocumentDOM().setElementProperty("antiAliasSharpness", 400);
fl.getDocumentDOM().setElementProperty("antiAliasThickness", -200);
```

See also

text.antiAliasSharpness, text.antiAliasThickness

text.getTextAttr()

Availability

Flash MX 2004.

Usage

```
text.getTextAttr(attrName [, startIndex [, endIndex]])
```

Parameters

attrName   A string that specifies the name of the TextAttrs object property to be returned.

> **NOTE** For a list of possible values for attrName, see Property summary for the TextAttrs object.

startIndex   An integer that is the index of first character. This parameter is optional.

endIndex   An integer that specifies the end of the range of text, which starts with startIndex and goes up to, but does not include, endIndex. This parameter is optional.

Returns

The value of the attribute specified in the attrName parameter.

Description

Method; retrieves the attribute specified by the *attrName* parameter for the text identified by the optional *startIndex* and *endIndex* parameters. If the attribute is not consistent for the specified range, Flash returns undefined. If you omit the optional parameters *startIndex* and *endIndex*, the method uses the entire text range. If you specify only *startIndex*, the range used is a single character at that position. If you specify both *startIndex* and *endIndex*, the range starts from *startIndex* and goes up to, but does not include, *endIndex*.

Example

The following example gets the font size of the currently selected text field and shows it:

```
var TheTextSize = fl.getDocumentDOM().selection[0].getTextAttr("size");
fl.trace(TheTextSize);
```

The following example gets the text fill color of the selected text field:

```
var TheFill = fl.getDocumentDOM().selection[0].getTextAttr("fillColor");
fl.trace(TheFill);
```

The following example gets the size of the third character:

```
var Char2 = fl.getDocumentDOM().selection[0].getTextAttr("size", 2);
fl.trace(Char2);
```

The following example gets the color of the selected text field from the third through the eighth character:

```
fl.getDocumentDOM().selection[0].getTextAttr("fillColor", 2, 8);
```

text.getTextString()

Availability

Flash MX 2004.

Usage

```
text.getTextString([startIndex [, endIndex] ])
```

Parameters

startIndex   An integer that specifies the index (zero-based) of the first character. This parameter is optional.

endIndex   An integer that specifies the end of the range of text, which starts from *startIndex* and goes up to, but does not include, *endIndex*. This parameter is optional.

Returns

A string of the text in the specified range.

Description

Method; retrieves the specified range of text. If you omit the optional parameters *startIndex* and *endIndex*, the whole text string is returned. If you specify only *startIndex*, the method returns the string starting at the index location and ending at the end of the field. If you specify both *startIndex* and *endIndex*, the method returns the string starts from *startIndex* and goes up to, but does not include, *endIndex*.

Example

The following example gets the character(s) from the fifth character through the end of the selected text field:

```
var myText = fl.getDocumentDOM().selection[0].getTextString(4);
fl.trace(myText);
```

The following example gets the fourth through the ninth characters starting in the selected text field:

```
var myText = fl.getDocumentDOM().selection[0].getTextString(3, 9);
fl.trace(myText);
```

text.length

Availability

Flash MX 2004.

Usage

```
text.length
```

Description

Read-only property; an integer that represents the number of characters in the text object.

Example

The following example returns the number of characters in the selected text:

```
var textLength = fl.getDocumentDOM().selection[0].length;
```

text.lineType

Availability

Flash MX 2004.

Usage

```
text.lineType
```

Description

Property; a string that sets the line type. Acceptable values are `"single line"`, `"multiline"`, `"multiline no wrap"`, and `"password"`.

This property works only with dynamic or input text and generates a warning if used with static text. The `"password"` value works only for input text.

Example

The following example sets the `lineType` property to the value `"multiline no wrap"`:

```
fl.getDocumentDOM().selection[0].lineType = "multiline no wrap";
```

text.maxCharacters

Availability

Flash MX 2004.

Usage

```
text.maxCharacters
```

Description

Property; an integer that specifies the maximum number of characters the user can enter in this text object.

This property works only with input text; if used with other text types, the property generates a warning.

Example

The following example sets the value of the `maxCharacters` property to 30:

```
fl.getDocumentDOM().selection[0].maxCharacters = 30;
```

text.orientation

Availability

Flash MX 2004.

Usage

```
text.orientation
```

Description

Property; a string that specifies the orientation of the text field. Acceptable values are
`"horizontal"`, `"vertical left to right"`, and `"vertical right to left"`.

This property works only with static text; it generates a warning if used with other text types.

Example

The following example sets the orientation property to `"vertical right to left"`:

```
fl.getDocumentDOM().getTimeline().layers[0].frames[0].elements[0].orientati
  on = "vertical right to left";
```

text.renderAsHTML

Availability

Flash MX 2004.

Usage

```
text.renderAsHTML
```

Description

Property; a Boolean value. If the value is `true`, Flash draws the text as HTML and interprets
embedded HTML tags.

This property works only with dynamic or input text; it generates a warning if used with other
text types.

Example

The following example sets the `renderAsHTML` property to `true`:

```
fl.getDocumentDOM().selection[0].renderAsHTML = true;
```

text.scrollable

Availability

Flash MX 2004.

Usage

```
text.scrollable
```

Description

Property; a Boolean value. If the value is `true`, the text can be scrolled.

This property works only with dynamic or input text; it generates a warning if used with static text.

Example

The following example sets the `scrollable` property to `false`:

```
fl.getDocumentDOM().selection[0].scrollable = false;
```

text.selectable

Availability

Flash MX 2004.

Usage

```
text.selectable
```

Description

Property; a Boolean value. If the value is `true`, the text can be selected.

Input text is always selectable. It generates a warning when set to `false` and used with input text.

Example

The following example sets the `selectable` property to `true`:

```
fl.getDocumentDOM().getTimeline().layers[0].frames[0].elements[0].selectabl
  e = true;
```

text.selectionEnd

Availability

Flash MX 2004.

Usage

```
text.selectionEnd
```

Description

Property; a zero-based integer that specifies the end of a text subselection. For more information, see `text.selectionStart`.

text.selectionStart

Availability

Flash MX 2004.

Usage

```
text.selectionStart
```

Description

Property; a zero-based integer that specifies the beginning of a text subselection. You can use this property with `text.selectionEnd` to select a range of characters. Characters up to, but not including, `text.selectionEnd` are selected. See `text.selectionEnd`.

- If there is an insertion point or no selection, `text.selectionEnd` is equal to `text.selectionStart`.
- If `text.selectionStart` is set to a value greater than `text.selectionEnd`, `text.selectionEnd` is set to `text.selectionStart`, and no text is selected.

Example

The following example sets the start of the text subselection to the sixth character:

```
fl.getDocumentDOM().getTimeline().layers[0].frames[0].elements[0].selection
    Start = 5;
```

The following example selects the characters "Barbara" from a text field that contains the text "My name is Barbara" and formats them as bold and green:

```
fl.getDocumentDOM().selection[0].selectionStart = 11;
fl.getDocumentDOM().selection[0].selectionEnd = 18;
var s = fl.getDocumentDOM().selection[0].selectionStart;
var e = fl.getDocumentDOM().selection[0].selectionEnd;
fl.getDocumentDOM().setElementTextAttr('bold', true, s, e);
fl.getDocumentDOM().setElementTextAttr("fillColor", "#00ff00", s, e);
```

text.setTextAttr()

Availability

Flash MX 2004.

Usage

```
text.setTextAttr(attrName, attrValue [, startIndex [, endIndex]])
```

Parameters

attrName   A string that specifies the name of the TextAttrs object property to change.

attrValue   The value for the TextAttrs object property.

<table>
<tr><td>N
O
T
E</td><td>For a list of possible values for attrName and attrValue, see "Property summary for the TextAttrs object" on page 457.</td></tr>
</table>

startIndex   An integer that is the index (zero-based) of the first character in the array. This parameter is optional.

endIndex   An integer that specifies the index of the end point in the selected text string, which starts at *startIndex* and goes up to, but does not include, *endIndex*. This parameter is optional.

Returns

Nothing.

Description

Method; sets the attribute specified by the *attrName* parameter associated with the text identified by *startIndex* and *endIndex* to the value specified by *attrValue*. This method can be used to change attributes of text that might span TextRun elements (see TextRun object), or that are portions of existing TextRun elements. Using it may change the position and number of TextRun elements within this object's `text.textRuns` array (see `text.textRuns`).

If you omit the optional parameters, the method uses the entire text object's character range. If you specify only *startIndex*, the range is a single character at that position. If you specify both *startIndex* and *endIndex*, the range starts from *startIndex* and goes up to, but does not include, the character located at *endIndex*.

Example

The following example sets the selected text field to italic:

```
fl.getDocumentDOM().selection[0].setTextAttr("italic", true);
```

The following example sets the size of the third character to 10:

```
fl.getDocumentDOM().selection[0].setTextAttr("size", 10, 2);
```

The following example sets the color to red for the third through the eighth character of the selected text:

```
fl.getDocumentDOM().selection[0].setTextAttr("fillColor", 0xff0000, 2, 8);
```

text.setTextString()

Availability

Flash MX 2004.

Usage

```
text.setTextString(text [, startIndex [, endIndex]])
```

Parameters

text   A string that consists of the characters to be inserted into this text object.

startIndex   An integer that specifies the index (zero-based) of the character in the string where the text will be inserted. This parameter is optional.

endIndex   An integer that specifies the index of the end point in the selected text string. The new text overwrites the text from *startIndex* up to, but not including, *endIndex*. This parameter is optional.

Returns

Nothing.

Description

Property; changes the text string within this text object. If you omit the optional parameters, the whole text object is replaced. If you specify only *startIndex*, the specified string is inserted at the *startIndex* position. If you specify both *startIndex* and *endIndex*, the specified string replaces the segment of text starting from *startIndex* up to, but not including, *endIndex*.

Example

The following example assigns the string "this is a string" to the selected text field:

```
fl.getDocumentDOM().selection[0].setTextString("this is a string");
```

The following example inserts the string "abc" beginning at the fifth character of the selected text field:

```
fl.getDocumentDOM().selection[0].setTextString("01234567890");
fl.getDocumentDOM().selection[0].setTextString("abc", 4);
// text field is now "0123abc4567890"
```

The following example replaces the text from the third through the eighth character of the selected text string with the string "abcdefghij". Characters between *startIndex* and *endIndex* are overwritten. Characters beginning with *endIndex* follow the inserted string.

```
fl.getDocumentDOM().selection[0].setTextString("01234567890");
fl.getDocumentDOM().selection[0].setTextString("abcdefghij", 2, 8);
// text field is now 01abcdefghij890"
```

text.shortcut

Availability

Flash MX 2004.

Usage

```
text.shortcut
```

Description

Property; a string that is equivalent to the Shortcut field in the Accessibility panel. The shortcut is read by the screen reader. This property cannot be used with dynamic text.

Example

The following example gets the shortcut key of the selected object and shows the value:

```
var theShortcut = fl.getDocumentDOM().selection[0].shortcut;
fl.trace(theShortcut);
```

The following example sets the shortcut key of the selected object:

```
fl.getDocumentDOM().selection[0].shortcut = "Ctrl+i";
```

text.silent

Availability

Flash MX 2004.

Usage

```
text.silent
```

Description

Property; a Boolean value that specifies whether the object is accessible. This is equivalent to the inverse logic of the Make Object Accessible setting in the Accessibility panel. That is, if silent is true, Make Object Accessible is deselected. If it is false, Make Object Accessible is selected.

Example

The following example determines if the object is accessible (a value of `false` means that it is accessible):

```
var isSilent =
  fl.getDocumentDOM().getTimeline().layers[0].frames[0].elements[0].silent
  ;
```

The following example sets the object to be accessible:

```
fl.getDocumentDOM().getTimeline().layers[0].frames[0].elements[0].silent =
  false;
```

text.tabIndex

Availability

Flash MX 2004.

Usage

```
text.tabIndex
```

Description

Property; an integer that is equivalent to the Tab Index field in the Accessibility panel. This value lets you determine the order in which objects are accessed when the user presses the Tab key.

Example

The following example gets the `tabIndex` of the currently selected object:

```
var theTabIndex = fl.getDocumentDOM().selection[0].tabIndex;
```

The following example sets the `tabIndex` of the currently selected object:

```
fl.getDocumentDOM().selection[0].tabIndex = 1;
```

text.textRuns

Availability

Flash MX 2004.

Usage

```
text.textRuns
```

Description

Read-only property; an array of TextRun objects (see TextRun object).

Example

The following example stores the value of the `textRuns` property in the `myTextRuns` variable:

```
var myTextRuns = fl.getDocumentDOM().selection[0].textRuns;
```

text.textType

Availability

Flash MX 2004.

Usage

```
text.textType
```

Description

Property; a string that specifies the type of text field. Acceptable values are `"static"`, `"dynamic"`, and `"input"`.

Example

The following example sets the `textType` property to `"input"`:

```
fl.getDocumentDOM().selection[0].textType = "input";
```

text.useDeviceFonts

Availability

Flash MX 2004.

Usage

```
text.useDeviceFonts
```

Description

Property; a Boolean value. A value of `true` causes Flash to draw text using device fonts.

Example

The following example causes Flash to use device fonts when drawing text.

```
fl.getDocumentDOM().selection[0].useDeviceFonts = true;
```

text.variableName

Availability

Flash MX 2004.

Usage

`text.variableName`

Description

Property; a string that contains the name of the variable associated with the text object. This property works only with dynamic or input text; it generates a warning if used with other text types.

TextAttrs object

Availability

Flash MX 2004.

Description

The TextAttrs object contains all the properties of text that can be applied to a subselection. This object is a property of the TextRun object (`textRun.textAttrs`).

Property summary for the TextAttrs object

The following properties are available for the TextAttrs object.

Property	Description
textAttrs.aliasText	A Boolean value that specifies that Flash should draw the text using a method optimized for increasing the legibility of small text.
textAttrs.alignment	A string that specifies paragraph justification. Acceptable values are `"left"`, `"center"`, `"right"`, and `"justify"`.
textAttrs.autoKern	A Boolean value that determines whether Flash uses (`true`) or ignores (`false`) pair kerning information in the font(s) to kern the text.
textAttrs.bold	A Boolean value. A value of `true` causes text to appear with the bold version of the font.
textAttrs.characterPosition	A string that determines the baseline for the text.
textAttrs.characterSpacing	Deprecated in favor of `textAttrs.letterSpacing`. An integer that represents the space between characters.
textAttrs.face	A string that represents the name of the font, such as `"Arial"`.
textAttrs.fillColor	A string, hexadecimal value, or integer that represents the fill color.
textAttrs.indent	An integer that specifies paragraph indentation.
textAttrs.italic	A Boolean value. A value of `true` causes text to appear with the italic version of the font.
textAttrs.leftMargin	An integer that specifies the paragraph's left margin.
textAttrs.letterSpacing	An integer that represents the space between characters.

Property	Description
textAttrs.lineSpacing	An integer that specifies the line spacing (leading) of the paragraph
textAttrs.rightMargin	An integer that specifies the paragraph's right margin.
textAttrs.rotation	A Boolean value. A value of `true` causes Flash to rotate the characters of the text 90º. The default value is `false`.
textAttrs.size	An integer that specifies the size of the font.
textAttrs.target	A string that represents the `target` property of the text field.
textAttrs.url	A string that represents the URL property of the text field.

textAttrs.aliasText

Availability

Flash MX 2004.

Usage

```
textAttrs.aliasText
```

Description

Property; a Boolean value that specifies that Flash should draw the text using a method optimized for increasing the legibility of small text.

Example

The following example sets the `aliasText` property to `true` for all the text in the currently selected text field:

```
fl.getDocumentDOM().setElementTextAttr('aliasText', true);
```

textAttrs.alignment

Availability

Flash MX 2004.

Usage

```
textAttrs.alignment
```

Description

Property; a string that specifies paragraph justification. Acceptable values are `"left"`, `"center"`, `"right"`, and `"justify"`.

Example

The following example sets the paragraphs that contain characters between index 0 up to, but not including, index 3 to justify. This can affect characters outside the specified range if they are in the same paragraph.

```
fl.getDocumentDOM().setTextSelection(0, 3);
fl.getDocumentDOM().setElementTextAttr('alignment', 'justify');
```

textAttrs.autoKern

Availability

Flash MX 2004.

Usage

```
textAttrs.autoKern
```

Description

Property; a Boolean value that determines whether Flash uses (`true`) or ignores (`false`) pair kerning information in the font(s) when it kerns the text.

Example

The following example selects the characters from index 2 up to, but not including, index 6 and sets the `autoKern` property to `true`:

```
fl.getDocumentDOM().setTextSelection(3, 6);
fl.getDocumentDOM().setElementTextAttr('autoKern', true);
```

textAttrs.bold

Availability

Flash MX 2004.

Usage

```
textAttrs.bold
```

Description

Property; a Boolean value. A value of `true` causes text to appear with the bold version of the font.

Example

The following example selects the first character of the selected text object and sets the `bold` property to `true`:

```
fl.getDocumentDOM().setTextSelection(0, 1);
fl.getDocumentDOM().setElementTextAttr('bold', true);
```

textAttrs.characterPosition

Availability

Flash MX 2004.

Usage

```
textAttrs.characterPosition
```

Description

Property; a string that determines the baseline for the text. Acceptable values are `"normal"`, `"subscript"`, and `"superscript"`. This property applies only to static text.

Example

The following example selects the characters from index 2 up to, but not including, index 6 of the selected text field and sets the `characterPosition` property to `"subscript"`:

```
fl.getDocumentDOM().setTextSelection(2, 6);
fl.getDocumentDOM().setElementTextAttr("characterPosition", "subscript");
```

textAttrs.characterSpacing

Availability

Flash MX 2004. Deprecated in Flash 8 in favor of `textAttrs.letterSpacing`.

Usage

```
textAttrs.characterSpacing
```

Description

Property; an integer that represents the space between characters. Acceptable values are -60 through 60.

This property applies only to static text; it generates a warning if used with other text types.

Example

The following example sets the character spacing of the selected text field to 10:

```
fl.getDocumentDOM().setElementTextAttr("characterSpacing", 10);
```

textAttrs.face

Availability

Flash MX 2004.

Usage

```
textAttrs.face
```

Description

Property; a string that represents the name of the font, such as `"Arial"`.

Example

The following example sets the font of the selected text field from the character at index 2 up to, but not including, the character at index 8 to `"Arial"`:

```
fl.getDocumentDOM().selection[0].setTextAttr("face", "Arial", 2, 8);
```

textAttrs.fillColor

Availability

Flash MX 2004.

Usage

```
textAttrs.fillColor
```

Description

Property; the color of the fill, in one of the following formats:

- a string in the format `"#RRGGBB"` or `"#RRGGBBAA"`
- a hexadecimal number in the format `0xRRGGBB`
- an integer that represents the decimal equivalent of a hexadecimal number

Example

The following example sets the color of the selected text field from the character at index 2 up to, but not including, the character at index 8 to red:

```
fl.getDocumentDOM().selection[0].setTextAttr("fillColor", 0xff0000, 2, 8);
```

textAttrs.indent

Availability

Flash MX 2004.

Usage

```
textAttrs.indent
```

Description

Property; an integer that specifies paragraph indentation. Acceptable values are -720 through 720.

Example

The following example sets the indentation of the selected text field from the character at index 2 up to, but not including, the character at index 8 to 100. This can affect characters outside the specified range if they are in the same paragraph.

```
fl.getDocumentDOM().selection[0].setTextAttr("indent", 100, 2, 8);
```

textAttrs.italic

Availability

Flash MX 2004.

Usage

```
textAttrs.italic
```

Description

Property; a Boolean value. A value of `true` causes text to appear with the italic version of the font.

Example

The following example sets the selected text field to italic:

```
fl.getDocumentDOM().selection[0].setTextAttr("italic", true);
```

textAttrs.leftMargin

Availability

Flash MX 2004.

Usage

```
textAttrs.leftMargin
```

Description

Property; an integer that specifies the paragraph's left margin. Acceptable values are 0 through 720.

Example

The following example sets the `leftMargin` property of the selected text field from the character at index 2 up to, but not including, the character at index 8 to 100. This can affect characters outside the specified range if they are in the same paragraph.

```
fl.getDocumentDOM().selection[0].setTextAttr("leftMargin", 100, 2, 8);
```

textAttrs.letterSpacing

Availability

Flash 8.

Usage

```
textAttrs.letterSpacing
```

Description

Property; an integer that represents the space between characters. Acceptable values are -60 through 60.

This property applies only to static text; it generates a warning if used with other text types.

Example

The following code selects the characters from index 0 up to but not including index 10 and sets the character spacing to 60:

```
fl.getDocumentDOM().setTextSelection(0, 10);
fl.getDocumentDOM().setElementTextAttr("letterSpacing", 60);
```

textAttrs.lineSpacing

Availability

Flash MX 2004.

Usage

```
textAttrs.lineSpacing
```

Description

Property; an integer that specifies the line spacing (*leading*) of the paragraph. Acceptable values are -360 through 720.

Example

The following example sets the selected text field's `lineSpacing` property to 100:

```
fl.getDocumentDOM().selection[0].setTextAttr("lineSpacing", 100);
```

textAttrs.rightMargin

Availability

Flash MX 2004.

Usage

```
textAttrs.rightMargin
```

Description

Property; an integer that specifies the paragraph's right margin. Acceptable values are 0 through 720.

Example

The following example sets the `rightMargin` property of the selected text field from the character at index 2 up to, but not including, the character at index 8 to 100. This can affect characters outside the specified range if they are in the same paragraph.

```
fl.getDocumentDOM().selection[0].setTextAttr("rightMargin", 100, 2, 8);
```

textAttrs.rotation

Availability

Flash MX 2004.

Usage

```
textAttrs.rotation
```

Description

Property; a Boolean value. A value of `true` causes Flash to rotate the characters of the text 90°. The default value is `false`. This property applies only to static text with a vertical orientation; it generates a warning if used with other text types.

Example

The following example sets the rotation of the selected text field to `true`:

```
fl.getDocumentDOM().setElementTextAttr("rotation", true);
```

textAttrs.size

Availability

Flash MX 2004.

Usage

```
textAttrs.size
```

Description

Property; an integer that specifies the size of the font.

Example

The following example retrieves the size of the character at index 2 and shows the result in the Output panel:

```
fl.outputPanel.trace(fl.getDocumentDOM().selection[0].getTextAttr("size",
   2));
```

textAttrs.target

Availability

Flash MX 2004.

Usage

```
textAttrs.target
```

Description

Property; a string that represents the `target` property of the text field. This property works only with static text.

Example

The following example gets the `target` property of the text field in the first frame of the top layer of the current scene and shows it in the Output panel:

```
fl.outputPanel.trace(fl.getDocumentDOM().getTimeline().layers[0].frames[0].
    elements[0].getTextAttr("target"));
```

textAttrs.url

Availability

Flash MX 2004.

Usage

```
textAttrs.url
```

Description

Property; a string that represents the URL property of the text field. This property works only with static text.

Example

The following example sets the URL of the selected text field to http://www.macromedia.com:

```
fl.getDocumentDOM().setElementTextAttr("url", "http://www.macromedia.com");
```

TextRun object

Availability

Flash MX 2004.

Description

The TextRun object represents a run of characters that have attributes that match all of the properties in the TextAttrs object. This object is a property of the Text object (`text.textRuns`).

Property summary for the TextRun object

In addition to the properties available for use with the Text object, the TextRun object provides the following properties.

Property	Description
textRun.characters	A string that represents the text contained in the TextRun object.
textRun.textAttrs	The TextAttrs object containing the attributes of the run of text.

textRun.characters

Availability

Flash MX 2004.

Usage

`textRun.characters`

Description

Property; the text contained in the TextRun object.

Example

The following example displays the characters that make up the first run of characters in the selected text field in the Output panel.

```
fl.trace(fl.getDocumentDOM().selection[0].textRuns[0].characters);
```

textRun.textAttrs

Availability

Flash MX 2004.

Usage

```
textRun.textAttrs
```

Description

Property; the TextAttrs object containing the attributes of the run of text.

Example

The following example displays the properties of the first run of characters in the selected text field in the Output panel.

```
var curTextAttrs = fl.getDocumentDOM().selection[0].textRuns[0].textAttrs;
for (var prop in curTextAttrs) {
  fl.trace(prop + " = " + curTextAttrs[prop]);
}
```

Timeline object

Availability

Flash MX 2004.

Description

The Timeline object represents the Flash timeline, which can be accessed for the current document by using `fl.getDocumentDOM().getTimeline()`. This method returns the timeline of the current scene or symbol that is being edited.

When you work with scenes, each scene's timeline has an index value, and can be accessed for the current document by `fl.getDocumentDOM().timelines[i]`. (In this example, `i` is the index of the value of the timeline.)

When you work with frames by using the methods and properties of the Timeline object, remember that the frame value is a zero-based index (not the actual frame number in the sequence of frames in the timeline). That is, the first frame has a frame index of 0.

Method summary for the Timeline object

The following methods are available for the Timeline object.

Method	Description
`timeline.addMotionGuide()`	Adds a motion guide layer above the current layer and attaches the current layer to the newly added guide layer.
`timeline.addNewLayer()`	Adds a new layer to the document and makes it the current layer.
`timeline.clearFrames()`	Deletes all the contents from a frame or range of frames on the current layer.
`timeline.clearKeyframes()`	Converts a keyframe to a regular frame and deletes its contents on the current layer.
`timeline.convertToBlankKeyframes()`	Converts frames to blank keyframes on the current layer.
`timeline.convertToKeyframes()`	Converts a range of frames to keyframes (or converts the selection if no frames are specified) on the current layer.
`timeline.copyFrames()`	Copies a range of frames on the current layer to the Clipboard.

Method	Description
timeline.createMotionTween()	Sets the frame.tweenType property to motion for each selected keyframe on the current layer, and converts each frame's contents to a single symbol instance if necessary.
timeline.cutFrames()	Cuts a range of frames on the current layer from the timeline and saves them to the Clipboard.
timeline.deleteLayer()	Deletes a layer.
timeline.expandFolder()	Expands or collapses the specified folder or folders.
timeline.findLayerIndex()	Finds an array of indexes for the layers with the given name.
timeline.getFrameProperty()	Retrieves the specified property's value for the selected frames.
timeline.getLayerProperty()	Retrieves the specified property's value for the selected layers.
timeline.getSelectedFrames()	Retrieves the currently selected frames in an array.
timeline.getSelectedLayers()	Retrieves the zero-based index values of the currently selected layers.
timeline.insertBlankKeyframe()	Inserts a blank keyframe at the specified frame index; if the index is not specified, inserts the blank keyframe by using the playhead/selection.
timeline.insertFrames()	Inserts the specified number of frames at the given frame number.
timeline.insertKeyframe()	Inserts a keyframe at the specified frame.
timeline.pasteFrames()	Pastes the range of frames from the Clipboard into the specified frames.
timeline.removeFrames()	Deletes the frame.
timeline.reorderLayer()	Moves the first specified layer before or after the second specified layer.
timeline.reverseFrames()	Reverses a range of frames.
timeline.selectAllFrames()	Selects all the frames in the current timeline.
timeline.setFrameProperty()	Sets the property of the Frame object for the selected frames.
timeline.setLayerProperty()	Sets the specified property on all the selected layers to a specified value.

Method	Description
`timeline.setSelectedFrames()`	Selects a range of frames in the current layer or sets the selected frames to the selection array passed into this method.
`timeline.setSelectedLayers()`	Sets the layer to be selected; also makes the specified layer the current layer.
`timeline.showLayerMasking()`	Shows the layer masking during authoring by locking the mask and masked layers.

Property summary for the Timeline object

The following methods are available for the Timeline object.

Property	Description
`timeline.currentFrame`	A zero-based index for the frame at the current playhead location.
`timeline.currentLayer`	A zero-based index for the currently active layer.
`timeline.frameCount`	Read-only; an integer that represents the number of frames in this timeline's longest layer.
`timeline.layerCount`	Read-only; an integer that represents the number of layers in the specified timeline.
`timeline.layers`	Read-only; an array of layer objects.
`timeline.name`	A string that represents the name of the current timeline.

timeline.addMotionGuide()

Availability

Flash MX 2004.

Usage

`timeline.addMotionGuide()`

Parameters

None.

Returns

An integer that represents the zero-based index of the newly added guide layer. If the current layer type is not of type "Normal", Flash returns -1.

Description

Method; adds a motion guide layer above the current layer and attaches the current layer to the newly added guide layer, converting the current layer to a layer of type "Guided".

This method functions only on a layer of type "Normal". It has no effect on a layer whose type is "Folder", "Mask", "Masked", "Guide", or "Guided".

Example

The following example adds a motion guide layer above the current layer, and converts the current layer to "Guided":

```
fl.getDocumentDOM().getTimeline().addMotionGuide();
```

timeline.addNewLayer()

Availability

Flash MX 2004.

Usage

```
timeline.addNewLayer([name] [, layerType [, bAddAbove]])
```

Parameters

name   A string that specifies the name for the new layer. If you omit this parameter, a new default layer name is assigned to the new layer ("Layer n," where *n* is the total number of layers). This parameter is optional.

layerType   A string that specifies the type of layer to add. If you omit this parameter, a "Normal" type layer is created. This parameter is optional.

bAddAbove   A Boolean value that, if set to true (the default), causes Flash to add the new layer above the current layer; false causes Flash to add the layer below the current layer. This parameter is optional.

Returns

An integer value of the zero-based index of the newly added layer.

Description

Method; adds a new layer to the document and makes it the current layer.

Example

The following example adds a new layer to the timeline with a default name generated by Flash:

```
fl.getDocumentDOM().getTimeline().addNewLayer();
```

The following example adds a new folder layer on top of the current layer and names it "Folder1":

```
fl.getDocumentDOM().getTimeline().addNewLayer("Folder1", "folder", true);
```

timeline.clearFrames()

Availability

Flash MX 2004.

Usage

```
timeline.clearFrames([startFrameIndex [, endFrameIndex]])
```

Parameters

startFrameIndex A zero-based index that defines the beginning of the range of frames to clear. If you omit *startFrameIndex*, the method uses the current selection. This parameter is optional.

endFrameIndex A zero-based index that defines the end of the range of frames to clear. The range goes up to, but does not include, *endFrameIndex*. If you specify only *startFrameIndex*, *endFrameIndex* defaults to the value of *startFrameIndex*. This parameter is optional.

Returns

Nothing.

Description

Method; deletes all the contents from a frame or range of frames on the current layer.

Example

The following example clears the frames from Frame 6 up to, but not including, Frame 11 (remember that index values are different from frame number values):

```
fl.getDocumentDOM().getTimeline().clearFrames(5, 10);
```

The following example clears Frame 15:

```
fl.getDocumentDOM().getTimeline().clearFrames(14);
```

timeline.clearKeyframes()

Availability

Flash MX 2004.

Usage

```
timeline.clearKeyframes([startFrameIndex [, endFrameIndex]])
```

Parameters

startFrameIndex   A zero-based index that defines the beginning of the range of frames to clear. If you omit *startFrameIndex*, the method uses the current selection. This parameter is optional.

endFrameIndex   A zero-based index that defines the end of the range of frames to clear. The range goes up to, but does not include, *endFrameIndex*. If you specify only *startFrameIndex*, *endFrameIndex* defaults to the value of *startFrameIndex*. This parameter is optional.

Returns

Nothing.

Description

Method; converts a keyframe to a regular frame and deletes its contents on the current layer.

Example

The following example clears the keyframes from Frame 5 up to, but not including, Frame 10 (remember that index values are different from frame number values):

```
fl.getDocumentDOM().getTimeline().clearKeyframes(4, 9);
```

The following example clears the keyframe at Frame 15 and converts it to a regular frame:

```
fl.getDocumentDOM().getTimeline().clearKeyframes(14);
```

timeline.convertToBlankKeyframes()

Availability

Flash MX 2004.

Usage

```
timeline.convertToBlankKeyframes([startFrameIndex [, endFrameIndex]])
```

Parameters

startFrameIndex   A zero-based index that specifies the starting frame to convert to keyframes. If you omit *startFrameIndex*, the method converts the currently selected frames. This parameter is optional.

endFrameIndex   A zero-based index that specifies the frame at which the conversion to keyframes will stop. The range of frames to convert goes up to, but does not include, *endFrameIndex*. If you specify only *startFrameIndex*, *endFrameIndex* defaults to the value of *startFrameIndex*. This parameter is optional.

Returns

Nothing.

Description

Method; converts frames to blank keyframes on the current layer.

Example

The following example converts Frame 2 up to, but not including, Frame 10 to blank keyframes (remember that index values are different from frame number values):

```
fl.getDocumentDOM().getTimeline().convertToBlankKeyframes(1, 9);
```

The following example converts Frame 5 to a blank keyframe:

```
fl.getDocumentDOM().getTimeline().convertToBlankKeyframes(4);
```

timeline.convertToKeyframes()

Availability

Flash MX 2004.

Usage

```
timeline.convertToKeyframes([startFrameIndex [, endFrameIndex]])
```

Parameters

startFrameIndex   A zero-based index that specifies the first frame to convert to keyframes. If you omit *startFrameIndex*, the method converts the currently selected frames. This parameter is optional.

endFrameIndex   A zero-based index that specifies the frame at which conversion to keyframes will stop. The range of frames to convert goes up to, but does not include, *endFrameIndex*. If you specify only *startFrameIndex*, *endFrameIndex* defaults to the value of *startFrameIndex*. This parameter is optional.

Returns

Nothing.

Description

Method; converts a range of frames to keyframes (or converts the selection if no frames are specified) on the current layer.

Example

The following example converts the selected frames to keyframes:

```
fl.getDocumentDOM().getTimeline().convertToKeyframes();
```

The following example converts to keyframes the frames from Frame 2 up to, but not including, Frame 10 (remember that index values are different from frame number values):

```
fl.getDocumentDOM().getTimeline().convertToKeyframes(1, 9);
```

The following example converts Frame 5 to a keyframe:

```
fl.getDocumentDOM().getTimeline().convertToKeyframes(4);
```

timeline.copyFrames()

Availability

Flash MX 2004.

Usage

```
timeline.copyFrames([startFrameIndex [, endFrameIndex]])
```

Parameters

startFrameIndex   A zero-based index that specifies the beginning of the range of frames to copy. If you omit *startFrameIndex*, the method uses the current selection. This parameter is optional.

endFrameIndex   A zero-based index that specifies the frame at which to stop copying. The range of frames to copy goes up to, but does not include, *endFrameIndex*. If you specify only *startFrameIndex*, *endFrameIndex* defaults to the value of *startFrameIndex*. This parameter is optional.

Returns

Nothing.

Description

Method; copies a range of frames on the current layer to the Clipboard.

Example

The following example copies the selected frames to the Clipboard:

```
fl.getDocumentDOM().getTimeline().copyFrames();
```

The following example copies Frame 2 up to, but not including, Frame 10, to the Clipboard (remember that index values are different from frame number values):

```
fl.getDocumentDOM().getTimeline().copyFrames(1, 9);
```

The following example copies Frame 5 to the Clipboard:

```
fl.getDocumentDOM().getTimeline().copyFrames(4);
```

timeline.createMotionTween()

Availability

Flash MX 2004.

Usage

```
timeline.createMotionTween([startFrameIndex [, endFrameIndex]])
```

Parameters

startFrameIndex   A zero-based index that specifies the beginning frame at which to create a motion tween. If you omit *startFrameIndex*, the method uses the current selection. This parameter is optional.

endFrameIndex   A zero-based index that specifies the frame at which to stop the motion tween. The range of frames goes up to, but does not include, *endFrameIndex*. If you specify only *startFrameIndex*, *endFrameIndex* defaults to the *startFrameIndex* value. This parameter is optional.

Returns

Nothing.

Description

Method; sets the frame.tweenType property to motion for each selected keyframe on the current layer, and converts each frame's contents to a single symbol instance if necessary. This property is the equivalent to the Create Motion Tween menu item in the Flash authoring tool.

Example

The following example converts the shape in the first frame up to, but not including, Frame 10 to a graphic symbol instance and sets the `frame.tweenType` to `motion` (remember that index values are different from frame number values):

```
fl.getDocumentDOM().getTimeline().createMotionTween(0, 9);
```

timeline.currentFrame

Availability

Flash MX 2004.

Usage

```
timeline.currentFrame
```

Description

Property; the zero-based index for the frame at the current playhead location.

Example

The following example sets the playhead of the current timeline to Frame 10 (remember that index values are different from frame number values):

```
fl.getDocumentDOM().getTimeline().currentFrame = 9;
```

The following example stores the value of the current playhead location in the `curFrame` variable:

```
var curFrame = fl.getDocumentDOM().getTimeline().currentFrame;
```

timeline.currentLayer

Availability

Flash MX 2004.

Usage

```
timeline.currentLayer
```

Description

Property; the zero-based index for the currently active layer. A value of 0 specifies the top layer, a value of 1 specifies the layer below it, and so on.

Example

The following example makes the top layer active:

```
fl.getDocumentDOM().getTimeline().currentLayer = 0;
```

The following example stores the index of the currently active layer in the curLayer variable:

```
var curLayer = fl.getDocumentDOM().getTimeline().currentLayer;
```

timeline.cutFrames()

Availability

Flash MX 2004.

Usage

```
timeline.cutFrames([startFrameIndex [, endFrameIndex]])
```

Parameters

startFrameIndex A zero-based index that specifies the beginning of a range of frames to cut. If you omit *startFrameIndex*, the method uses the current selection. This parameter is optional.

endFrameIndex A zero-based index that specifies the frame at which to stop cutting. The range of frames goes up to, but does not include, *endFrameIndex*. If you specify only *startFrameIndex*, *endFrameIndex* defaults to the *startFrameIndex* value. This parameter is optional.

Returns

Nothing.

Description

Method; cuts a range of frames on the current layer from the timeline and saves them to the Clipboard.

Example

The following example cuts the selected frames from the timeline and saves them to the Clipboard:

```
fl.getDocumentDOM().getTimeline().cutFrames();
```

The following example cuts Frame 2 up to, but not including, Frame 10 from the timeline and saves them to the Clipboard (remember that index values are different from frame number values):

```
fl.getDocumentDOM().getTimeline().cutFrames(1, 9);
```

The following example cuts Frame 5 from the timeline and saves it to the Clipboard:

```
fl.getDocumentDOM().getTimeline().cutFrames(4);
```

timeline.deleteLayer()

Availability

Flash MX 2004.

Usage

```
timeline.deleteLayer([index])
```

Parameters

index   A zero-based index that specifies the layer to be deleted. If there is only one layer in the timeline, this method has no effect. This parameter is optional.

Returns

Nothing.

Description

Method; deletes a layer. If the layer is a folder, all layers within the folder are deleted. If you do not specify the layer index, Flash deletes the currently selected layers.

Example

The following example deletes the second layer from the top:

```
fl.getDocumentDOM().getTimeline().deleteLayer(1);
```

The following example deletes the currently selected layers:

```
fl.getDocumentDOM().getTimeline().deleteLayer();
```

timeline.expandFolder()

Availability

Flash MX 2004.

Usage

```
timeline.expandFolder(bExpand [, bRecurseNestedParents [, index]])
```

Parameters

bExpand   A Boolean value that, if set to true, causes the method to expand the folder; false causes the method to collapse the folder.

bRecurseNestedParents   A Boolean value that, if set to true, causes all the layers within the specified folder to be opened or closed, based on the *bExpand* parameter. This parameter is optional.

index   A zero-based index of the folder to expand or collapse. Use -1 to apply to all layers (you also must set *bRecurseNestedParents* to true). This property is equivalent to the Expand All/Collapse All menu items in the Flash authoring tool. This parameter is optional.

Returns

Nothing.

Description

Method; expands or collapses the specified folder or folders. If you do not specify a layer, this method operates on the current layer.

Example

The following examples use this folder structure:

```
Folder 1 ***
--layer 7
--Folder 2 ****
----Layer 5
```

The following example expands Folder 1 only:

```
fl.getDocumentDOM().getTimeline().currentLayer = 1;
fl.getDocumentDOM().getTimeline().expandFolder(true);
```

The following example expands Folder 1 only (assuming that Folder 2 collapsed when Folder 1 last collapsed; otherwise, Folder 2 appears expanded):

```
fl.getDocumentDOM().getTimeline().expandFolder(true, false, 0);
```

The following example collapses all folders in the current timeline:

```
fl.getDocumentDOM().getTimeline().expandFolder(false, true, -1);
```

timeline.findLayerIndex()

Availability

Flash MX 2004.

Usage

```
timeline.findLayerIndex(name)
```

Parameters

name   A string that specifies the name of the layer to find.

Returns

An array of index values for the specified layer. If the specified layer is not found, Flash returns `undefined`.

Description

Method; finds an array of indexes for the layers with the given name. The layer index is flat, so folders are considered part of the main index.

Example

The following example shows the index values of all layers named Layer 7 in the Output panel:

```
var layerIndex = fl.getDocumentDOM().getTimeline().findLayerIndex("Layer
    7");
fl.trace(layerIndex);
```

The following example illustrates how to pass the values returned from this method back to `timeline.setSelectedLayers()`:

```
var layerIndex = fl.getDocumentDOM().getTimeline().findLayerIndex("Layer
    1");
fl.getDocumentDOM().getTimeline().setSelectedLayers(layerIndex[0], true);
```

timeline.frameCount

Availability

Flash MX 2004.

Usage

```
timeline.frameCount
```

Description

Read-only property; an integer that represents the number of frames in this timeline's longest layer.

Example

The following example uses a `countNum` variable to store the number of frames in the current document's longest layer:

```
var countNum = fl.getDocumentDOM().getTimeline().frameCount;
```

timeline.getFrameProperty()

Availability

Flash MX 2004.

Usage

```
timeline.getFrameProperty(property [, startframeIndex [, endFrameIndex]])
```

Parameters

property   A string that specifies the name of the property for which to get the value. See "Property summary for the Frame object" on page 273 for a complete list of properties.

startFrameIndex   A zero-based index that specifies the starting frame number for which to get the value. If you omit *startFrameIndex*, the method uses the current selection. This parameter is optional.

endFrameIndex   A zero-based index that specifies the end of the range of frames to select. The range goes up to, but does not include, *endFrameIndex*. If you specify only *startFrameIndex*, *endFrameIndex* defaults to the value of *startFrameIndex*. This parameter is optional.

Returns

A value for the specified property, or `undefined` if all the selected frames do not have the same property value.

Description

Method; retrieves the specified property's value for the selected frames.

Example

The following example retrieves the name of the first frame in the current document's top layer and displays the name in the Output panel:

```
fl.getDocumentDOM().getTimeline().currentLayer = 0;
fl.getDocumentDOM().getTimeline().setSelectedFrames(0, 0, true);
var frameName = fl.getDocumentDOM().getTimeline().getFrameProperty("name");
fl.trace(frameName);
```

timeline.getLayerProperty()

Availability

Flash MX 2004.

Usage

```
timeline.getLayerProperty(property)
```

Parameters

property   A string that specifies the name of the property whose value you want to retrieve. For a list of properties, see "Property summary for the Layer object" on page 305.

Returns

The value of the specified property. Flash looks at the layer's properties to determine the type. If all the specified layers don't have the same property value, Flash returns undefined.

Description

Method; retrieves the specified property's value for the selected layers.

Example

The following example retrieves the name of the top layer in the current document and displays it in the Output panel:

```
fl.getDocumentDOM().getTimeline().currentLayer = 0;
var layerName = fl.getDocumentDOM().getTimeline().getLayerProperty("name");
fl.trace(layerName);
```

timeline.getSelectedFrames()

Availability

Flash MX 2004.

Parameters

None.

Returns

An array containing $3n$ integers, where n is the number of selected regions. The first integer in each group is the layer index, the second integer is the start frame of the beginning of the selection, and the third integer specifies the ending frame of that selection range. The ending frame is not included in the selection.

Description

Method; retrieves the currently selected frames in an array.

Example

With the top layer being the current layer, the following example displays $0,5,10,0,20,25$ in the Output panel:

```
var timeline = fl.getDocumentDOM().getTimeline();
timeline.setSelectedFrames(5,10);
timeline.setSelectedFrames(20,25,false);
var theSelectedFrames = timeline.getSelectedFrames();
fl.trace(theSelectedFrames);
```

See also

```
timeline.setSelectedFrames()
```

timeline.getSelectedLayers()

Availability

Flash MX 2004.

Parameters

None.

Returns

An array of the zero-based index values of the selected layers.

Description

Method; gets the zero-based index values of the currently selected layers.

Example

The following example displays $1,0$ in the Output panel:

```
fl.getDocumentDOM().getTimeline().setSelectedLayers(0);
fl.getDocumentDOM().getTimeline().setSelectedLayers(1, false);
var layerArray = fl.getDocumentDOM().getTimeline().getSelectedLayers();
fl.trace(layerArray);
```

`timeline.setSelectedLayers()`

timeline.insertBlankKeyframe()

Availability

Flash MX 2004.

Usage

`timeline.insertBlankKeyframe([frameNumIndex])`

Parameters

frameNumIndex   A zero-based index that specifies the frame at which to insert the keyframe. If you omit *frameNumIndex*, the method uses the current playhead frame number. This parameter is optional.

If the specified or selected frame is a regular frame, the keyframe is inserted at the frame. For example, if you have a span of 10 frames numbered 1-10 and you select Frame 5, this method makes Frame 5 a blank keyframe, and the length of the frame span is still 10 frames. If Frame 5 is selected and is a keyframe with a regular frame next to it, this method inserts a blank keyframe at Frame 6. If Frame 5 is a keyframe and the frame next to it is already a keyframe, no keyframe is inserted but the playhead moves to Frame 6.

Returns

Nothing.

Description

Method; inserts a blank keyframe at the specified frame index; if the index is not specified, the method inserts the blank keyframe by using the playhead/selection. See also `timeline.insertKeyframe()`.

Example

The following example inserts a blank keyframe at Frame 20 (remember that index values are different from frame number values):

`fl.getDocumentDOM().getTimeline().insertBlankKeyframe(19);`

The following example inserts a blank keyframe at the currently selected frame (or playhead location if no frame is selected):

`fl.getDocumentDOM().getTimeline().insertBlankKeyframe();`

timeline.insertFrames()

Availability

Flash MX 2004.

Usage

```
timeline.insertFrames([numFrames [, bAllLayers [, frameNumIndex]]])
```

Parameters

numFrames An integer that specifies the number of frames to insert. If you omit this parameter, the method inserts frames at the current selection in the current layer. This parameter is optional.

bAllLayers A Boolean value that, if set to `true` (the default), causes the method to insert the specified number of frames in the *numFrames* parameter into all layers; if set to `false`, the method inserts frames into the current layer. This parameter is optional.

frameNumIndex A zero-based index that specifies the frame at which to insert a new frame. This parameter is optional.

Returns

Nothing.

Description

Method; inserts the specified number of frames at the specified index.

If no parameters are specified, this method works as follows:

- If one or more frames are selected, the method inserts the selected number of frames at the location of the first selected frame in the current layer. That is, if frames 6 through 10 are selected (a total of five frames), the method adds five frames at Frame 6 in the layer containing the selected frames.
- If no frames are selected, the method inserts one frame at the current frame on all layers.

If parameters are specified, the method works as follows:

- If only *numFrames* is specified, inserts the specified number of frames at the current frame on the current layer.
- If *numFrames* is specified and *bAllLayers* is `true`, inserts the specified number of frames at the current frame on all layers.
- If all three parameters are specified, inserts the specified number of frames at the specified index (*frameIndex*); the value passed for *bAllLayers* determines if the frames are added only to the current layer or to all layers.

If the specified or selected frame is a regular frame, the frame is inserted at that frame. For example, if you have a span of 10 frames numbered 1-10 and you select Frame 5 (or pass a value of 4 for *frameIndex*), this method adds a frame at Frame 5, and the length of the frame span becomes 11 frames. If Frame 5 is selected and it is a keyframe, this method inserts a frame at Frame 6 regardless of whether the frame next to it is also a keyframe.

Example

The following example inserts a frame (or frames, depending on the selection) at the current selection in the current layer:

```
fl.getDocumentDOM().getTimeline().insertFrames();
```

The following example inserts five frames at the current frame in all layers:

```
fl.getDocumentDOM().getTimeline().insertFrames(5);
```

 NOTE If you have multiple layers with frames in them, and you select a frame in one layer when using the previous command, Flash inserts the frames in the selected layer only. If you have multiple layers with no frames selected in them, Flash inserts the frames in all layers.

The following example inserts three frames in the current layer only:

```
fl.getDocumentDOM().getTimeline().insertFrames(3, false);
```

The following example inserts four frames in all layers, starting from the first frame:

```
fl.getDocumentDOM().getTimeline().insertFrames(4, true, 0);
```

timeline.insertKeyframe()

Availability

Flash MX 2004.

Usage

```
timeline.insertKeyframe([frameNumIndex])
```

Parameters

frameNumIndex   A zero-based index that specifies the frame index at which to insert the keyframe in the current layer. If you omit *frameNumIndex*, the method uses the frame number of the current playhead or selected frame. This parameter is optional.

Returns

Nothing.

Description

Method; inserts a keyframe at the specified frame. If you omit the parameter, the method inserts a keyframe using the playhead or selection location.

This method works the same as `timeline.insertBlankKeyframe()` except that the inserted keyframe contains the contents of the frame it converted (that is, it's not blank).

Example

The following example inserts a keyframe at the playhead or selected location:

```
fl.getDocumentDOM().getTimeline().insertKeyframe();
```

The following example inserts a keyframe at Frame 10 of the second layer (remember that index values are different from frame or layer number values):

```
fl.getDocumentDOM().getTimeline().currentLayer = 1;
fl.getDocumentDOM().getTimeline().insertKeyframe(9);
```

timeline.layerCount

Availability

Flash MX 2004.

Usage

```
timeline.layerCount
```

Description

Read-only property; an integer that represents the number of layers in the specified timeline.

Example

The following example uses the `NumLayer` variable to store the number of layers in the current scene:

```
var NumLayer = fl.getDocumentDOM().getTimeline().layerCount;
```

timeline.layers

Availability

Flash MX 2004.

Usage

```
timeline.layers
```

Description

Read-only property; an array of layer objects.

Example

The following example uses the `currentLayers` variable to store the array of layer objects in the current document:

```
var currentLayers = fl.getDocumentDOM().getTimeline().layers;
```

timeline.name

Availability

Flash MX 2004.

Usage

```
timeline.name
```

Description

Property; a string that specifies the name of the current timeline. This name is the name of the current scene, screen (slide or form), or symbol that is being edited.

Example

The following example retrieves the first scene name:

```
var sceneName = fl.getDocumentDOM().timelines[0].name;
```

The following example sets the first scene name to `FirstScene`:

```
fl.getDocumentDOM().timelines[0].name = "FirstScene";
```

timeline.pasteFrames()

Availability

Flash MX 2004.

Usage

```
timeline.pasteFrames([startFrameIndex [, endFrameIndex]])
```

Parameters

startFrameIndex   A zero-based index that specifies the beginning of a range of frames to paste. If you omit *startFrameIndex*, the method uses the current selection. This parameter is optional.

endFrameIndex   A zero-based index that specifies the frame at which to stop pasting frames. The method pastes up to, but not including, *endFrameIndex*. If you specify only *startFrameIndex*, *endFrameIndex* defaults to the *startFrameIndex* value. This parameter is optional.

Returns

Nothing.

Description

Method; pastes the range of frames from the Clipboard into the specified frames.

Example

The following example pastes the frames on the Clipboard to the currently selected frame or playhead location:

```
fl.getDocumentDOM().getTimeline().pasteFrames();
```

The following example pastes the frames on the Clipboard at Frame 2 up to, but not including, Frame 10 (remember that index values are different from frame number values):

```
fl.getDocumentDOM().getTimeline().pasteFrames(1, 9);
```

The following example pastes the frames on the Clipboard starting at Frame 5:

```
fl.getDocumentDOM().getTimeline().pasteFrames(4);
```

timeline.removeFrames()

Availability

Flash MX 2004.

Usage

```
timeline.removeFrames([startFrameIndex [, endFrameIndex]])
```

Parameters

startFrameIndex A zero-based index that specifies the first frame at which to start removing frames. If you omit *startFrameIndex*, the method uses the current selection; if there is no selection, all frames at the current playhead on all layers are removed. This parameter is optional.

endFrameIndex A zero-based index that specifies the frame at which to stop removing frames; the range of frames goes up to, but does not include, *endFrameIndex*. If you specify only *startFrameIndex*, *endFrameIndex* defaults to the *startFrameIndex* value. This parameter is optional.

Returns

Nothing.

Description

Method; deletes the frame.

Example

The following example deletes Frame 5 up to, but not including, Frame 10 of the top layer in the current scene (remember that index values are different from frame number values):

```
fl.getDocumentDOM().getTimeline().currentLayer = 0;
fl.getDocumentDOM().getTimeline().removeFrames(4, 9);
```

The following example deletes Frame 8 on the top layer in the current scene:

```
fl.getDocumentDOM().getTimeline().currentLayer = 0;
fl.getDocumentDOM().getTimeline().removeFrames(7);
```

timeline.reorderLayer()

Availability

Flash MX 2004.

Usage

```
timeline.reorderLayer(layerToMove, layerToPutItBy [, bAddBefore])
```

Parameters

layerToMove   A zero-based index that specifies which layer to move.

layerToPutItBy   A zero-based index that specifies which layer you want to move the layer next to. For example, if you specify 1 for *layerToMove* and 0 for *layerToPutItBy*, the second layer is placed next to the first layer.

bAddBefore   Specifies whether to move the layer before or after *layerToPutItBy*. If you specify `false`, the layer is moved after *layerToPutItBy*. The default value is `true`. This parameter is optional.

Returns

Nothing.

Description

Method; moves the first specified layer before or after the second specified layer.

Example

The following example moves the layer at index 2 to the top (on top of the layer at index 0):

```
fl.getDocumentDOM().getTimeline().reorderLayer(2, 0);
```

The following example places the layer at index 3 after the layer at index 5:

```
fl.getDocumentDOM().getTimeline().reorderLayer(3, 5, false);
```

timeline.reverseFrames()

Availability

Flash MX 2004.

Usage

```
timeline.reverseFrames([startFrameIndex [, endFrameIndex]])
```

Parameters

startFrameIndex   A zero-based index that specifies the first frame at which to start reversing frames. If you omit *startFrameIndex*, the method uses the current selection. This parameter is optional.

endFrameIndex   A zero-based index that specifies the first frame at which to stop reversing frames; the range of frames goes up to, but does not include, *endFrameIndex*. If you specify only *startFrameIndex*, *endFrameIndex* defaults to the value of *startFrameIndex*. This parameter is optional.

Returns

Nothing.

Description

Method; reverses a range of frames.

Example

The following example reverses the positions of the currently selected frames:

```
fl.getDocumentDOM().getTimeline().reverseFrames();
```

The following example reverses frames from Frame 10 up to, but not including, Frame 15 (remember that index values are different from frame number values):

```
fl.getDocumentDOM().getTimeline().reverseFrames(9, 14);
```

timeline.selectAllFrames()

Availability

Flash MX 2004.

Usage

```
timeline.selectAllFrames()
```

Parameters

None.

Returns

Nothing.

Description

Method; selects all the frames in the current timeline.

Example

The following example selects all the frames in the current timeline.

```
fl.getDocumentDOM().getTimeline().selectAllFrames();
```

timeline.setFrameProperty()

Availability

Flash MX 2004.

Usage

```
timeline.setFrameProperty(property, value [, startFrameIndex [,
  endFrameIndex]])
```

Parameters

property   A string that specifies the name of the property to be modified. For a complete list of properties and values, see "Property summary for the Frame object" on page 273.

 NOTE You can't use this method to set values for read-only properties such as `frame.duration` and `frame.elements`.

value   Specifies the value to which you want to set the property. To determine the appropriate values and type, see "Property summary for the Frame object" on page 273.

startFrameIndex   A zero-based index that specifies the starting frame number to modify. If you omit *startFrameIndex*, the method uses the current selection. This parameter is optional.

endFrameIndex   A zero-based index that specifies the first frame at which to stop. The range of frames goes up to, but does not include, *endFrameIndex*. If you specify *startFrameIndex* but omit *endFrameIndex*, *endFrameIndex* defaults to the value of *startFrameIndex*. This parameter is optional.

Returns

Nothing.

Description

Method; sets the property of the Frame object for the selected frames.

Example

The following example assigns the ActionScript `stop()` command to the first frame of the top layer in the current document:

```
fl.getDocumentDOM().getTimeline().currentLayer = 0;
fl.getDocumentDOM().getTimeline().setSelectedFrames(0,0,true);
fl.getDocumentDOM().getTimeline().setFrameProperty("actionScript",
  "stop();");
```

The following example sets a motion tween from Frame 2 up to, but not including, Frame 5, of the current layer (remember that index values are different from frame number values):

```
fl.getDocumentDOM().getTimeline().setFrameProperty("tweenType","motion",1,4
  );
```

timeline.setLayerProperty()

Availability

Flash MX 2004.

Usage

```
timeline.setLayerProperty(property, value [, layersToChange])
```

Parameters

property   A string that specifies the property to set. For a list of properties, see "Layer object" on page 305.

value   The value to which you want to set the property. Use the same type of value you would use when setting the property in the layer object.

layersToChange   A string that identifies which layers should be modified. Acceptable values are `"selected"`, `"all"`, and `"others"`. The default value is `"selected"` if you omit this parameter. This parameter is optional.

Returns

Nothing.

Description

Method; sets the specified property on all the selected layers to a specified value.

Example

The following example makes the selected layer(s) invisible:

```
fl.getDocumentDOM().getTimeline().setLayerProperty("visible", false);
```

The following example sets the name of the selected layer(s) to "selLayer":

```
fl.getDocumentDOM().getTimeline().setLayerProperty("name", "selLayer");
```

timeline.setSelectedFrames()

Availability

Flash MX 2004.

Usage

```
timeline.setSelectedFrames(startFrameIndex, endFrameIndex [,
  bReplaceCurrentSelection])
timeline.setSelectedFrames(selectionList [, bReplaceCurrentSelection])
```

Parameters

startFrameIndex   A zero-based index that specifies the beginning frame to set.

endFrameIndex   A zero-based index that specifies the end of the selection; *endFrameIndex* is the frame after the last frame in the range to select.

bReplaceCurrentSelection   A Boolean value that, if it is set to true, causes the currently selected frames to be deselected before the specified frames are selected. The default value is true.

selectionList   An array of three integers, as returned by timeline.getSelectedFrames().

Returns

Nothing.

Description

Method; selects a range of frames in the current layer or sets the selected frames to the selection array passed into this method.

Example

The following example selects the top layer, Frame 1, up to, but not including, Frame 10; it then adds Frame 12 up to, but not including, Frame 15 on the same layer to the current selection (remember that index values are different from frame number values):

```
fl.getDocumentDOM().getTimeline().setSelectedFrames(0, 9);
fl.getDocumentDOM().getTimeline().setSelectedFrames(11, 14, false);
```

The following example first stores the array of selected frames in the `savedSelectionList` variable, and then uses the array later in the code to reselect those frames after a command or user interaction has changed the selection:

```
var savedSelectionList =
    fl.getDocumentDOM().getTimeline().getSelectedFrames();
// Do something that changes the selection.
fl.getDocumentDOM().getTimeline().setSelectedFrames(savedSelectionList);
```

The following example selects the top layer, Frame 1, up to, but not including, Frame 10, then adds Frame 12, up to, but not including, Frame 15, on the same layer to the current selection:

```
fl.getDocumentDOM().getTimeline().setSelectedFrames([0, 0, 9]);
fl.getDocumentDOM().getTimeline().setSelectedFrames([0, 11, 14], false);
```

See also

`timeline.getSelectedFrames()`

timeline.setSelectedLayers()

Availability

Flash MX 2004.

Usage

`timeline.setSelectedLayers(index [, bReplaceCurrentSelection])`

Parameters

index   A zero-based index for the layer to select.

bReplaceCurrentSelection   A Boolean value that, if it is set to `true`, causes the method to replace the current selection; `false` causes the method to extend the current selection. The default value is `true`. This parameter is optional.

Returns

Nothing.

Description

Method; sets the layer to be selected, and also makes the specified layer the current layer. Selecting a layer also means that all the frames in the layer are selected.

Example

The following example selects the top layer:

```
fl.getDocumentDOM().getTimeline().setSelectedLayers(0);
```

The following example adds the next layer to the selection:

```
fl.getDocumentDOM().getTimeline().setSelectedLayers(1, false);
```

See also

```
timeline.getSelectedLayers()
```

timeline.showLayerMasking()

Availability

Flash MX 2004.

Usage

```
timeline.showLayerMasking([layer])
```

Parameters

layer   A zero-based index of a mask or masked layer to show masking during authoring. This parameter is optional.

Returns

Nothing.

Description

Method; shows the layer masking during authoring by locking the mask and masked layers. This method uses the current layer if no layer is specified. If you use this method on a layer that is not of type Mask or Masked, Flash displays an error in the Output panel.

Example

The following example specifies that the layer masking of the first layer should show during authoring.

```
fl.getDocumentDOM().getTimeline().showLayerMasking(0);
```

ToolObj object

Availability

Flash MX 2004.

Description

A ToolObj object represents an individual tool in the Tools panel. To access a ToolObj object, use properties of the Tools object: either the `tools.toolObjs` array or `tools.activeTool`.

Method summary for the ToolObj object

The following methods are available for the ToolObj object.

 The following methods are used only when creating extensible tools.

Method	Description
`toolObj.enablePIControl()`	Enables or disables the specified control in a Property inspector. Used only when creating extensible tools.
`toolObj.setIcon()`	Identifies a PNG file to use as a tool icon in the Flash Tools panel.
`toolObj.setMenuString()`	Sets the string that appears in the pop-up menu as the name for the tool.
`toolObj.setOptionsFile()`	Associates an XML file with the tool.
`toolObj.setPI()`	Sets a particular Property inspector to be used when the tool is activated.
`toolObj.setToolName()`	Assigns a name to the tool for the configuration of the Tools panel.
`toolObj.setToolTip()`	Sets the tooltip that appears when the mouse is held over the tool icon.
`toolObj.showPIControl()`	Shows or hides a control in the Property inspector.
`toolObj.showTransformHandles()`	Called in the `configureTool()` method of an extensible tool's JavaScript file to indicate that the free transform handles should appear when the tool is active.

Property summary for the ToolObj object

The following property is available for the ToolObj object:

Property	Description
toolObj.depth	An integer that specifies the depth of the tool in the pop-up menu in the Tools panel.
toolObj.iconID	An integer that specifies the resource ID of the tool.
toolObj.position	Read-only; an integer specifying the position of the tool in the Tools panel.

toolObj.depth

Availability

Flash MX 2004.

Usage

```
toolObj.depth
```

Description

Read-only property; an integer that specifies the depth of the tool in the pop-up menu in the Tools panel. This property is used only when creating extensible tools.

Example

The following example specifies that the tool has a depth of 1, which means one level under a tool in the Tools panel.

```
fl.tools.activeTool.depth = 1;
```

toolObj.enablePIControl()

Availability

Flash MX 2004.

Usage

```
toolObj.enablePIControl( control, bEnable )
```

Parameters

control   A string that specifies the name of the control to enable or disable. Legal values depend on the Property inspector invoked by this tool (see `toolObj.setPI()`).

A shape Property inspector has the following controls:

stroke   fill

A text Property inspector has the following controls:

type	font	pointsize
color	bold	italic
direction	alignLeft	alignCenter
alignRight	alignJustify	spacing
position	autoKern	small
rotation	format	lineType
selectable	html	border
deviceFonts	varEdit	options
link	maxChars	target

A movie Property inspector has the following controls:

size	publish	background
framerate	player	profile

bEnable   A Boolean value that determines whether to enable (`true`) or disable (`false`) the control.

Returns

Nothing.

Description

Method; enables or disables the specified control in a Property inspector. Used only when creating extensible tools.

Example

The following command in an extensible tool's JavaScript file will set Flash to not show the stroke options in the Property inspector for that tool:

```
theTool.enablePIControl( "stroke", false);
```

toolObj.iconID

Availability

Flash MX 2004.

Usage

```
toolObj.iconID
```

Description

Read-only property; an integer with a value of -1. This property is used only when you create extensible tools. An `iconID` value of -1 means that Flash will not try find an icon for the tool. Instead, the script for the tool should specify the icon to display in the Tools panel; see `toolObj.setIcon()`.

Example

The following example assigns a value of -1 (the icon ID of the current tool) to the `toolIconID` variable:

```
var toolIconID = fl.tools.activeTool.iconID
```

toolObj.position

Availability

Flash MX 2004.

Usage

```
toolObj.position
```

Description

Read-only property; an integer that specifies the position of the tool in the Tools panel. This property is used only when you create extensible tools.

Example

The following commands in the `mouseDown()` method of a tool's JavaScript file will show that tool's position in the Tools panel as an integer in the Output panel:

```
myToolPos = fl.tools.activeTool.position;
fl.trace(myToolPos);
```

toolObj.setIcon()

Availability

Flash MX 2004.

Usage

```
toolObj.setIcon( file )
```

Parameters

file A string that specifies the name of the PNG file to use as the icon. The PNG file must be placed in the same folder as the JSFL file.

Returns

Nothing.

Description

Method; identifies a PNG file to use as a tool icon in the Tools panel. This method is used only when you create extensible tools.

Example

The following example specifies that the image in the PolyStar.png file should be used as the icon for the tool named PolyStar. This code is taken from the sample PolyStar.jsfl file (see "Sample PolyStar tool" on page 20):

```
theTool = fl.tools.activeTool;
theTool.setIcon("PolyStar.png");
```

toolObj.setMenuString()

Availability

Flash MX 2004.

Usage

```
toolObj.setMenuString( menuStr )
```

Parameters

menuStr A string that specifies the name that appears in the pop-up menu as the name for the tool.

Returns

Nothing.

Description

Method; sets the string that appears in the pop-up menu as the name for the tool. This method is used only when you create extensible tools.

Example

The following example specifies that the tool named `theTool` should display the name "PolyStar Tool" in its pop-up menu. This code is taken from the sample PolyStar.jsfl file (see "Sample PolyStar tool" on page 20):

```
theTool = fl.tools.activeTool;
theTool.setMenuString("PolyStar Tool");
```

toolObj.setOptionsFile()

Availability

Flash MX 2004.

Usage

```
toolObj.setOptionsFile( xmlFile )
```

Parameters

xmlFile   A string that specifies the name of the XML file that has the description of the tool's options. The XML file must be placed in the same folder as the JSFL file.

Returns

Nothing.

Description

Method; associates an XML file with the tool. The file specifies the options to appear in a modal panel that is invoked by an Options button in the Property inspector. You would usually use this method in the `configureTool()` function inside your JSFL file. See `configureTool()`.

For example, the PolyStar.xml file specifies three options associated with the Polygon tool:

```
<properties>
  <property name="Style"
    variable="style"
    list="polygon,star"
    defaultValue="0"
    type="Strings"  />

  <property name="Number of Sides"
    variable="nsides"
    min="3"
    max="32"
    defaultValue="5"
    type="Number"   />

  <property name="Star point size"
    variable="pointParam"
    min="0"
    max="1"
    defaultValue=".5"
    type="Double"   />

</properties>
```

Example

The following example specifies that the file named PolyStar.xml is associated with the currently active tool. This code is taken from the sample PolyStar.jsfl file (see "Sample PolyStar tool" on page 20):

```
theTool = fl.tools.activeTool;
theTool.setOptionsFile( "PolyStar.xml" );
```

toolObj.setPI()

Availability

Flash MX 2004.

Usage

```
toolObj.setPI( pi )
```

Parameters

pi   A string that specifies the Property inspector to invoke for this tool.

Returns

Nothing.

Description

Method; specifies which Property inspector should be used when the tool is activated. This method is used only when you create extensible tools. Acceptable values are `"shape"` (the default), `"text"`, and `"movie"`.

Example

The following example specifies that the shape Property inspector should be used when the tool is activated. This code is taken from the sample PolyStar.jsfl file (see "Sample PolyStar tool" on page 20):

```
theTool = fl.tools.activeTool;
theTool.setPI( "shape" );
```

toolObj.setToolName()

Availability

Flash MX 2004.

Usage

```
toolObj.setToolName( name )
```

Parameters

name   A string that specifies the name of the tool.

Returns

Nothing.

Description

Method; assigns a name to the tool for the configuration of the Tools panel. This method is used only when you create extensible tools. The name is used only by the XML layout file that Flash reads to construct the Tools panel. The name does not appear in the Flash user interface.

Example

The following example assigns the name "polystar" to the tool named `theTool`. This code is taken from the sample PolyStar.jsfl file (see "Sample PolyStar tool" on page 20):

```
theTool = fl.tools.activeTool;
theTool.setToolName("polystar");
```

toolObj.setToolTip()

Availability

Flash MX 2004.

Usage

```
toolObj.setToolTip( toolTip )
```

Parameters

toolTip   A string that specifies the tooltip to use for the tool.

Returns

Nothing.

Description

Method; sets the tooltip that appears when the mouse is held over the tool icon. This method is used only when you create extensible tools.

Example

The following example specifies that the tooltip for the tool should be "PolyStar Tool." This code is taken from the sample PolyStar.jsfl file (see "Sample PolyStar tool" on page 20):

```
theTool = fl.tools.activeTool;
theTool.setToolTip("PolyStar Tool");
```

toolObj.showPIControl()

Availability

Flash MX 2004.

Usage

```
toolObj.showPIControl( control, bShow )
```

Parameters

control   A string that specifies the name of the control to show or hide. This method is used only when you create extensible tools. Valid values depend on the Property inspector invoked by this tool (see `toolObj.setPI()`).

A shape Property inspector has the following controls:

stroke   fill

A text Property inspector has the following controls:

type	font	pointsize
color	bold	italic
direction	alignLeft	alignCenter
alignRight	alignJustify	spacing
position	autoKern	small
rotation	format	lineType
selectable	html	border
deviceFonts	varEdit	options
link	maxChars	target

The movie Property inspector has the following controls:

size	publish	background
framerate	player	profile

bShow   A Boolean value that determines whether to show or hide the specified control (`true` shows the control; `false` hides the control).

Returns
Nothing.

Description
Method; shows or hides a control in the Property inspector. This method is used only when you create extensible tools.

Example
The following command in an extensible tool's JavaScript file will set Flash to not show the fill options in the Property inspector for that tool:

```
fl.tools.activeTool.showPIControl( "fill", false );
```

toolObj.showTransformHandles()

Availability

Flash MX 2004.

Usage

```
toolObj.showTransformHandles( bShow )
```

Parameters

bShow　A Boolean value that determines whether to show or hide the free transform handles for the current tool (`true` shows the handles; `false` hides them).

Returns

Nothing.

Description

Method; called in the `configureTool()` method of an extensible tool's JavaScript file to indicate that the free transform handles should appear when the tool is active. This method is used only when you create extensible tools.

Example

See `configureTool()`.

Tools object

Availability

Flash MX 2004.

Description

The Tools object is accessible from the flash object (`fl.tools`). The `tools.toolObjs` property contains an array of ToolObj objects, and the `tools.activeTool` property returns the ToolObj object for the currently active tool. (See also "ToolObj object" on page 500 and "Extensible tools" on page 24.)

 NOTE The following methods and properties are used only when creating extensible tools.

Method summary for the Tools object

The following methods are available for the Tools object.

Method	Description
`tools.constrainPoint()`	Takes two points and returns a new adjusted or *constrained* point.
`tools.getKeyDown()`	Returns the most recently pressed key.
`tools.setCursor()`	Sets the pointer to a specified appearance.
`tools.snapPoint()`	Takes a point as input and returns a new point that may be adjusted or *snapped* to the nearest geometric object.

Property summary for the Tools object

The following properties are available for the Tools object.

Property	Description
`tools.activeTool`	Read-only; returns the ToolObj object for the currently active tool.
`tools.altIsDown`	Read-only; a Boolean value that identifies if the Alt key is being pressed.
`tools.ctlIsDown`	Read-only; a Boolean value that identifies if the Control key is being pressed.
`tools.mouseIsDown`	Read-only; a Boolean value that identifies if the left mouse button is currently pressed.

Property	Description
tools.penDownLoc	Read-only; a point that represents the position of the last mouse-down event on the Stage.
tools.penLoc	Read-only; a point that represents the current location of the mouse.
tools.shiftIsDown	Read-only; a Boolean value that identifies if the Shift key is being pressed.
tools.toolObjs	Read-only; an array of ToolObj objects.

tools.activeTool

Availability

Flash MX 2004.

Usage

```
tools.activeTool
```

Description

Read-only property; returns the ToolObj object for the currently active tool.

Example

The following example saves an object that represents the currently active tool in the theTool variable.

```
var theTool = fl.tools.activeTool;
```

tools.altIsDown

Availability

Flash MX 2004.

Usage

```
tools.altIsDown
```

Description

Read-only property; a Boolean value that identifies if the Alt key is being pressed. The value is `true` if the Alt key is pressed, and `false` otherwise.

Example

The following example determines whether the Alt key is being pressed.

```
var isAltDown = fl.tools.altIsDown;
```

tools.constrainPoint()

Availability

Flash MX 2004.

Usage

```
tools.constrainPoint(pt1, pt2)
```

Parameters

pt1 and *pt2*   specify the starting-click point and the drag-to point.

Returns

A new adjusted or constrained point.

Description

Method; takes two points and returns a new adjusted or constrained point. If the Shift key is pressed when the command is run, the returned point is constrained to follow either a 45° constrain (useful for something such as a line with an arrowhead) or to constrain an object to maintain its aspect ratio (such as pulling out a perfect square with the rectangle tool).

Example

The following example returns a constrained point:

```
pt2 = fl.tools.constrainPoint(pt1, tempPt);
```

tools.ctlIsDown

Availability

Flash MX 2004.

Usage

```
tools.ctlIsDown
```

Description

Read-only property; a Boolean value that is `true` if the Control key is pressed; `false` otherwise.

Example

The following example determines whether the Control key is being pressed.

```
var isCtrldown = fl.tools.ctrlIsDown;
```

tools.getKeyDown()

Availability

Flash MX 2004.

Usage

```
tools.getKeyDown()
```

Parameters

None.

Returns

The integer value of the key.

Description

Method; returns the most recently pressed key.

Example

The following example displays the integer value of the most recently pressed key in the Output panel.

```
var theKey = fl.tools.getKeyDown();
fl.trace(theKey);
```

tools.mouseIsDown

Availability

Flash MX 2004.

Usage

```
tools.mouseIsDown
```

Description

Read-only property; a Boolean value that is `true` if the left mouse button is currently down; `false` otherwise.

Example

The following example determines whether the left mouse button is pressed.

```
var isMouseDown = fl.tools.mouseIsDown;
```

tools.penDownLoc

Availability

Flash MX 2004.

Usage

```
tools.penDownLoc
```

Description

Read-only property; a point that represents the position of the last mouse-down event on the Stage. The `tools.penDownLoc` property comprises two properties, *x* and *y*, corresponding to the *x*, *y* location of the mouse pointer.

Example

The following example determines the position of the last mouse-down event on the Stage and displays the *x* and *y* values in the Output panel.

```
var pt1 = fl.tools.penDownLoc;
fl.trace("x,y location of last mouseDown event was " + pt1.x + ", " + pt1.y)
```

See also

```
tools.penLoc
```

tools.penLoc

Availability

Flash MX 2004.

Usage

```
tools.penLoc
```

Description

Read-only property; a point that represents the current location of the mouse pointer. The tools.penLoc property comprises two properties, x and y, corresponding to the x, y location of the mouse pointer.

Example

The following example determines the current location of the mouse.

```
var tempPt = fl.tools.penLoc;
```

See also

```
tools.penDownLoc
```

tools.setCursor()

Availability

Flash MX 2004.

Usage

```
tools.setCursor( cursor )
```

Parameters

cursor An integer that defines the pointer appearance, as described in the following list:

- 0 Plus cursor (+)
- 1 black arrow
- 2 white arrow
- 3 four-way arrow
- 4 two-way horizontal arrow
- 5 two-way vertical arrow
- 6 X
- 7 hand cursor

Returns

Nothing.

Description

Method; sets the pointer to a specified appearance.

Example

The following example sets the pointer to a black arrow.

```
fl.tools.setCursor(1);
```

tools.shiftIsDown

Availability

Flash MX 2004.

Usage

```
tools.shiftIsDown
```

Description

Read-only property; a Boolean value that is `true` if the Shift key is pressed; `false` otherwise.

Example

The following example determines whether the Shift key is being pressed.

```
var isShiftDown = fl.tools.shiftIsDown;
```

tools.snapPoint()

Availability

Flash MX 2004.

Usage

```
tools.snapPoint(pt)
```

Parameters

pt   specifies the location of the point for which you want to return a snap point.

Returns

A new point that may be adjusted or snapped to the nearest geometric object.

Description

Method; takes a point as input and returns a new point that may be adjusted or *snapped* to the nearest geometric object. If snapping is disabled in the View menu in the Flash user interface, the point returned is the original point.

Example

The following example returns a new point that may be snapped to the nearest geometric object.

```
var theSnapPoint = fl.tools.snapPoint(pt1);
```

tools.toolObjs

Availability

Flash MX 2004.

Usage

```
tools.toolObjs
```

Description

Read-only property; an array of ToolObj objects (see ToolObj object).

Vertex object

Availability

Flash MX 2004.

Description

The Vertex object is the part of the shape data structure that holds the coordinate data.

Method summary for the Vertex object

You can use the following methods with the Vertex object.

Method	Description
vertex.getHalfEdge()	Gets a HalfEdge object that shares this vertex.
vertex.setLocation()	Sets the location of the vertex.

Property summary for the Vertex object

The following properties are available for the Vertex object:

Property	Description
vertex.x	Read-only; the x location of the vertex in pixels.
vertex.y	Read-only; the y location of the vertex in pixels.

vertex.getHalfEdge()

Availability

Flash MX 2004.

Usage

vertex.getHalfEdge()

Parameters

None.

Returns

A HalfEdge object.

Description

Method; gets a HalfEdge object that shares this vertex.

Example

The following example shows how to get other half edges that share the same vertex.

```
var shape = fl.getDocumentDOM().selection[0];
var hEdge = shape.edges[0].getHalfEdge(0);
var theVertex = hEdge.getVertex();
var someHEdge = theVertex.getHalfEdge(); // Not necessarily the same half
  edge
var theSameVertex = someHEdge.getVertex();
fl.trace('the same vertex: ' + theSameVertex);
```

vertex.setLocation()

Availability

Flash MX 2004.

Usage

```
vertex.setLocation( x, y )
```

Parameters

x A floating-point value that specifies the *x* coordinate of where the vertex should be positioned, in pixels.

y A floating-point value that specifies the *y* coordinate of where the vertex should be positioned, in pixels.

Returns

Nothing.

Description

Method; sets the location of the vertex. You must call `shape.beginEdit()` before using this method.

Example

The following example sets the vertex to the origin point.

```
var shape = fl.getDocumentDOM().selection[0];
var hEdge = shape.edges[0].getHalfEdge(0);
var vertex = hEdge.getVertex();

// Move the vertex to the origin.
vertex.setLocation(0.0, 0.0);
```

vertex.x

Availability

Flash MX 2004.

Usage

```
vertex.x
```

Description

Read-only property; the *x* location of the vertex in pixels.

Example

The following example displays the location of the *x* and *y* values of the vertex in the Output panel.

```
var shape = fl.getDocumentDOM().selection[0];
var hEdge = shape.edges[0].getHalfEdge(0);
var vertex = hEdge.getVertex();

fl.trace('x location of vertex is: ' +  vertex.x);
fl.trace('y location of vertex is: ' + vertex.y);
```

vertex.y

Availability

Flash MX 2004.

Usage

```
vertex.y
```

Description

Read-only property; the *y* location of the vertex, in pixels.

Example

See `vertex.x`.

XMLUI object

Availability

Flash MX 2004.

Description

Flash 8 supports custom dialog boxes written in a subset of the XML User Interface Language (XUL). An XML User Interface (XMLUI) dialog box can be used by several Flash features, such as commands and behaviors, to provide a user interface for features that you build using extensibility. The XMLUI object provides the ability to get and set properties of an XMLUI dialog box, and accept or cancel out of one. The XMLUI methods can be used in callbacks, such as `oncommand` handlers in buttons.

You can write a dialog.xml file and invoke it from the JavaScript API using the `document.xmlPanel()` method. To retrieve an object representing the current XMLUI dialog box, use `fl.xmlui`.

For more information, see Appendix B, "XML to UI" in *Using Flash* in Flash Help.

Method summary for the XMLUI object

The following methods are available for the XMLUI object:

Method	Description
`xmlui.accept()`	Closes the current XMLUI dialog box with an accept state.
`xmlui.cancel()`	Closes the current XMLUI dialog box exit with a cancel state.
`xmlui.get()`	Retrieves the value of the specified property of the current XMLUI dialog box.
`xmlui.getControlItemElement()`	Returns the current control item for the specified control.
`xmlui.getEnabled()`	Returns a Boolean value that specifies whether the control is enabled or disabled (dimmed).
`xmlui.getVisible()`	Returns a Boolean value that specifies whether the control is visible or hidden.
`xmlui.set()`	Modifies the value of the specified property of the current XMLUI dialog box.
`xmlui.setControlItemElement()`	Sets the label and value for the current item.

Method	Description
xmlui.setControlItemElements()	Sets the label, value pairs of the current item.
xmlui.setEnabled()	Enables or disables (dims) a control.
xmlui.setVisible()	Shows or hides a control.

xmlui.accept()

Availability

Flash MX 2004.

Usage

```
xmlui.accept()
```

Parameters

None.

Returns

Nothing.

Description

Method; closes the current XMLUI dialog box with an accept state, which is equivalent to the user clicking the OK button.

See also

```
fl.xmlui, document.xmlPanel(), xmlui.cancel()
```

xmlui.cancel()

Availability

Flash MX 2004.

Usage

```
xmlui.cancel()
```

Parameters

None.

Returns

Nothing.

Description

Method; closes the current XMLUI dialog box with a cancel state, which is equivalent to the user clicking the Cancel button.

See also

`fl.xmlui, document.xmlPanel(), xmlui.accept()`

xmlui.get()

Availability

Flash MX 2004.

Usage

`xmlui.get( controlPropertyName )`

Parameters

`controlPropertyName`   A string that specifies the name of the XMLUI property whose value you want to retrieve.

Returns

A string that represents the value of the specified property. In cases where you might expect a Boolean value of `true` or `false`, it returns the string `"true"` or `"false"`.

Description

Method; retrieves the value of the specified property of the current XMLUI dialog box.

Example

The following example returns the value of a property named "URL":

`fl.xmlui.get("URL");`

See also

`fl.xmlui, document.xmlPanel(), xmlui.getControlItemElement(), xmlui.set()`

xmlui.getControlItemElement()

Availability

Flash 8.

Usage

`xmlui.getControlItemElement( controlPropertyName )`

Parameters

controlPropertyName   A string that specifies the property whose control item element you want to retrieve.

Returns

An object that represents the current control item for the control specified by *controlPropertyName*.

Description

Method; returns the label and value of the line selected in a ListBox or ComboBox control for the control specified by *controlPropertyName*.

Example

The following example returns the label and value of the currently selected line for the myListBox control :

```
var elem = new Object();
elem = fl.xmlui.getControlItemElement("myListBox");
fl.trace("label = " + elem.label + " value = " + elem.value);
```

See also

fl.xmlui, document.xmlPanel(), xmlui.get(), xmlui.setControlItemElement(), xmlui.setControlItemElements()

xmlui.getEnabled()

Availability

Flash 8.

Usage

xmlui.getEnabled(*controlID*)

Parameters

controlID   A string that specifies the ID attribute of the control whose status you want to retrieve.

Returns

A Boolean value of true if the control is enabled; false otherwise.

Description

Method; returns a Boolean value that specifies whether the control is enabled or disabled (dimmed).

Example

The following example returns a value that indicates whether the control with the ID attribute myListBox is enabled:

```
var isEnabled = fl.xmlui.getEnabled("myListBox");
fl.trace(isEnabled);
```

See also

fl.xmlui, document.xmlPanel(), xmlui.setEnabled()

xmlui.getVisible()

Availability

Flash 8.

Usage

xmlui.getVisible(*controlID*)

Parameters

controlID   A string that specifies the ID attribute of the control whose visibility status you want to retrieve.

Returns

A Boolean value of true if the control is visible, or false if it is invisible (hidden).

Description

Method; returns a Boolean value that specifies whether the control is visible or hidden.

Example

The following example returns a value that indicates whether the control with the ID attribute myListBox is visible:

```
var isVisible = fl.xmlui.getVisible("myListBox");
fl.trace(isVisible);
```

See also

xmlui.setVisible()

xmlui.set()

Availability

Flash MX 2004.

Usage

```
xmlui.set( controlPropertyName, value )
```

Parameters

controlPropertyName   A string that specifies the name of XMLUI property to modify.

value   A string that specifies the value to which you want to set the XMLUI property.

Returns

Nothing.

Description

Method; modifies the value of the specified property of the current XMLUI dialog box.

Example

The following example sets the value of a property named "URL" to "www.macromedia.com":

```
fl.xmlui.set("URL", "www.macromedia.com");
```

See also

fl.xmlui, document.xmlPanel(), xmlui.get(), xmlui.setControlItemElement(), xmlui.setControlItemElements()

xmlui.setControlItemElement()

Availability

Flash 8.

Usage

```
xmlui.setControlItemElement( controlPropertyName, elementItem )
```

Parameters

controlPropertyName   A string that specifies the control item element to set.

elementItem   A JavaScript object with a string property named label and an optional string property named value. If the value property does not exist, then it is created and assigned the same value as label.

Returns

Nothing.

Description

Method; sets the label and value of the currently selected line in the ListBox or ComboBox control specified by *controlPropertyName*.

Example

The following example sets the label and value for the current item of the control property named "PhoneNumber":

```
var elem = new Object();
elem.label = "Fax";
elem.value = "707-555-5555";
fl.xmlui.setControlItemElement("PhoneNumber",elem);
```

See also

fl.xmlui, document.xmlPanel(), xmlui.getControlItemElement(), xmlui.set(), xmlui.setControlItemElements()

xmlui.setControlItemElements()

Availability

Flash 8.

Usage

xmlui.setControlItemElements(*controlID, elementItemArray*)

Parameters

controlID   A string that specifies the ID attribute of the control you want to set.

elementItemArray   An array of JavaScript objects, where each object has a string property named label and an optional string property named value. If the value property does not exist, then it is created and assigned the same value as label.

Returns

Nothing.

Description

Method; clears the values of the ListBox or ComboBox control specified by *controlID* and replaces the list or menu items with the label, value pairs specified by *elementItemArray*.

Example

The following example sets the label and value of items in the the control with the ID attribute myControlID to the label, value pairs specified:

```
var nameArray = new Array("January", "February", "March");
var monthArray = new Array();
for (i=0;i<nameArray.length;i++){
  elem = new Object();
  elem.label = nameArray[i];
  elem.value = i;
  monthArray[i] = elem;
}
fl.xmlui.setControlItemElements("myControlID", monthArray);
```

See also

xmlui.getControlItemElement(), xmlui.set(), xmlui.setControlItemElement()

xmlui.setEnabled()

Availability

Flash 8.

Usage

xmlui.setEnabled(controlID, enable)

Parameters

controlID   A string that specifies the ID attribute of the control you want to enable or disable.

enable   A Boolean value of true if you want to enable the control, or false if you want to disable (dim) it.

Returns

Nothing.

Description

Method; enables or disables (dims) a control.

Example

The following example dims the control with the ID attribute myControl:

fl.xmlui.setEnabled("myControl", false);

See also

xmlui.getEnabled()

xmlui.setVisible()

Availability

Flash 8.

Usage

```
xmlui.setVisible(controlID, visible)
```

Parameters

controlID   A string that specifies the ID attribute of the control you want to show or hide.

visible   A Boolean value of `true` if you want to show the control; `false` if you want to hide it.

Returns

Nothing.

Description

Method; shows or hides a control.

Example

The following example hides the control with the ID attribute `myControl`:

```
fl.xmlui.setVisible("myControl", false);
```

See also

```
xmlui.getVisible()
```

VideoItem object

Inheritance Item object > VideoItem object

Availability

Flash MX 2004.

Description

The VideoItem object is a subclass of the Item object.

Property summary for the VideoItem object

In addition to the Item object properties, you can use the following properties with the VideoItem object:

Property	Description
videoItem.sourceFilePath	Read-only; a string that specifies the path to the video item.
videoItem.videoType	Read-only; a string that specifies the type of video the item represents.

videoItem.sourceFilePath

Availability

Flash 8.

Usage

videoItem.sourceFilePath

Description

Read-only property; a string, expressed as a file:/// URI that specifies the path to the video item.

Example

The following example displays the name and source file path of any items in the library that
are of type "video":

```
for ( idx in fl.getDocumentDOM().library.items ) {
  if ( fl.getDocumentDOM().library.items[idx].itemType == "video" ) {
    var myItem = fl.getDocumentDOM().library.items[idx];
    fl.trace( myItem.name + " source is " + myItem.sourceFilePath );
  }
}
```

See also

library.items

videoItem.videoType

Availability

Flash 8.

Usage

videoItem.videoType

Description

Read-only property; a string that specifies the type of video the item represents. Possible
values are "embedded video", "linked video", and "video".

Example

The following example displays the name and type of any items in the library that are of type
"video":

```
for ( idx in fl.getDocumentDOM().library.items ) {
  if ( fl.getDocumentDOM().library.items[idx].itemType == "video" ) {
    var myItem = fl.getDocumentDOM().library.items[idx];
    fl.trace( myItem.name + " is " + myItem.videoType );
  }
}
```

See also

library.items

## CHAPTER 3

C-Level Extensibility

The C-level extensibility mechanism lets you implement Macromedia Flash extensibility files using a combination of JavaScript and custom C code. You define functions using C, bundle them in a dynamic linked library (DLL) or a shared library, save the library in the appropriate directory, and then call the functions from JavaScript using the Macromedia Flash JavaScript API.

For example, you might want to define a function that performs intense calculations more efficiently than JavaScript does, which improves performance, or when you want to create more advanced tools or effects.

This extensibility mechanism is a subset of the Macromedia Dreamweaver API. If you are familiar with that API, you might recognize the functions in this API. However, this API differs from the Dreamweaver API in the following ways:

- This API does not contain all the commands in the Dreamweaver API.

- All declarations of type `wchar_t` and `char` in the Dreamweaver API are implemented as `unsigned short` declarations in this API, to support Unicode when strings are passed.

- The `JSVal JS_BytesToValue()` function in this API is not part of the Dreamweaver API.

- The location where DLL or shared library files must be stored is different (see "Integrating C functions" on page 534).

Integrating C functions

The C-level extensibility mechanism lets you implement Flash extensibility files using a combination of JavaScript and C code. The process for implementing this capability is summarized in the following steps:

1. Define functions using the C or C++ language.
2. Bundle them in a DLL file (Windows) or a shared library (Macintosh).
3. Save the DLL file or library in the appropriate location:
   - Windows 2000 or Windows XP:

     boot drive\Documents and Settings*user*\Local Settings\Application Data\Macromedia\ Flash 8*language*\Configuration\External Libraries
   - Macintosh OS X:

     Macintosh HD/Users/*userName*/Library/Application Support/Macromedia/Flash 8/*language*/Configuration/External Libraries
4. Create a JSFL file that calls the functions.
5. Run the JSFL file from the Commands menu in the Flash authoring environment.

For more information, see "Sample DLL implementation" on page 540.

C-level extensibility and the JavaScript interpreter

The C code in the DLL or shared library interacts with the Flash JavaScript API at three different times:

- At startup, to register the library's functions
- When the C function is called, to unpack the arguments that are being passed from JavaScript to C
- Before the C function returns, to package the return value

To accomplish these tasks, the interpreter defines several data types and exposes an API. Definitions for the data types and functions that are listed in this section appear in the mm_jsapi.h file. For your library to work properly, you must include the mm_jsapi.h file at the top of each file in your library, with the following line:

```
#include "mm_jsapi.h"
```

Including the mm_jsapi.h file includes the mm_jsapi_environment.h file, which defines the MM_Environment structure.

To get a copy of the mm_jsapi.h file, extract it from the sample ZIP or SIT file (see "Sample DLL implementation" on page 540), or copy the following code into a file that you name mm_jsapi.h:

```
#ifndef _MM_JSAPI_H_
#define _MM_JSAPI_H_

/
 ************************************************************************
 *****
 * Public data types

 ************************************************************************
 ****/

typedef struct JSContext JSContext;
typedef struct JSObject JSObject;
typedef long jsval;
#ifndef JSBool
typedef long JSBool;
#endif

typedef JSBool (*JSNative)(JSContext *cx, JSObject *obj, unsigned int argc,
    jsval *argv, jsval *rval);

/* Possible values for JSBool */
#define JS_TRUE 1
#define JS_FALSE 0




/
 ************************************************************************
 *****
 * Public functions

 ************************************************************************
 ****/

/* JSBool JS_DefineFunction(unsigned short *name, JSNative call, unsigned
   int nargs) */
#define JS_DefineFunction(n, c, a) \
    (mmEnv.defineFunction ? (*(mmEnv.defineFunction))(mmEnv.libObj, n, c,
   a) \
                          : JS_FALSE)

/* unsigned short *JS_ValueToString(JSContext *cx, jsval v, unsigned int
   *pLength) */
#define JS_ValueToString(c, v, l) \
```

```
      (mmEnv.valueToString  ? (*(mmEnv.valueToString))(c, v, l) : (unsigned
    short *)0)

/* unsigned char *JS_ValueToBytes(JSContext *cx, jsval v, unsigned int
   *pLength) */
#define JS_ValueToBytes(c, v, l) \
      (mmEnv.valueToBytes  ? (*(mmEnv.valueToBytes))(c, v, l) : (unsigned char
   *)0)

/* JSBool JS_ValueToInteger(JSContext *cx, jsval v, long *lp); */
#define JS_ValueToInteger(c, v, l) \
      (mmEnv.valueToInteger ? (*(mmEnv.valueToInteger))(c, v, l) : JS_FALSE)

/* JSBool JS_ValueToDouble(JSContext *cx, jsval v, double *dp); */
#define JS_ValueToDouble(c, v, d) \
      (mmEnv.valueToDouble  ? (*(mmEnv.valueToDouble))(c, v, d) : JS_FALSE)

/* JSBool JS_ValueToBoolean(JSContext *cx, jsval v, JSBool *bp); */
#define JS_ValueToBoolean(c, v, b) \
      (mmEnv.valueToBoolean ? (*(mmEnv.valueToBoolean))(c, v, b) : JS_FALSE)

/* JSBool JS_ValueToObject(JSContext *cx, jsval v, JSObject **op); */
#define JS_ValueToObject(c, v, o) \
      (mmEnv.valueToObject  ? (*(mmEnv.valueToObject))(c, v, o) : JS_FALSE)

/* JSBool JS_StringToValue(JSContext *cx, unsigned short *bytes, uint sz,
   jsval *vp); */
#define JS_StringToValue(c, b, s, v) \
      (mmEnv.stringToValue  ? (*(mmEnv.stringToValue))(c, b, s, v) : JS_FALSE)

/* JSBool JS_BytesToValue(JSContext *cx, unsigned char *bytes, uint sz,
   jsval *vp); */
#define JS_BytesToValue(c, b, s, v) \
      (mmEnv.bytesToValue  ? (*(mmEnv.bytesToValue))(c, b, s, v) : JS_FALSE)

/* JSBool JS_DoubleToValue(JSContext *cx, double dv, jsval *vp); */
#define JS_DoubleToValue(c, d, v) \
      (mmEnv.doubleToValue  ? (*(mmEnv.doubleToValue))(c, d, v) : JS_FALSE)

/* jsval JS_IntegerToValue(long lv); */
#define JS_IntegerToValue(lv)         (((jsval)(lv) << 1) | 0x1)

/* jsval JS_BooleanToValue(JSBool bv); */
#define JS_BooleanToValue(bv)         (((jsval)(bv) << 3) | 0x6)

/* jsval JS_ObjectToValue(JSObject *obj); */
#define JS_ObjectToValue(ov)          ((jsval)(ov))

/* unsigned short *JS_ObjectType(JSObject *obj); */
#define JS_ObjectType(o) \
```

```
    (mmEnv.objectType      ? (*(mmEnv.objectType))(o) : (unsigned short *)0)

/* JSObject *JS_NewArrayObject(JSContext *cx, unsigned int length, jsval
   *v) */
#define JS_NewArrayObject(c, l, v) \
    (mmEnv.newArrayObject ? (*(mmEnv.newArrayObject))(c, l, v) : (JSObject
    *)0)


/* long JS_GetArrayLength(JSContext *cx, JSObject *obj) */
#define JS_GetArrayLength(c, o) \
    (mmEnv.getArrayLength ? (*(mmEnv.getArrayLength))(c, o) : -1)


/* JSBool JS_GetElement(JSContext *cx, JSObject *obj, jsint idx, jsval *vp)
   */
#define JS_GetElement(c, o, i, v) \
    (mmEnv.getElement     ? (*(mmEnv.getElement))(c, o, i, v) : JS_FALSE)


/* JSBool JS_SetElement(JSContext *cx, JSObject *obj, jsint idx, jsval *vp)
   */
#define JS_SetElement(c, o, i, v) \
    (mmEnv.setElement     ? (*(mmEnv.setElement))(c, o, i, v) : JS_FALSE)


/* JSBool JS_ExecuteScript(JSContext *cx, JSObject *obj, unsigned short
   *script,
 *      unsigned int sz, jsval *rval) */
#define JS_ExecuteScript(c, o, s, z, r) \
    (mmEnv.executeScript  ? (*(mmEnv.executeScript))(c, o, s, z,
   _T(__FILE__), \
        __LINE__, r) : JS_FALSE)


/* JSBool JS_ReportError(JSContext *cx, unsigned short *error, unsigned int
   sz) */
#define JS_ReportError(c, e, s) \
    (mmEnv.reportError    ? (*(mmEnv.reportError))(c, e, s) : JS_FALSE)




/
    *******************************************************************
    *****
 * Private data types, macros, and globals

    *******************************************************************
    ****/

typedef struct {
    JSObject *libObj;
    JSBool (*defineFunction)(JSObject *libObj, unsigned short *name,
   JSNative call,
        unsigned int nargs);
```

```c
    unsigned short *(*valueToString)(JSContext *cx, jsval v, unsigned int
  *pLength);
    unsigned char *(*valueToBytes)(JSContext *cx, jsval v, unsigned int
  *pLength);
    JSBool (*valueToInteger)(JSContext *cx, jsval v, long *lp);
    JSBool (*valueToDouble)(JSContext *cx, jsval v, double *dp);
    JSBool (*valueToBoolean)(JSContext *cx, jsval v, JSBool *bp);
    JSBool (*valueToObject)(JSContext *cx, jsval v, JSObject **op);
    JSBool (*stringToValue)(JSContext *cx, unsigned short *b, unsigned int
  sz, jsval *vp);
    JSBool (*bytesToValue)(JSContext *cx, unsigned char *b, unsigned int sz,
  jsval *vp);
    JSBool (*doubleToValue)(JSContext *cx, double dv, jsval *vp);
    unsigned short *(*objectType)(JSObject *obj);
    JSObject *(*newArrayObject)(JSContext *cx, unsigned int length, jsval
  *vp);
    long (*getArrayLength)(JSContext *cx, JSObject *obj);
    JSBool (*getElement)(JSContext *cx, JSObject *obj, unsigned int idx,
        jsval *vp);
    JSBool (*setElement)(JSContext *cx, JSObject *obj, unsigned int idx,
        jsval *vp);
    JSBool (*executeScript)(JSContext *cx, JSObject *obj, unsigned short
  *script,
        unsigned int sz, unsigned short *file, unsigned int lineNum, jsval
  *rval);
    JSBool (*reportError)(JSContext *cx, unsigned short *error, unsigned int
  sz);
} MM_Environment;

extern MM_Environment mmEnv;

// Declare the external entry point and linkage.
#ifdef _WIN32
#   ifndef _MAC
    // Windows
__declspec( dllexport ) void MM_InitWrapper( MM_Environment *env, unsigned
  int envSize );
#   else
    // Mac with MSVC++ Win32 portability lib
    extern void MM_InitWrapper( MM_Environment *env, unsigned int envSize );
#   endif
#else
    // Codewarrior
#   pragma export on
    extern void MM_InitWrapper( MM_Environment *env, unsigned int envSize );
#   pragma export off
#endif


#define MM_STATE                                                            \
```

```
    /* Definitions of global variables */
\
    MM_Environment mmEnv;                                                      \
                                                                               \
    void                                                                       \
    MM_InitWrapper(MM_Environment *env, unsigned int envSize)
\
    {                                                                          \
        extern void MM_Init();                                                 \
                                                                               \
        char **envPtr = (char **)env;
\
        char **mmPtr =  (char **)(&mmEnv);
\
        char **envEnd = (char **)((char *)envPtr + envSize);
\
        char **mmEnd =  (char **)((char *)mmPtr  + sizeof(MM_Environment));
\
                                                                               \
        /* Copy fields from env to mmEnv, one pointer at a time */
\
        while (mmPtr < mmEnd && envPtr < envEnd)
\
            *mmPtr++ = *envPtr++;                                              \
                                                                               \
    /* If env doesn't define all of mmEnv's fields, set extras to NULL */
\
        while (mmPtr < mmEnd)                                                  \
            *mmPtr++ = (char *)0;                                             \
                                                                               \
    /* Call user's MM_Init function */
\
        MM_Init();                                                             \
    }                                                                          \

#endif /* _MM_JSAPI_H_ */
```

Sample DLL implementation

A sample DLL implementation is located in ZIP and SIT files in the ExtendingFlash/dllSampleComputeSum folder (see "Sample implementations" on page 19). To see how the process works without actually building the DLL, you can do the following:

- Store the Sample.jsfl file in the Commands directory (see "Saving JSFL files" on page 7).

- Store the Sample.dll file in the External Libraries directory (see "Integrating C functions" on page 534).

- In the Flash authoring environment, select Commands > Sample. The trace statement in the JSFL file sends the results of the function defined in Sample.dll to the Output panel.

This section discusses the development of the sample. In this case, the DLL contains only one function, which adds two numbers. The C code is shown in the following example:

```c
// Source code in C
// Save the DLL or shared library with the name "Sample".
#include <windows.h>
#include <stdlib.h>

#include "mm_jsapi.h"

// A sample function
// Every implementation of a JavaScript function must have this signature.
JSBool computeSum(JSContext *cx, JSObject *obj, unsigned int argc, jsval
  *argv, jsval *rval)
{
  long a, b, sum;

  // Make sure the right number of arguments were passed in.
  if (argc != 2)
    return JS_FALSE;

  // Convert the two arguments from jsvals to longs.
  if (JS_ValueToInteger(cx, argv[0], &a) == JS_FALSE ||
    JS_ValueToInteger(cx, argv[1], &b) == JS_FALSE)
      return JS_FALSE;

  /* Perform the actual work. */
  sum = a + b;

  /* Package the return value as a jsval. */
  *rval = JS_IntegerToValue(sum);

  /* Indicate success. */
  return JS_TRUE;
}
```

After writing this code, build the DLL file or shared library, and store it in the appropriate External Libraries directory (see "Integrating C functions" on page 534). Then create a JSFL file with the following code, and store it in the Commands directory (see "Saving JSFL files" on page 7).

```
// JSFL file to run C function defined above.
var a = 5;
var b = 10;
var sum = Sample.computeSum(a, b);
fl.trace("The sum of " + a + " and " + b + " is " + sum );
```

To run the function defined in the DLL, select Commands > Sample in the Flash authoring environment.

Data types

The JavaScript interpreter defines the following data types:

- `JSContext`
- `JSObject`
- `jsval`
- `JSBool`

typedef struct JSContext JSContext

A pointer to this opaque data type passes to the C-level function. Some functions in the API accept this pointer as one of their arguments.

typedef struct JSObject JSObject

A pointer to this opaque data type passes to the C-level function. This data type represents an object, which might be an array object or some other object type.

typedef struct jsval jsval

An opaque data structure that can contain an integer, or a pointer to a float, string, or object. Some functions in the API can read the values of function arguments by reading the contents of a `jsval` structure, and some can be used to write the function's return value by writing a `jsval` structure.

typedef enum { JS_FALSE = 0, JS_TRUE = 1 } JSBool

A simple data type that stores a Boolean value.

The C-level API

The C-level extensibility API consists of the `JSBool (*JSNative)` function signature and the following functions:

- `JSBool JS_DefineFunction()`
- `unsigned short *JS_ValueToString()`
- `JSBool JS_ValueToInteger()`
- `JSBool JS_ValueToDouble()`
- `JSBool JS_ValueToBoolean()`
- `JSBool JS_ValueToObject()`
- `JSBool JS_StringToValue()`
- `JSBool JS_DoubleToValue()`
- `JSVal JS_BooleanToValue()`
- `JSVal JS_BytesToValue()`
- `JSVal JS_IntegerToValue()`
- `JSVal JS_ObjectToValue()`
- `unsigned short *JS_ObjectType()`
- `JSObject *JS_NewArrayObject()`
- `long JS_GetArrayLength()`
- `JSBool JS_GetElement()`
- `JSBool JS_SetElement()`
- `JSBool JS_ExecuteScript()`

typedef JSBool (*JSNative)(JSContext *cx, JSObject *obj, unsigned int argc, jsval *argv, jsval *rval)

Description

Method; describes C-level implementations of JavaScript functions in the following situations:

- The *cx* pointer is a pointer to an opaque JSContext structure, which must be passed to some of the functions in the JavaScript API. This variable holds the interpreter's execution context.

- The *obj* pointer is a pointer to the object in whose context the script executes. While the script is running, the this keyword is equal to this object.

- The *argc* integer is the number of arguments being passed to the function.

- The *argv* pointer is a pointer to an array of jsval structures. The array is argc elements in length.

- The *rval* pointer is a pointer to a single jsval structure. The function's return value should be written to *rval.

The function returns JS_TRUE if successful; JS_FALSE otherwise. If the function returns JS_FALSE, the current script stops executing and an error message appears.

JSBool JS_DefineFunction()

Usage

```
JSBool JS_DefineFunction(unsigned short *name, JSNative call, unsigned int
  nargs)
```

Description

Method; registers a C-level function with the JavaScript interpreter in Flash. After the JS_DefineFunction() function registers the C-level function that you specify in the *call* argument, you can invoke it in a JavaScript script by referring to it with the name that you specify in the *name* argument. The *name* argument is case-sensitive.

Typically, this function is called from the MM_Init() function, which Flash calls during startup.

Arguments

unsigned short *name, JSNative call, unsigned int nargs

- The name argument is the name of the function as it is exposed to JavaScript.
- The call argument is a pointer to a C-level function. The function must return a JSBool, which indicates success or failure.
- The nargs argument is the number of arguments that the function expects to receive.

Returns

A Boolean value: JS_TRUE indicates success; JS_FALSE indicates failure.

unsigned short *JS_ValueToString()

Usage

unsigned short *JS_ValueToString(JSContext *cx, jsval v,
  unsigned int *pLength)

Description

Method; extracts a function argument from a jsval structure, converts it to a string, if possible, and passes the converted value back to the caller.

 | Do not modify the returned buffer pointer or you might corrupt the data structures of the JavaScript interpreter. To change the string, you must copy the characters into another buffer and create a new JavaScript string.

Arguments

JSContext *cx, jsval v, unsigned int *pLength

- The cx argument is the opaque JSContext pointer that passes to the JavaScript function.
- The v argument is the jsval structure from which the string is to be extracted.
- The pLength argument is a pointer to an unsigned integer. This function sets *plength equal to the length of the string in bytes.

Returns

A pointer that points to a null-terminated string if successful or to a null value on failure. The calling routine must not free this string when it finishes.

JSBool JS_ValueToInteger()

Usage

```
JSBool JS_ValueToInteger(JSContext *cx, jsval v, long *lp);
```

Description

Method; extracts a function argument from a `jsval` structure, converts it to an integer (if possible), and passes the converted value back to the caller.

Arguments

`JSContext *cx`, `jsval v`, `long *lp`

- The *cx* argument is the opaque `JSContext` pointer that passes to the JavaScript function.
- The *v* argument is the `jsval` structure from which the integer is to be extracted.
- The *lp* argument is a pointer to a 4-byte integer. This function stores the converted value in `*lp`.

Returns

A Boolean value: `JS_TRUE` indicates success; `JS_FALSE` indicates failure.

JSBool JS_ValueToDouble()

Usage

```
JSBool JS_ValueToDouble(JSContext *cx, jsval v, double *dp);
```

Description

Method; extracts a function argument from a `jsval` structure, converts it to a double (if possible), and passes the converted value back to the caller.

Arguments

`JSContext *cx`, `jsval v`, `double *dp`

- The *cx* argument is the opaque `JSContext` pointer that passed to the JavaScript function.
- The *v* argument is the `jsval` structure from which the double is to be extracted.
- The *dp* argument is a pointer to an 8-byte double. This function stores the converted value in `*dp`.

Returns

A Boolean value: `JS_TRUE` indicates success; `JS_FALSE` indicates failure.

JSBool JS_ValueToBoolean()

Usage

```
JSBool JS_ValueToBoolean(JSContext *cx, jsval v, JSBool *bp);
```

Description

Method; extracts a function argument from a `jsval` structure, converts it to a Boolean value (if possible), and passes the converted value back to the caller.

Arguments

`JSContext *cx`, `jsval v`, `JSBool *bp`

- The *cx* argument is the opaque `JSContext` pointer that passes to the JavaScript function.
- The *v* argument is the `jsval` structure from which the Boolean value is to be extracted.
- The *bp* argument is a pointer to a `JSBool` Boolean value. This function stores the converted value in `*bp`.

Returns

A Boolean value: `JS_TRUE` indicates success; `JS_FALSE` indicates failure.

JSBool JS_ValueToObject()

Usage

```
JSBool JS_ValueToObject(JSContext *cx, jsval v, JSObject **op);
```

Description

Method; extracts a function argument from a `jsval` structure, converts it to an object (if possible), and passes the converted value back to the caller. If the object is an array, use `JS_GetArrayLength()` and `JS_GetElement()` to read its contents.

Arguments

`JSContext *cx`, `jsval v`, `JSObject **op`

- The *cx* argument is the opaque `JSContext` pointer that passes to the JavaScript function.
- The *v* argument is the `jsval` structure from which the object is to be extracted.
- The *op* argument is a pointer to a `JSObject` pointer. This function stores the converted value in `*op`.

Returns

A Boolean value: `JS_TRUE` indicates success; `JS_FALSE` indicates failure.

JSBool JS_StringToValue()

Usage

```
JSBool JS_StringToValue(JSContext *cx, unsigned short *bytes, uint sz,
  jsval *vp);
```

Description

Method; stores a string return value in a jsval structure. It allocates a new JavaScript string object.

Arguments

JSContext *cx*, unsigned short *bytes*, size_t *sz*, jsval *vp*

- The *cx* argument is the opaque JSContext pointer that passes to the JavaScript function.
- The *bytes* argument is the string to be stored in the jsval structure. The string data is copied, so the caller should free the string when it is not needed. If the string size is not specified (see the *sz* argument), the string must be null-terminated.
- The *sz* argument is the size of the string, in bytes. If *sz* is 0, the length of the null-terminated string is computed automatically.
- The *vp* argument is a pointer to the jsval structure into which the contents of the string should be copied.

Returns

A Boolean value: JS_TRUE indicates success; JS_FALSE indicates failure.

JSBool JS_DoubleToValue()

Usage

```
JSBool JS_DoubleToValue(JSContext *cx, double dv, jsval *vp);
```

Description

Method; stores a floating-point number return value in a jsval structure.

Arguments

JSContext *cx*, double *dv*, jsval *vp*

- The *cx* argument is the opaque JSContext pointer that passes to the JavaScript function.
- The *dv* argument is an 8-byte floating-point number.
- The *vp* argument is a pointer to the jsval structure into which the contents of the double should be copied.

Returns

A Boolean value: JS_TRUE indicates success; JS_FALSE indicates failure.

JSVal JS_BooleanToValue()

Usage

```
jsval JS_BooleanToValue(JSBool bv);
```

Description

Method; stores a Boolean return value in a jsval structure.

Arguments

JSBool *bv*

■ The *bv* argument is a Boolean value: JS_TRUE indicates success; JS_FALSE indicates failure.

Returns

A JSVal structure that contains the Boolean value that passes to the function as an argument.

JSVal JS_BytesToValue()

Usage

```
JSBool JS_BytesToValue(JSContext *cx, unsigned short *bytes, uint sz, jsval
   *vp);
```

Description

Method; converts bytes to a JavaScript value.

Arguments

JSContext *cx*, unsigned short *bytes*, uint *sz*, jsval *vp*

■ The *cx* argument is the JavaScript context.

■ The *bytes* argument is the string of bytes to convert to a JavaScript object.

■ The *sz* argument is the number of bytes to be converted.

■ The *vp* argument is the JavaScript value.

Returns

A Boolean value: JS_TRUE indicates success; JS_FALSE indicates failure.

JSVal JS_IntegerToValue()

Usage

```
jsval JS_IntegerToValue(long lv);
```

Description

Method; converts a long integer value to JSVal structure.

Arguments

lv

- The *lv* argument is the long integer value that you want to convert to a jsval structure.

Returns

A JSVal structure that contains the integer that passed to the function as an argument.

JSVal JS_ObjectToValue()

Usage

```
jsval JS_ObjectToValue(JSObject *obj);
```

Description

Method; stores an object return value in a JSVal. Use JS_ NewArrayObject() to create an array object; use JS_SetElement() to define its contents.

Arguments

JSObject *obj*

- The *obj* argument is a pointer to the JSObject object that you want to convert to a JSVal structure.

Returns

A JSVal structure that contains the object that you passed to the function as an argument.

unsigned short *JS_ObjectType()

Usage

```
unsigned short *JS_ObjectType(JSObject *obj);
```

Description

Method; given an object reference, returns the class name of the object. For example, if the object is a DOM object, the function returns "Document". If the object is a node in the document, the function returns "Element". For an array object, the function returns "Array".

 Do not modify the returned buffer pointer, or you might corrupt the data structures of the JavaScript interpreter.

Arguments

JSObject *obj

- Typically, this argument is passed in and converted using the JS_ValueToObject() function.

Returns

A pointer to a null-terminated string. The caller should not free this string when it finishes.

JSObject *JS_NewArrayObject()

Usage

```
JSObject *JS_NewArrayObject( JSContext *cx, unsigned int length [, jsval *v
    ] )
```

Description

Method; creates a new object that contains an array of JSVals.

Arguments

`JSContext *cx`, `unsigned int length`, `jsval *v`

- The *cx* argument is the opaque `JSContext` pointer that passes to the JavaScript function.
- The *length* argument is the number of elements that the array can hold.
- The *v* argument is an optional pointer to the `jsvals` to be stored in the array. If the return value is not `null`, *v* is an array that contains *length* elements. If the return value is `null`, the initial content of the array object is undefined and can be set using the `JS_SetElement()` function.

Returns

A pointer to a new array object or the value `null` upon failure.

long JS_GetArrayLength()

Usage

`long JS_GetArrayLength(JSContext *cx, JSObject *obj)`

Description

Method; given a pointer to an array object, gets the number of elements in the array.

Arguments

`JSContext *cx`, `JSObject *obj`

- The *cx* argument is the opaque `JSContext` pointer that passes to the JavaScript function.
- The *obj* argument is a pointer to an array object.

Returns

The number of elements in the array or -1 upon failure.

JSBool JS_GetElement()

Usage
JSBool JS_GetElement(JSContext *cx, JSObject *obj, jsint idx, jsval *vp)

Description
Method; reads a single element of an array object.

Arguments
JSContext *cx, JSObject *obj, unsigned int index, jsval *v

- The cx argument is the opaque JSContext pointer that passes to the JavaScript function.
- The obj argument is a pointer to an array object.
- The index argument is an integer index into the array. The first element is index 0, and the last element is index (length - 1).
- The v argument is a pointer to a jsval where the contents of the jsval structure in the array should be copied.

Returns
A Boolean value: JS_TRUE indicates success; JS_FALSE indicates failure.

JSBool JS_SetElement()

Usage
JSBool JS_SetElement(JSContext *cx, JSObject *obj, jsint idx, jsval *vp)

Description
Method; writes a single element of an array object.

Arguments
JSContext *cx, JSObject *obj, unsigned int index, jsval *v

- The cx argument is the opaque JSContext pointer that passes to the JavaScript function.
- The obj argument is a pointer to an array object.
- The index argument is an integer index into the array. The first element is index 0, and the last element is index (length - 1).
- The v argument is a pointer to a jsval structure whose contents should be copied to the jsval in the array.

Returns

A Boolean value: JS_TRUE indicates success; JS_FALSE indicates failure.

JSBool JS_ExecuteScript()

Usage

```
JS_ExecuteScript (JSContext *cx, JSObject *obj, unsigned short *script,
    unsigned int sz, jsval *rval)
```

Description

Method; compiles and executes a JavaScript string. If the script generates a return value, it returns in *rval.

Arguments

JSContext *cx, JSObject *obj, unsigned short *script, unsigned int sz, jsval *rval

- The cx argument is the opaque JSContext pointer that passes to the JavaScript function.

- The obj argument is a pointer to the object in whose context the script executes. While the script is running, the this keyword is equal to this object. Usually this is the JSObject pointer that passes to the JavaScript function.

- The script argument is a string that contains JavaScript code. If the string size is not specified (see the sz argument), the string must be null-terminated.

- The sz argument is the size of the string, in bytes. If sz is 0, the length of the null-terminated string is computed automatically.

- The rval argument is a pointer to a single jsval structure. The function's return value is stored in *rval.

Returns

A Boolean value: JS_TRUE indicates success; JS_FALSE indicates failure.

Training from the Source

Macromedia's *Training from the Source* series is one of the best-selling series on the market. This series offers you a unique self-paced approach that introduces you to the major features of the software and guides you step by step through the development of real-world projects.

Each book is divided into a series of lessons. Each lesson begins with an overview of the lesson's content and learning objectives and is divided into short tasks that break the skills into bite-size units. All the files you need for the lessons are included on the CD that comes with the book.

Macromedia Flash 8: Training from the Source
ISBN 0-321-33629-1

Macromedia Flash Professional 8: Training from the Source
ISBN 0-321-38403-2

Macromedia Flash 8 ActionScript: Training from the Source
ISBN 0-321-33619-4

Macromedia Studio 8: Training from the Source
ISBN 0-321-33620-8

Macromedia Dreamweaver 8: Training from the Source
ISBN 0-321-33626-7

Macromedia Dreamweaver 8 with ASP, PHP and ColdFusion: Training from the Source
ISBN 0-321-33625-9

Macromedia Fireworks 8: Training from the Source
ISBN 0-321-33591-0

macromedia®
PRESS

www.macromediapress.com